Irene Ofteringer
with Chris Turner, Lewis Lansford, Anthony Cosgrove and Alison Bewsher

STARTER

Total English

Teacher's Resource Book

PEARSON
Longman

Contents

Syllabus outline

	UNIT	LESSON 1	LESSON 2	LESSON 3	COMMUNICATION
1	**Arrivals** page 9	**Grammar:** *I'm/you're* **Vocabulary:** numbers 0–9 **Can do:** check in to a hotel **Skills:** **listening:** listen to and identify correct information **speaking:** role play: checking into a hotel	**Grammar:** *he's/she's/it's* **Vocabulary:** letters **Can do:** greet someone at an airport **Skills:** **pronunciation:** syllables **listening and reading:** listen to and read about where people are from and where they are now **speaking:** say where famous people are from **Lifelong learning:** keep a vocabulary notebook	**Grammar:** *Where are you from?* **Vocabulary:** common phrases **Can do:** introduce someone; start a conversation **Skills:** **listening:** listen to people being introduced to each other **pronunciation:** the main stress in question words **speaking:** ask and answer questions about where people are from	**Can do:** understand and say phone numbers
		Film bank material: page 116 and Teacher's Resource Book pages 132 and 142 **Photocopiable material:** Vocabulary, Grammar and Communication (Teacher's Resource Book page 84)			
2	**My life** page 19	**Grammar:** *Who ...?; my* **Vocabulary:** numbers 10–99? *How old ...?* **Can do:** give basic information about your family **Skills:** **listening:** listen to Sabrina talking about her family **pronunciation:** numbers **speaking:** talk about five members of your family or five friends **Lifelong learning:** use English to talk about your family, your life, etc.	**Grammar:** *What's your ...?* **Vocabulary:** *great, good, OK, bad, awful* **Can do:** ask for and give personal details **Skills:** **listening:** listen to and identify correct addresses **speaking:** ask for names and addresses	**Grammar:** *his/her; a/an* **Vocabulary:** jobs **Can do:** give information about other people; write a short personal profile **Skills:** **reading and listening:** read and listen to short profiles about people **speaking:** asking for and giving information about people **writing:** write a short profile about yourself	**Can do:** talk about favourite people and things
		Film bank material: page 117 and Teacher's Resource Book pages 133 and 142 **Photocopiable material:** Vocabulary, Grammar and Communication (Teacher's Resource Book page 87)			
3	**Travel** page 29	**Grammar:** *we're/they're*; affirmative of *to be*; *our/their* **Vocabulary:** adjectives for describing places **Can do:** write a simple holiday email **Skills:** **reading:** read a holiday email **pronunciation:** *they're* or *their* **writing:** write about your holiday	**Grammar:** plural nouns; negative of *to be* **Vocabulary:** holiday things **Can do:** say what's in your suitcase **Skills:** **listening:** listen to people describing what's in their suitcases **pronunciation:** /s/, /z/ or /ɪz/ **Lifelong learning:** record important pronunciation **speaking:** ask and answer questions about what's in your suitcase	**Grammar:** *Yes/No* questions with *to be* **Vocabulary:** days of the week **Can do:** ask for tourist information **Skills:** **reading:** read and identify addresses, telephone numbers and email addresses **listening:** listen to people giving directions **speaking:** ask for and give information about tourist attractions	**Can do:** have an extended phone conversation
		Film bank material: page 118 and Teacher's Resource Book pages 134 and 143 **Photocopiable material:** Vocabulary, Grammar and Communication (Teacher's Resource Book page 90)			
4	**In town** page 39	**Grammar:** *Can I have ...?* **Vocabulary:** food and drink; prices **Can do:** order food in a café or coffee shop **Skills:** **pronunciation:** /kæ–naɪ–hæ–və/ ...? **speaking:** asking for and giving information about food and drink prices	**Grammar:** *this, that, these, those* **Vocabulary:** clothes and colours **Can do:** ask for and understand prices **Skills:** **reading:** read about Portobello market **listening and speaking:** listen to and ask about prices **writing:** write about your favourite market/shop	**Grammar:** possessive *'s* **Vocabulary:** irregular plurals **Can do:** ask about things and make simple transactions **Skills:** **reading and listening:** read and listen to transactional dialogues **speaking:** ask and give information about possessions	**Can do:** ask for and give locations
		Film bank material: page 119 and Teacher's Resource Book pages 135 and 143 **Photocopiable material:** Vocabulary, Grammar and Communication (Teacher's Resource Book page 93)			

Syllabus outline

	UNIT	LESSON 1	LESSON 2	LESSON 3	COMMUNICATION
5	**Places** page 49	**Grammar:** *there is/are* **Vocabulary:** *some, a lot of* **Can do:** give a simple description of a place **Skills:** **reading:** read about favourite places for a holiday **speaking:** talk about three things that make a good holiday **writing:** write about your favourite place	**Grammar:** *Is/Are there; there isn't/aren't; some, any* **Vocabulary:** nationalities **Can do:** ask about a new town and where important places are **Skills:** **listening:** listen to information about a town map **speaking:** ask for and give information about amenities in town	**Grammar:** *can/can't* **Vocabulary:** telling the time **Can do:** talk about general abilities **Skills:** **listening:** listen to a conversation giving information about abilities **pronunciation:** *can/can't* **speaking:** ask and answer questions about ability	**Can do:** check into a Bed and Breakfast **Lifelong learning:** learn new vocabulary in short phrases
		Film bank material: page 120 and Teacher's Resource Book pages 136 and 144 **Photocopiable material:** Vocabulary, Grammar and Communication (Teacher's Resource Book page 96)			
6	**People** page 59	**Grammar:** Present Simple (1): *I/You ...;* object pronouns: *me, you, him, her, it, us, them* **Can do:** say what you like/don't like **Skills:** **listening:** listen to a 60-second interview with Cynthia Castro **pronunciation:** questions with *like* **speaking:** ask and answer questions about what you like/don't like	**Grammar:** Present Simple (2): *we/they; Wh-* questions **Vocabulary:** jobs and activities **Can do:** start and continue a conversation with someone you don't know **Skills:** **listening:** listen to people talking about their jobs **reading:** read a magazine article about best friends **speaking:** role play a conversation in a restaurant	**Grammar:** Present Simple (3): *he/she/it* **Vocabulary:** verbs of routine **Can do:** talk about the routines of people you know **Skills:** **reading:** read about people's routines **speaking:** talk about a member of your family or a friend **listening:** listen to Adam's song **writing:** write a letter to a friend about your life	**Can do:** ask and answer questions about a friend **Lifelong learning:** revise grammar and vocabulary regularly
		Film bank material: page 121 and Teacher's Resource Book pages 137 and 144 **Photocopiable material:** Vocabulary, Grammar and Communication (Teacher's Resource Book page 99)			
7	**Work** page 69	**Grammar:** imperatives **Vocabulary:** months **Can do:** understand simple written and spoken instructions **Skills:** **listening and vocabulary:** listen to a teacher applying for a new job **speaking:** role play a business phone call **reading:** read about Tim Clarke's day **Lifelong learning:** try to use your English in a real communicative situation	**Grammar:** adverbs of frequency **Vocabulary:** work phrases **Can do:** say how often you do something **Skills:** **listening:** listen to a radio games show **pronunciation:** *often* and *usually* **writing:** write request notes	**Grammar:** *would like* **Vocabulary:** ordinal numbers **Can do:** welcome a visitor to your place of work **Skills:** **listening:** listen to a secretary telling the manager about visits for the month **listening and vocabulary:** listen to a conversation about a staff canteen **speaking:** role play welcoming visitors to your office and offer food and drink	**Can do:** understand and give directions in a building
		Film bank material: page 122 and Teacher's Resource Book pages 138 and 145 **Photocopiable material:** Vocabulary, Grammar and Communication (Teacher's Resource Book page 103)			
8	**Leisure** page 79	**Grammar:** *like + -ing; want + infinitive* **Vocabulary:** adjectives for describing activities **Can do:** explain why you want to do something **Skills:** **speaking:** talk about things to do at hotels **listening:** listen to Gary and Annie choosing a hotel **writing:** write an email to a hotel asking for information	**Grammar:** *have got/has got* **Vocabulary:** rooms and furniture **Can do:** say what things you possess **Skills:** **listening:** listen to Paul and Jo talking about Paul's sister's wedding **pronunciation:** *I've, we've* and *she's* **reading:** do a technology quiz	**Grammar:** question words **Vocabulary:** food **Can do:** suggest a restaurant; book a restaurant; order food in a restaurant **Skills:** **reading:** read about different restaurants **listening:** listen to Mark and Alda choosing and booking a restaurant **speaking:** role play ordering food at a restaurant	**Can do:** ask for and give information about people
		Film bank material: page 123 and Teacher's Resource Book pages 139 and 145 **Photocopiable material:** Vocabulary, Grammar and Communication (Teacher's Resource Book page 107)			

	UNIT	LESSON 1	LESSON 2	LESSON 3	COMMUNICATION
9	**The past** page 89	**Grammar:** past of *to be*: affirmative **Vocabulary:** occupations **Can do:** make simple statements about people from history **Skills:** **reading:** read texts about 20th-century icons **listening and vocabulary:** listen to a radio game show	**Grammar:** past of *to be*: negatives and questions **Vocabulary:** *yesterday, last, ago* **Can do:** give a short description of a past experience **Skills:** **speaking:** talk about different board games **listening:** listen to people playing *My first, my last* **pronunciation:** *was/wasn't* **writing:** write about your first teacher or your last holiday	**Grammar:** *Can/Could you ...?; Can/Could I ...?* **Vocabulary:** housework **Can do:** make a simple request and ask permission **Skills:** **reading:** read an article about housework **listening:** listen to Jeff's week **speaking:** ask for help to complete a *to do* list	**Can do:** talk about school days **Lifelong learning:** when you listen to English, pay attention to stressed words
		Film bank material: page 124 and Teacher's Resource Book pages 140 and 146 **Photocopiable material:** Vocabulary, Grammar and Communication (Teacher's Resource Book page 111)			
10	**Stories** page 99	**Grammar:** Past Simple: regular verbs **Can do:** understand a simple narrative of past events **Skills:** **speaking:** talk about the *Mona Lisa* **reading:** read about the *Mona Lisa* **pronunciation:** *-ed* endings of verbs **listening:** listen to *The story of the Mona Lisa*	**Grammar:** Past Simple: irregular verbs **Vocabulary:** high numbers **Can do:** give a simple summary of a news event **Skills:** **reading:** read about current news stories **speaking:** ask people about their week **writing:** write a news story about a good week/bad week	**Grammar:** *going to* **Vocabulary:** future plans **Can do:** talk about immediate and long term plans **Skills:** **listening:** listen to people talking about last week and their plans **speaking:** talk about future plans **pronunciation:** *going to*	**Can do:** talk about past and future holidays
		Film bank material: page 125 and Teacher's Resource Book pages 141 and 146 **Photocopiable material:** Vocabulary, Grammar and Communication (Teacher's Resource Book page 115)			

Test A: Units 1–5 (Teacher's Resource Book page 148)
Test B: Units 1–5 (Teacher's Resource Book page 152)
Test A: Units 6–10 (Teacher's Resource Book page 156)
Test B: Units 6–10 (Teacher's Resource Book page 160)

Introduction

Teaching and learning are unpredictable experiences. Learners can be dynamic and engaged one lesson and then demotivated, tired or even absent the next. The aim of *Total English* is two-fold: firstly to set new standards in terms of interest level, teachability and range of support materials; and secondly to address the reality of most people's unpredictable teaching experience as it is, not as we hope it will be. Research for *Total English* suggested three classroom 'realities' that need to be addressed in a coursebook: 1) learners often lack direction and purpose – they are often not sure about the relevance of what they are learning and where they are going with English; 2) learners need to be genuinely engaged in coursebook content just as they are in the newspapers, TV programmes and films that they see around them; 3) learners often miss lessons and this creates extra work for the teacher to make sure that no one falls behind.

Finding direction and purpose

Learners need a clear sense of where they are going and how they are going to get there. They need to know what they are learning, why they are learning it and how it can be applied outside the classroom. Clear goals and objectives are crucial. *Total English* contains a clear grammar syllabus and plenty of practice. Each input lesson is organised on a double-page spread and has a grammar and *Can do* learning objective clearly stated at the start. The *Can do* objectives give a purpose and reason for learning and mean that students know why they are studying that lesson and how they can use the new language.

The learning objectives in *Total English* are derived from the *Can do* statements in the Common European Framework, which means teachers can feel confident that *Total English* covers the language areas their students need. The levels of *Total English* correlate to the Common European Framework in the following way:

Starter	Introduces A1
Elementary	Covers A1 and goes towards A2
Pre-intermediate	Covers A2 and goes towards B1
Intermediate	Covers B1 and goes towards B2
Upper Intermediate	Covers B2
Advanced	Covers C1

Engaging learners' interest

Motivation through engagement is equally important for successful language learning. *Total English* lessons give a new twist to familiar topics – topics that reflect learners' needs and interests. This ensures that learners will always have something to say about the content of the lesson. There are frequent opportunities for learners to exchange ideas and opinions and engage with the material on a personal level. Activities have been designed to be as realistic as possible so that learners can see how the language they're learning can be applied outside the classroom.

In addition to the wide range of topics, texts and activities, each level of the *Total English* Students' Books has a DVD, which adds an extra dimension to the course. The DVDs expose learners to a variety of different English media and give them a feel for how the language is used in real life. Each unit of the Students' Books has a corresponding DVD extract and the Film banks at the back of the Students' Books offer material to use in class or at home while watching the DVD.

Helping learners catch up

One of the most common problems that teachers face is irregular attendance. Learners often have busy lives with work, study or family commitments, and attending English classes on a regular basis is not always possible. *Total English* recognises this problem and has been designed to help learners catch up easily if they miss lessons. In addition to the practice exercises in each lesson, there is a Reference page and a Review and practice page at the end of each unit. These provide an accessible summary of the main grammar and vocabulary covered.

The *Total English* Workbooks also have freestanding CD-ROMs that include interactive self-study 'catch-up' material to present and practise language from any lessons learners have missed. With this extensive range of animated presentations, interactive practice exercises and games, *Total English* ensures your students don't get left behind if they miss lessons.

The course package

Total English has six levels and takes learners from Starter to Advanced. Each level consists of the following:

- **Students' Book**
The *Total English* Students' Books are divided into 10–12 units and contain approximately 80–120 hours of teaching material. Each unit contains a balanced mix of grammar, vocabulary, pronunciation and skills work including writing.

- **DVD**
The 'with DVD' version of the Students' Books has a freestanding DVD which provides additional listening practice linked to the topic areas in the Students' Books.

- **Video**
The DVD material is also available on video (PAL and NTSC).

- **Class Cassettes/CDs**
The *Total English* Class Cassettes/CDs contain all the recorded material from the Students' Books.

- **Workbook**
The *Total English* Workbooks contain further practice of language areas covered in the corresponding units of the Students' Books.

- **Workbook 'Catch-up' CD-ROM**
The *Total English* Workbook CD-ROMs provide extra support for students who miss lessons. In addition to the recorded material from the Workbooks, the Workbook CD-ROMs feature 'catch-up' material related to the key grammar areas covered in the Students' Books.

- **Teacher's Resource Book**
The *Total English* Teacher's Resource Books provide all the support teachers need to get the most out of the course. The Teacher's Resource Books contain teaching notes, photocopiable worksheets, DVD worksheets and tests.

- **Website**
Total English has its own dedicated website. In addition to background information about the course and authors, the website features teaching tips, downloadable worksheets, links to other useful websites as well as special offers and competitions. Join us online at www.longman.com/totalenglish.

The Students' Book

Each unit of the *Total English* Students' Books follows the same structure, making the material very easy to use:

- **Lead-in page**
  - acts as a springboard into the topic of the unit and engages students' interest.
  - introduces essential vocabulary related to the topic so that students start with the same basic grounding.

- **Input lessons**
  - three double-page input lessons, thematically linked, offer interesting angles on the unit topic.
  - each input lesson leads towards a *Can do* learning objective in line with the Council of Europe's *Can do* statements.
  - each 90-minute lesson focuses on a specific grammar area and includes vocabulary, pronunciation and skills work.
  - each unit contains at least two reading texts and a substantial listening element.
  - How to ... boxes develop students' competence in using language, in line with the Common European Framework.
  - Lifelong learning boxes offer tips and strategies for developing students' study skills.

- **Communication page**
  - revises language taught in the previous three lessons in a freer, more communicative context.
  - each communication task practises a range of skills and has a measurable goal or outcome.

- **Reference page**
  - summarises the main grammar points covered in each unit and provides a list of key vocabulary.
  - helps learners to catch up if they miss lessons and is an essential revision tool.

- **Review and practice page**
  - provides a range of exercises to consolidate key grammar and vocabulary covered in the unit.
  - can be used to check progress, enabling teachers to identify areas that need further practice.

- **Film bank pages**
  - support the DVD which is attached to the back of the 'with DVD' version of the Students' Books.
  - feature a range of exercises designed to stimulate interest in each DVD extract and make the authentic material contained on the DVD accessible to students.

The *Total English* Students' Books also feature the following:

- **Do you know?**
  - an optional section to be covered before learners start the course, which teaches basic language areas such as the alphabet, numbers and classroom language.

- **Writing bank**
  - provides models and tips on how to write emails, letters and postcards, as well as guidance on different writing skills such as punctuation, spelling and paragraph construction.

- **Pronunciation bank**
  - provides a list of English phonemes, guidance on sound-spelling correspondences and weak forms.

The Workbook

The *Total English* Workbooks contain 10–12 units which correspond to the Students' Book material. Each Workbook contains:

- **Additional practice material**
  Extra grammar, vocabulary, skills and pronunciation exercises practise language covered in the corresponding units of the Students' Books.

- **Review and consolidation sections**
  At Starter level these occur after every two units and contain additional practice of the grammar and vocabulary covered in the unit.

- **Vocabulary bank**
  This provides further practice in the key vocabulary areas covered in each unit of the Students' Books. Students can refer to this after studying a particular topic and record the new vocabulary they have learned. They can also add new items as they come across them.

The Workbook CD-ROM

In addition to the recorded material from the Workbook, the 'catch-up' section of the CD-ROM contains the following:

- **Grammar presentations**
  Simple, accessible grammar explanations summarise the target language of each unit in a succinct and memorable way.

- **Self-check practice exercises**
  A range of practice exercises (two for each grammar point) enable students to practise the target language.

- **'Can do' game**
  This provides communicative practice of the target language.

The Teacher's Resource Book

The Teacher's Resource Books are divided into the following sections:

- **Introduction**
  This explains the aims and rationale of the course and provides a complete description of the course package. In this Starter level Teacher's Resource Book there are additional tips on teaching beginners and ideas for warmer activities.

- **Teaching notes**
  These provide step by step instructions on how to exploit each unit as well as background notes and suggestions for warm-up, lead-in and extension activities.

- **Photocopiable resource banks**
  The photocopiable resource banks contain 35 photocopiable worksheets at Starter level (three each for Units 1–5, four each for Units 6–10). The worksheets are designed to practise the grammar and vocabulary covered in the Students' Book units in a freer, less structured and enjoyable context. Detailed instructions on how to use each worksheet are also provided in the Teacher's Resource Book.

- **DVD worksheets**
  In addition to the Film bank pages in the Students' Books, the Teacher's Resource Books also have a DVD worksheet for each unit. Containing Before viewing, While viewing and Post viewing activities, the DVD worksheets

provide more detailed exploitation of the DVD material. Instructions on how to use each worksheet including warm-up and extension activities are also provided.

- **Tests**
  Two photocopiable progress tests (each with A and B versions) are included in this Teacher's Resource Book at Starter level. Each test covers grammar, vocabulary, reading, listening and writing skills.

The Test Master CD-ROM

The Teacher's Resource Book includes a Test Master CD-ROM which provides an additional teaching resource.

Easy to use

- The tests are based strictly on the content of *Total English Starter*, providing a fair measure of learners' progress.
- An interactive menu makes it easy to find the tests you want.
- Keys and audio scripts are provided to help marking.
- Most tests have A and B versions to make it harder for learners to copy from each other.
- The audio files for the listening tests are on the same CD.

Types of test

The Test Master CD-ROM contains five types of test: Placement Test/s, Module Test, Progress Tests, Mid-Course Test, End of Course Test.

Flexible

The tests can be used as they are or edited using Microsoft® Word. These are possible adaptations to suit your teaching situation:

- Delete or add exercises to make the test shorter or longer.
- Delete exercises or items which you omitted.
- Add in exercises to cover extra content you introduced.
- Edit exercises to make them harder/easier.
- Edit the format of exercises to match other exams.
- Personalise the content to bring exercises to life.
- Use audio scripts to create extra listening exercises, e.g. creating gap fills, introducing deliberate errors for learners to find.
- Add your school name to the top of the test.

Using this CD

It is best to treat it as a master. Copy the test to the hard drive of your computer (using the installation wizard) and burn the audio files to CD or copy them on to cassette. If you don't have a CD burner or prefer to teach with cassettes, put the Test Master CD into the CD drive of a hi-fi and copy the audio files on to a blank cassette.

Teaching approaches

Grammar

Total English covers all the main language areas you would expect at each level and gives learners a thorough foundation in grammar based on the following principles:

- **Clear presentation/analysis**
  Each double-page lesson has a clear grammar aim which is stated at the top of the page. New language items are presented in context via reading and/or listening texts and grammar rules are then analysed and explained via the Active grammar boxes which are a key feature of each lesson.

Total English takes a 'guided discovery' approach to grammar and learners are actively invited to think about grammar and work out the rules for themselves.

- **Varied, regular practice**
  Once learners have grasped the important rules, all new language is then practised in a variety of different ways so that learners are able to use the grammar with confidence. Practice activities include form-based exercises designed to help learners manipulate the new structures as well as more meaningful, personalised practice. Additional grammar practice exercises can be found in the Review and practice sections at the end of each unit as well as in the Workbooks and on the Workbook CD-ROMs. The Teacher's Resource Books also contain an extensive bank of photocopiable grammar activities which are designed to practise the language in freer, more communicative contexts.

- **Accessible reference material**
  In addition to the explanations contained in the Active Grammar boxes, there is a Reference section at the end of each unit which summarises the rules in greater detail and provides extra information and examples.

Vocabulary

Total English recognises the central role that vocabulary plays in successful communication. The emphasis is on providing learners with high-frequency, useful vocabulary which is regularly practised and revised. New vocabulary is presented and practised in a variety of different ways – via the Lead-in pages which provide a springboard into the topic of each unit, enabling teachers to elicit vocabulary that learners already know as well as pre-teach essential vocabulary for the rest of the unit; via the reading and listening texts and related exercises; via special vocabulary sections in the main lessons. Additional vocabulary practice is provided in the Review and practice sections of the Students' Book, in the practice exercises in the Workbook and special vocabulary worksheets in the Teacher's Resource Book.

Speaking

The key aim for most learners is spoken fluency but low level learners cannot express themselves easily without support. *Total English* develops spoken fluency in a number of ways – by giving learners discussion topics they want to talk about; by setting up situations where they are motivated to communicate in order to complete a specific task; by providing clear models and examples of how to structure

discourse and by encouraging them, wherever possible, to express their own ideas and opinions. All lessons feature some speaking practice and there are regular How to ... boxes throughout the course which focus on the words and expressions learners need to carry out specific functions.

Communication pages at the end of each unit engage learners in a variety of problem-solving tasks and involve learners in a number of different skills – including speaking. The photocopiable activities in the Teacher's Resource Book are also specifically designed to promote speaking practice.

Listening

Listening is one of the most difficult skills to master and *Total English* pays particular emphasis to developing learners' confidence in this area. Listening texts include short dialogues as well as longer texts (conversations, interviews, stories and songs). There are lots of simple 'Listen and check your answer' exercises as well as more challenging activities where learners have to listen to longer extracts in order to find specific information. The recorded material features a variety of accents including British, American, Australian and some non-native speakers. There is additional listening practice in the Workbooks, and the DVDs further enhance learners' confidence in understanding the spoken word.

Pronunciation

Total English pays particular attention to pronunciation, which is integrated into all the lessons which present new language. The pronunciation syllabus includes word and sentence stress, weak forms, intonation and difficult sounds. The Pronunciation banks at the back of the Students' Books include a list of English phonemes, guidance on sound-spelling correspondences and weak forms. There is additional pronunciation practice in the Workbooks and on the Workbook CD-ROMs.

Reading

There is a wide variety of reading texts in *Total English*, ranging from simple forms and advertisements to short texts from newspapers and magazines. Texts have been chosen for their intrinsic interest as well as for their usefulness in providing a vehicle for the particular grammar and vocabulary points in focus. Many of the texts have been adapted from authentic, real-life sources (magazines, websites, etc.) and related tasks have been carefully selected to develop learners' confidence in dealing with written texts. Activities include comprehension and vocabulary work as well as practice in dealing with different reading sub-skills such as reading for gist. There are a number of jigsaw readings where learners work together and share information. The length and complexity of the texts get more challenging as the course progresses.

Writing

With the growth of email, writing is becoming an increasingly important skill. *Total English* acknowledges this by including regular writing tasks in the Students' Books. These are carefully structured with exercises and examples designed to ensure that learners are actually able to carry out the tasks. Models of different types of writing – emails, postcards, formal and informal letters are provided in the Writing bank at the back of the Students' Books as well as additional advice and guidance on different writing sub-skills such as punctuation, spelling and paragraph construction.

Revision and testing

There are plenty of opportunities for revision in *Total English* and language is constantly recycled throughout the course. At the end of every unit, there are special Review and practice pages which take the form of mini-progress checks enabling learners to identify areas where they might need further practice.

In addition to the Review and practice pages, there are Review and consolidation sections in the accompanying Workbooks, and a whole range of additional practice material on the 'Catch-up' CD-ROMs. The Teacher's Resource Books include photocopiable progress tests.

Learner training

Total English places a strong emphasis on learner training and good study habits are encouraged and developed via the Lifelong learning boxes which are a featured in many lessons. The Lifelong learning boxes provide useful tips and suggestions on how to continue learning outside the classroom. In addition, the Vocabulary banks in the Workbooks not only encourage students to record vocabulary from particular lessons, but also to revisit and add further vocabulary items as they arise.

Lifelong learning

Personalise it!
When you want to learn new words, it is useful to write them in a personal sentence.
fridge – *My fridge is very old – it's useless!*
cupboard – *I have a big cupboard in my bedroom.*

Teaching beginner classes

Learning processes are more effective if links are made between the known and the new, i.e. activating learners' prior knowledge is essential to successful learning and teaching processes. Even beginners of English bring some knowledge of English to the classroom. A lot of people are familiar with English words and phrases through popular culture and international expressions in business, computing, science, etc. Others have learnt some English before but want to start from scratch. Someone who has learnt other foreign languages has acquired language learning strategies. Last but not least, all learners know (about) their own language.

The activation of learners' prior knowledge is built into *Total English* through the 'Active grammar' approach. Further ideas are offered in the unit notes, but words that come up on the news, titles of current films or songs can often be used to build a bridge between the familiar and the new.

Make learners active

Whenever possible, try to set up learning scenarios in which learners construct knowledge actively. They will remember what they've worked out for themselves better than something that's been presented to them.

False beginners – real beginners – refreshers

Total English provides materials that can be used either with real beginners or with students who have had some experience of English.

In the teaching notes in this book *real beginners* refers to students who have never learnt any English. They may have picked up internationally-used expressions, etc. Real beginners who have learnt other foreign languages are likely to learn much faster than those for whom English is their first foreign language.

False beginners refers to students who have had about 60–80 teaching hours of English (a maximum of 180 hours) and who would like to take it up again after a break of a year or more.

The material can be used flexibly to accommodate real and false beginners. The unit notes provide ideas for real and false beginners and include suggestions for extra activities for all learners.

How to speak to beginners

Here are some 'do's and 'don'ts' about controlling language so that learners can understand:

- Give learners time and speak slowly. Use repetition. If possible, visualise/act out what you want to say.

- Use short sentences and simple structures (Simple Present, if possible), but do not hesitate to use words or structures they haven't come across if they are clear from the context or communicative situation. Input should be at what Stephen Krashen has dubbed 'n+1'-level, i.e. slightly higher than what the learners know actively.

- Give instructions and conduct the lesson in English as far as possible – again, use simple English, and use the same phrases again and again. Teach 'classroom phrases'. If learners ask questions in their own language, rephrase them in simple English.

Warmers, starters, activity formats 'for all seasons'

Warmers help to focus learners' attention, refresh their memories or introduce a new topic. Fun, movement, music and visuals are important ingredients. None of these suggestions requires much preparation.

▶ Name games

1 Learners stand in circle. You introduce yourself by taking a step towards the middle and saying, *My name is Irene and I like Indian food./ My name is Fred, and I like football.* All learners repeat your sentence and movement. Each student introduces him/herself that way, and everybody repeats.

2 Sit/stand in a circle or U. Teacher: *My name is X*; student 1: *this is x and my name is Y*, student 2: *that is x, this is y and my name is z'* etc. Go round the class. You are first and last, i.e. you have to say all the names!

▶ Do your students play ball with you?

Many exercises are more fun if you stand in a circle and, rather than nominating a learner, you throw them a ball. Use a soft, medium-sized ball. Short question-and-answer exercises, vocabulary revision, etc. can be done like this. You start off by asking a question and throwing the ball to a student who answers and then asks a new question, throws the ball to another student, etc.

▶ Cocktail party

This is a bit like 'musical chairs'. Play some music and ask students to walk around the classroom. When you stop the music, they stop and talk to the person standing nearest to them. This is a good way to get learners moving around and talking to other learners. It can be played in pairs.

▶ 'Find someone who ...'

You can either prepare a list of five ideas or put them on the board. This can be used to introduce any topic and is good for practising question formation. For example, 'Find someone who likes Prince Charles'. Q: *Do you like ...?* Clarify how to use negatives before the game: *Find someone who doesn't like chocolate* requires the question *Do you* but a negative answer. Students circulate and ask each other questions. Ask them to find at least three people for each idea and/or to find a different person for each idea.

▶ The classics

Hangman, bingo, memory, trivial pursuit, board games, competitive activities, noughts and crosses, scrabble, etc. TV quiz shows provide useful formats for quizzes because students are familiar with formats and focus on content.

▶ Partner/group finding activities

Always have a pack of cards on you. Take out the cards necessary to form groups or pairs, students pick one of these cards and form groups accordingly.

Create your own word–picture or word/phrase–word/phrase matches. You can use virtually any linguistic structure, e.g. synonyms, antonyms, irregular verbs. Put the items on flash cards and ask students to find their partner, e.g. 'hot'-'cold'.

Total English and exams

The table below shows how the different levels of *Total English* relate to the Common European Framework levels and the University of Cambridge ESOL main suite examinations in terms of the language taught and the topics covered.

Starter	Introduces A1	Builds foundations for KET
Elementary	Covers A1 and goes towards A2	Useful for KET
Pre-Intermediate	Covers A2 and goes towards B1	Useful for PET
Intermediate	Covers B1 and goes towards B2	Useful for FCE
Upper Intermediate	Covers B2	
Advanced	Covers C1	Useful for CAE

While *Total English* is not an examination preparation course, a student who has, for example, completed the Upper Intermediate level would have sufficient language to attempt the Cambridge ESOL FCE (First Certificate in English) examination. Many of the exercises in the *Total English* Students' Books, Workbooks and photocopiable tests are similar in format to those found in the Cambridge ESOL main suite examinations but specific training is required for all EFL examinations and we would strongly recommend this. For further information on the University of Cambridge ESOL examinations, contact:

Cambridge ESOL
1 Hills Road
Cambridge
CB1 2EU

Tel. +44 (0) 1223 553355
Fax. +44 (0) 1223 460278
Email: ESOL@ucles.org.uk
www.CambridgeESOL.org

Overview

Lead-in	**Vocabulary:** greetings and introducing yourself
1.1	**Grammar:** *I'm, you're*
	Vocabulary: numbers 0–9
	Can do: check in to a hotel
1.2	**Grammar:** *he's/she's/it's*
	Vocabulary: alphabet, countries
	Can do: greet someone at an airport
1.3	**Grammar:** *Where are you from?*
	Vocabulary: common phrases
	Can do: introduce someone; start a conversation
Com. Focus	Find a phone number

Summary

Lesson 1: Sts hear people checking into hotels. They learn numbers and then role play checking into a hotel.

Lesson 2: Sts talk about countries and learn how to greet someone at an airport.

Lesson 3: Sts learn how to introduce someone and use conversational phrases when meeting people.

Communication: Sts listen to how phone numbers are said, then practise asking for hotel phone numbers.

> **Film bank: Saying hello**
>
> A series of extracts showing people introducing themselves both formally and informally in social and work contexts.
>
> Possible places to use this short film are:
> ▶ after 1.3
> ▶ at the end of the unit
>
> For ways to use this short film in class, see Students' Book page 116 and Teacher's Resource Book pages 132 and 142.

Introductory lesson and Lead-in

The purpose of this lesson is not only to introduce sts to the language, but also to make them feel comfortable in their learning environment.

> **OPTIONAL WELCOME WARMER**
>
> Don't ask sts to introduce themselves to the group before you 'really begin'. They'll be curious to meet the other students – an authentic motivation for classroom communication.
>
> Before the class starts, write *Welcome to the English course* on the board or prepare an OHT. Greet the sts:
> *Good morning/afternoon/evening*, and introduce yourself: *Hello, I'm ... .* Try to arrange the class in a U-shape, so that everyone can see each other.

Walk round the class and address each student: *Hello, I'm ... . What's your name?* They might just give their names, or even continue with *Hello, I'm ... .*

At this stage, use your full name (first and last name).

Write on the board *Hello, I'm ... . What's your name?* Model and ask the whole class to repeat. Ask sts to introduce themselves to the person sitting next to them. You'll have to demonstrate this so that sts understand. Then ask them to get up and talk to five other sts. Circulate and monitor. False beginners will probably try to start conversations. At this stage, listen in so that you get some idea of the sts in your class.

Tip Watch pronunciation/intonation right from the start, as it is very difficult to un-learn mistakes later. Don't interrupt, but correct gently after sts have finished their sentences.

1a/b ▶ If sts haven't got the course book yet, you could bring in pictures showing similar situations to the photos on page 9. Ask sts to listen and decide which conversation matches photo A, B, C and D. Play recording 1.1. Play it again and stop it after each dialogue. Ask sts which picture it matches.

> **Answers:** Photo A   Photo D   Photo B   Photo C

▶ Play the recording again, pausing after each sentence. Ask sts to repeat as a class. Add *Nice to meet you* to the phrases on the board. Repeat round the class, practising *Welcome to the English course, What's your name?* and *Nice to meet you.*

▶ Elicit or explain that the dialogues differ in formality. Elicit what makes them formal or less formal.

2 ▶ Explain that sts will have to respond to the phrases on the recording. Demonstrate an example. Say: *Welcome to the English course.* Elicit *Thank you.* Play recording 1.2 item by item and ask sts to respond together. Explain the meaning of, and point out the difference in meaning and pronunciation between *to* and *too.*

> **Answers:** 1 Good morning.   2 Thank you.   3 Hello.   4 Nice to meet you, too.   5 Hello. My name's ... .

3 ▶ Ask sts to mingle and welcome five other sts to the English class, asking their names and introducing themselves.

▶ Teach *Goodbye, see you next week* by going round the class and addressing each student directly: *Goodbye, Toni. See you next week.* Sts will be impressed if you remember all their names!

1.1 Hotel check-in

In this lesson sts learn numbers 0–9 and have brief exchanges checking into a hotel. Grammar: *I'm/You're.*

Vocabulary

1a ▶ Real beginners Books closed. Write figures 0–9 on the board and elicit how to say them in English (both false and real beginners are likely to know at least some of them). Then ask sts to listen and repeat. Play recording 1.3.

b ▶ Ask sts to write the figures against the words. Circulate and monitor. Then ask 10 sts to write one number each as a word and a figure on the board to check the answers.

▶ False beginners Write numbers 0–9 in words, but with the letters jumbled, on the board, or prepare an OHT. Ask sts to rearrange the letters. Elicit the answers and write the correct version and numbers on the board/OHT.

Language note Silent *gh* and *w*, voiced *v* and *z* and *th* may cause problems. Listen carefully and correct, but don't focus on them unless sts' pronunciation could interfere with meaning.

Answers: four – 4 five – 5 three – 3 eight – 8 seven – 7 zero – 0 one – 1 six – 6 nine – 9 two – 2

2 ▶ Ask sts to practise in pairs. After a few minutes, ask them to look at Ex. 1b again, then close their books. Dictate numbers 0–9 and ask sts to write them out. They check their answers on page 7.

3a ▶ Ask: *Where is this? Doors with numbers?* Elicit *hotel, room, door.* Ask sts to read the How to ... box and then cover both the How to ... box and Ex. 1 before they write the numbers. Clean the board. As sts write, circulate and correct any mistakes you see. Ask sts to check their work against Ex. 1. For real beginners or slower learners, write all answers on the board.

Answers: 1 Room one two nine 2 Room four three eight 3 Room five one seven 4 Room two oh nine 5 Room six oh eight 6 Room three four five

b ▶ Read the How to ... box out loud, modelling the rhythm of room numbers. Ask a few sts to read the room numbers from **a** out loud. Correct pronunciation and rhythm. To practise rhythm, ask sts to make a gesture or conduct as they speak, to help them understand that you say the numbers together, almost as one word.

Tip Use simple classroom English from the beginning and support your words by visualising/gesturing (e.g. opening or closing books) or by pointing to sections in the book you are referring to. You are introducing numbers here and letters in the next lesson. Use them!

Listening

4 ▶ Ask sts to read the forms first, then listen and decide which one is correct. Play recording 1.4. Ask sts to write the correct number on a piece of paper (as a word). You could have a vote on the answer by asking sts to hold up their paper as you say *number 3, 1, 2.*

Answer: 2

Language note Married women are addressed as *Mrs* /ˈmɪsɪz/, or *Ms* /məz/ if they don't take their husband's surname. Unmarried women are addressed as *Ms* or *Miss* /mɪs/. If it's not clear whether a woman is married, *Mrs, Ms* or *Miss* are all used – there aren't clear rules. English learners would be advised to use *Mrs* or *Ms* and ensure that their tone of voice is polite. Sts tend to find it difficult to differentiate between *Miss* and *Ms* in both comprehension and pronunciation.

5 ▶ Sts work in new pairs. With their partner, ask them to read through the How to ... box. Explain or elicit *Mrs/Ms/Miss* and discuss how you address a woman you don't know. Then ask sts to practise the dialogue using their own names, changing roles once and then changing partners.

Grammar

6 ▶ As this is the first Active grammar box, explain that sts will construct grammar rules in the course (because that way they learn more effectively). Ask them to fill in the gaps and elicit the answers, then ask them to look at Reference page 17 (verb *to be*). Explain the use of contractions (spoken, informal) and full forms (written, except in personal letters).

Answers: 'm 're

7a ▶ Point out that the dialogues are spoken language. Elicit/explain that sts should use contractions. As sts fill these in individually, circulate and correct any mistakes you see. Go over the answers by having pairs of sts read out dialogues 1–5. As sts read, write the answers on the board.

Answers: 1 're 2 'm/'re 3 'm/'m 4 're 5 'm/'m

b ▶ Ask sts to take it in turns to be the receptionist and guest. Alternatively, ask each student to pick one of the given identities. Ask them to walk around the room with their books and talk to five different people, checking in and playing the receptionist with each partner. Sts mingle and have check-in conversations. Circulate and correct as necessary. With false beginners or confident sts, encourage them to extend their conversations with the phrases from the unit.

Tip Correction vs fluency: make notes of mistakes during fluency-oriented activities and discuss them with the class afterwards (i.e. give feedback without interrupting!). Only correct on the spot if you feel it is necessary and not too demoralising.

Vocabulary

8a/b▶ Ask sts to shout out the answers. Play recording 1.5. Then practise pronunciation. Clarify that *Good day* isn't used in this way.

> **Answers:** 1 morning 2 afternoon 3 evening 4 night

c▶ Encourage sts to exaggerate intonation as they greet each other.

Speaking

9▶ Sts choose to be A or B. Ask Sts A to think of a name for their hotel and note it down. Sts A stand in different parts of the room and welcome Sts B to their hotel, and use the room numbers given. Sts B walk around and check into different hotels.

> **OPTIONAL WRAP-UP**
>
> Ask sts to write a page for their vocabulary folders with three sections: *How to say names, How to greet people, How to react to greetings.*

1.2 Airport arrivals

In this lesson sts learn the alphabet and talk about countries and how to greet people at the airport. Grammar: *he's/she's/it's.*

> **OPTIONAL WARMER**
>
> This activity reviews numbers and introduces countries (for comprehension only). If you can, bring in a selection of five to eight songs (different styles and current or well-known). Alternatively, write up the names of well-known or current songs and their singers/bands. Explain that the class is the jury at an international song contest. Allocate countries to pairs of sts (using flags or symbols, if possible) and make sure they know what country it is. Explain that pairs can give each song between 0–9 points. Play about 15 seconds of each song, then call on each 'country' to tell you how many points they give it. Draw a table on the board in which you enter countries, song titles and scores. Add up the scores, announce the winner and play the song.

Vocabulary

1a▶ Books closed. Write *a, b, c* on the board and elicit the alphabet. Write the letters sts give you on the board to make sure they mean what they say – they may mispronounce some. Add any missing letters.

▶ **Real beginners** Ask sts to listen, and play recording 1.6, pointing at each letter on the board.

b/c▶ Books closed. Play recording 1.6 in sections of about five letters, pointing at the relevant letters on the board. Ask sts to repeat as a class. Ask them to practise the alphabet with a partner. Listen in closely.

2a▶ Ask sts (individually or in pairs) to open their books and find letters that rhyme.

> **Answers:** /eɪ/ (eight) = a h j k /iː/ (three) = b c d e g p t v /e/ (ten) = f l m n s x z /aɪ/ (five) = i y /əʊ/ (zero) o /uː/ (two) q u w /ɑː/ (are) r

b▶ Ask sts to listen and check their answers. Play recording 1.7. Write the answers on the board. Sts may still confuse some letters.

> **OPTIONAL EXTENSION**
>
> Ask sts in groups of three to write an alphabet poem or rap. They can either write an abstract poem, using solely the letters and their names, or they can play with words they already know plus their names.

3▶ Ask sts to look at the picture and ask them: *Where is this?* Elicit *airport.* Explain *arrivals* (e.g. use an icon with a plane touching down). Elicit/explain that flight numbers are a combination of letters (indicating the airline) and numbers. Elicit airlines and their abbreviations (e.g. *IB* for *Iberia*).

▶ **Real beginners** Read the flight numbers and cities to sts and ask them to repeat as a class.

▶ Repeat around the classroom with one student saying a flight number and the next one giving the city it is arriving from. Correct the pronunciation of flight numbers and places.

Vocabulary

4a/b▶ Ask sts, in pairs, to match the cities and countries. Play recording 1.8 and ask them to listen and check. Ask them to underline the stressed vowel as they listen. Play the recording again and ask sts to repeat. Be aware that unstressed vowels, especially initial unstressed vowels, may be mispronounced (e.g. *Australia*).

Language note Some sts may be unaware that England isn't Britain unless they are football fans. Explain that *UK* stands for *United Kingdom*, which comprises Great Britain (England, Wales, Scotland) and Northern Ireland.

> **Answers:** 1 Delhi – India   2 Sydney – Australia
> 3 Buenos Aires – Argentina   4 Tokyo – Japan
> 5 New York – the US   6 Rio de Janeiro – Brazil
> 7 London – the UK   8 Berlin – Germany   9 Rome –
> Italy   10 Warsaw – Poland

Pronunciation

5a▶ This exercise makes sts aware of syllables, important for pronunciation and placing stress. Looking at individual syllables may tempt them to stress each syllable in turn, however, resulting in incorrect pronunciation. Play recording 1.8 item by item and ask: *How many syllables?* Then write the word, indicating the syllables, and model pronunciation. Underline the stressed syllable in each country.

> **Answers:** 1 India – 3 syllables   2 Australia – 4
> 3 Argentina – 4   4 Japan – 2   5 the US – 3   6 Brazil
> – 2   7 the UK – 3   8 Germany – 3   9 Italy – 3
> 10 Poland – 2

b▶ If you have fewer than 15 sts in your group, you can do this activity standing in a circle, with one student saying a city and throwing a ball to another student, who then gives the country, etc. Have everybody repeat all cities and countries, stamping their feet or bending their knees as they say the stressed syllable.

▶ **False beginners** Encourage them to try cities/ countries that weren't in the exercise, and help as necessary (see c below). Note these down and write them on the board afterwards.

c▶ Ask sts to shout out other countries they know, and write them on the board. Be careful – sts may give you languages/adjectives. Reject them, but don't explain at this stage (except possibly to false beginners). Point out that countries always start with a capital letter.

Lifelong learning

Encourage sts to keep a vocabulary folder, ideally an A4 ring binder. This is more flexible than a notebook they just add words to at random because they can add to and reorder the contents in order to organise their vocabulary in a meaningful and ultimately learner-friendly and useful way. Suggest to sts that they record vocabulary by themes or topics, giving a translation and example sentence. Writing new words in groups, e.g. with their opposites or related adjectives, nouns, etc. will also help.

> **OPTIONAL EXTENSION**
>
> Encourage sts to write a countries page for their vocabulary folders. Ask them to copy all the items from the board and from Ex. 4a onto a separate sheet, with the heading *Countries*. Collect them to correct at home. (*Alternative*: Bring in a map and ask sts to label as many countries as they can.)

Listening and reading

6a/b▶ Have a short exchange like the one in the How to … box with one of your sts (without telling them to look at the How to … box). Explain that sts will hear three short dialogues, and that they need to note down places. You may need to tell sts that the sentences in the exercise are not exactly what they'll hear in the dialogues.

▶ Play recording 1.9 for sts to make notes. Play it again item by item and ask: *Who is it? Where is it?* Sts will understand these questions. Don't write them on the board.

> **Answers:** 1 the UK   2 Brazil, Germany
> 3 Australia, the US

c▶ **Real beginners** Write *1 Martin – the UK, 2 Rachel – Germany, 3 Abby – the US* on the board. Ask sts to look at the How to … box. Play the beginning of each dialogue, press *pause*, and ask the class to say Martin's, Rachel's and Abby's line respectively.

▶ **All students** Ask sts to read the How to … box out loud with their partner. Then ask each student to write their name on two separate pieces of paper. Collect them and redistribute them. Ask sts to find and greet the two people whose names they've got. Before they start, deliberately address a student by a wrong name and elicit/demonstrate *Sorry, no* from that student. As sts mingle and interact, circulate and make sure everyone is active. Join in and/or correct as necessary. It doesn't matter whether sts know each other's names for this activity – if they don't, they'll learn them.

Grammar

7▶ Ask sts to go back to their seats, taking their two bits of paper with them. Ask individual sts to show you the names they had. Point to these sts and say *He's …* or *She's … .* Ask other sts to show the class the sts they talked to in Ex. 6c. Correct *He* and *She*.

▶ Ask sts to complete the Active grammar box, then ask a student to write the answers on the board. Draw male and female symbols next to *he* and *she*. Draw items, e.g. a table, a lamp, a cat, and write *Paris, New York* next to *it*.

> **Answers:** is   's   's

8a▶ Ask sts to complete the sentences. Explain that they shouldn't use the words in brackets but *He's, She's* or *It's*. Circulate and correct any mistakes you see. Go over the answers with the class by calling on individual sts to read out their sentences.

> **Answers:** 1 He's   2 She's   3 It's   4 She's   5 She's
> 6 It's   7 He's   8 It's

b▶ Write *True or false?* on the board and draw a happy face under *True* and an unhappy face under *False*. Say: *Sydney is in Australia – true or false?* If necessary, use more examples to establish meaning. Then ask sts to work in pairs, one of them giving a statement, the other commenting (and correcting if necessary).

c ▶ Sts need to know each other a little bit to talk about each other. If you feel they don't, put sts in groups of four and ask them to introduce themselves to the group while the others make notes. Then pair up members of different groups who exchange information about each other's group members.

Speaking

9 ▶ Ask sts to briefly discuss with a partner who the people in the picture are and where they are from. Elicit answers from the class. With false beginners, encourage sts to add ideas. Provide vocabulary.

> Answers: A She's Gisele Bündchen. She's from Brazil.
> B He's Michael Schumacher. He's from Germany.
> C She's Condoleezza Rice. She's from the US.   D He's Thierry Henry. He's from France.   E She's Penelope Cruz. She's from Spain.   F He's Prince William. He's from the UK.

1.3 Nice to meet you

In this lesson sts learn how to introduce someone and use conversational phrases when meeting people. You could bring in CDs for the 'cocktail party' suggestion in Ex. 4b. Grammar: *Where are you from?*

> **OPTIONAL WARMER**
>
> Play hangman with countries. Before you tell sts whether the letter is in the word, write it on the board to check if they meant what they said. To do this as a competitive game, form teams. A team can keep guessing as long as they guess correct letters. If they guess letters not in the country name, or say something that has already been said, or mispronounce a letter, it is the other team's turn.

Vocabulary

1a/b ▶ Ask sts to match the phrases and pictures. Play recording 1.10 and ask sts to check their answers. Go over the answers by asking individual sts to say the full phrase and imitate the intonation of the speaker. Play the recording again item by item and ask sts to repeat the phrases as a class.

Language note Differentiating *Pardon*, *Sorry* and *Excuse me* can be difficult for learners. Use this exercise to clarify the meanings and usage.

> Answers: 1 Yes, please.   2 No, thank you.   3 Nice to meet you.   4 Excuse me.   5 Sorry.   6 Pardon?

2 ▶ Ask sts to listen and note down (not say) the phrase they think appropriate. Play recording 1.11, then ask them to compare their ideas with a partner.

▶ This time ask sts to say the phrase they think is appropriate. Play recording 1.11 again, item by item, and invite sts to call out phrases. In a large group, call on individual sts. Once you have established the correct answer, model intonation again and have the whole class repeat the correct phrase.

> Answers: 1 Pardon?   2 Nice to meet you.
> 3 Yes, please./No, thanks.

Listening

3a ▶ **Real beginners** Ask sts to listen and number the sentences in the order they hear them. Play recording 1.12.

▶ **False beginners** Ask sts to read the sentences and decide on the correct order.

> Answers: 1 Hi, Boris.   2 Hi, Andy. This is Luisa.
> 3 Nice to meet you, Luisa.   4 Nice to meet you, too.

b ▶ Ask sts to listen (again) and check their answers. Play recording 1.12. Ask: *How many people are talking?* Draw three stick people on the board to demonstrate the conversation.

4a ▶ **Real beginners** Sts read the conversation in Ex. 3a in groups of three.

▶ **False beginners** Go to 4b.

b ▶ Ask the class to read the How to ... box and review *What's your name?* Write *I'm ...* , *This is ...* , *Nice to meet you* on the board. Ask sts to find a partner and introduce themselves. Make sure everyone is standing up. Explain that sts are at a cocktail party. When there is music playing, people move around the room with their partner. When the music stops, people talk to the pair next to them and introduce their partner. Pairs should try to meet as many other pairs as possible. Play some music (anything suitable), after about 15 seconds press *pause* for 30 seconds or so, and keep repeating this pattern. The activity should take about eight minutes (depending on class size).

Tip Get sts used to 'speaking on their feet'. What they've said without 'hiding' behind tables or books they are likely to remember when they need to speak spontaneously.

5a ▶ **Real beginners** Give sts 30 seconds to read the text, then ask them to listen and fill in the gaps. Play recording 1.13. Go over the answers by asking individual sts. Write the answers on the board. Explain that these words make a question, but the words are in the wrong order. Elicit *Where are you from?* and write this on the board. Ask a few sts: *Where are you from?* Elicit *I'm from ...* and write this on the board, too.

> Answers: 1 'm   2 are   3 you   4 from

b ▶ **Real beginners** Ensure that sts understand 'true or false'. Ask them to read the sentences and mark them true or false, then compare with a partner. Go over the answers by asking individual sts to read the statement and say *True* or *False*.

▶ Now ask two sts to read the dialogue out loud. Explain *Where are you from in ...?* by practising a few examples with sts, including *Where are you from in (name of city)?*, as this is what may be relevant to sts' conversations in Ex. 6.

> **Answers:** 1 F   2 W   3 F   4 F   5 W

5a/b ▶ False beginners Books closed. Explain that sts are going to listen to a conversation between Andy and Luisa about where they are from, and take notes. Play recording 1.13. If necessary, play the recording again. Read the statements from b and ask sts to note down whether they are true or false. Then go through the statements one by one, checking the answers – see above.

▶ Now ask sts to open the book and look at the dialogue. Ask them to fill in the gaps from memory. Go over the answers – see above, then ask two sts to read the dialogue to the class. Point out 'normal' intonation (*Where are you from?*) vs contrastive stress (*Where are you from?*). Encourage individual sts to ask other sts where they are from. Correct as necessary.

6a ▶ Real beginners In pairs, ask sts to read the dialogue from Ex. 5a.

▶ **False beginners** Go straight to 6b.

b ▶ Put sts in groups of three. Ask them to ask each other where they are from. Call on groups and ask sts to tell the class about the other two people in their group.

Grammar

7 ▶ Ask sts to match the questions, then go over the answers with the class. Explain that for question 1, both answers are possible, but that question 2 requires answer a.

> **Answers:** 1 a or b   2 a

8a/b ▶ Ask sts to work individually. For real beginners, it may be a good idea to write the exercise out in full. Ask sts to compare answers with a partner. To check the answers, ask one pair to read each dialogue. Correct as necessary.

> **Answers a:** 1 Where   2 I'm   3 Where   4 from   5 you
> 6 from   7 are   8 from

> **Answers b:** 1 Where are you from?   2 Where are you from   3 I'm from   4 Where are you from in

Pronunciation

9a/b ▶ Say: *Where are you from?* with the intonation of an automated voice, stressing each syllable to demonstrate that that is very difficult to understand. Ask sts to look at the sentences and decide which words should be stressed. Play recording 1.14 item by item and ask sts to repeat as a class or individually (depending on class size). Demonstrate reduced vowels (e.g. *from* /frəm/ in item 3).

Language note Rhythm and intonation are more important than exact pronunciation for sts to make themselves understood – it is difficult to follow rhythm-less speech, especially if it is fast.

> **Answers:** 1 Where are you from?   2 Where are you from in Poland?   3 I'm from Warsaw.

Speaking

10 ▶ Explain that sts will work in groups of three. Ask them to ask each other their names and where they are from. Remind them that when they speak English, they should be polite. After three minutes, ask one student from each group to move to the next group. That way you create an authentic situation in which someone introduces someone else to the newcomer. Again, sts exchange information for three minutes. Repeat twice. Circulate and correct as necessary.

1 Communication: Find a phone number

In this lesson sts learn how to find out a phone number from directory enquiries.

> **OPTIONAL WARMER**
>
> This activity revises numbers. Prepare a menu with 10 items numbered 0–9, each of which should be typical of one of the countries in the unit. Put it on an OHT or give each student a copy. Use words sts will probably know (e.g. *hamburger, vodka, paella, nasi goreng,* etc.). Elicit the countries associated with each dish: *Where is number 1 from? It's from Austria.*

1a ▶ Ask sts in pairs to identify the countries, then check the answers with the class.

> **Answers:** a Russia   b Mexico   c Spain   d Turkey
> e China   f Australia

b ▶ Ask sts to look at the table. Elicit/explain *country code* (by explaining *area code* first and giving the local area code as an example, and then the country code). Ask them to note down the country codes as they listen. Play recording 1.15. Note the codes down on an OHT, or write them on the board and cover them with a large sheet of paper. Ask individual sts to read the answers. Show the answers one by one for sts to check.

> **Answers:** Australia 61   China 86   Mexico 52
> Russia 7   Spain 34   Turkey 90

c ▶ Ask: *What's the country code for Japan?* Sts may say *eighty-one.* Explain that in English you use single numbers when you give telephone numbers. Ask for the country code for Brazil. Point out *double five.* Then ask for the UK code. Sts should manage *double four.*

▶ Point to *UK* and *US* on your OHT/the board and ask sts how to say these (*the UK, the US*). Then point to Turkey and ask a student to tell you the country code (90). Refer sts to the How to … box and explain *oh* vs. *zero.*

2a ▶ Ask: *Where do you find phone numbers?* Sts will probably say *the Internet, telephone/phone book, the telephone* (meaning directory enquiries). Ask for the number they call, write it on the board and explain that this is called *directory enquiries*. Ask sts to read the lines of the dialogue first, then listen and number them in order. Play recording 1.16.

> **Answers:** Rome   00 39 6812 941

b ▶ Ask sts to listen again and complete the information. Replay recording 1.16 .

> **Answers:** 1 A: Directory enquiries.   2 B: The Lamden Hotel, please.   3 A: Where is it?   4 B: It's in Rome, in Italy.   5 A: Thank you.   6 C: The number is: double 0 ...

3 ▶ Put sts in pairs and explain that they are going to role play a *directory enquiries* dialogue using the model in Ex. 2. Circulate and support as necessary.

> **OPTIONAL WRAP-UP**
>
> Ask sts to write a How to ... box with the heading *How to call directory enquiries* to add to their vocabulary folder.

Review and practice

1 ▶

> **Answers:** 1 A: I'm Maggie May. B: You're in room 511. 2 A: I'm Ruby Tuesday. B: You're in room 147.   3 A: I'm Peggy Sue. B: You're in room 312.

2 ▶

> **Answers:** 1 I'm, You're   2 You're   3 I'm, You're   4 I'm, You're

3 ▶

> **Answers:** 1 He's from   2 She's from   3 It's from   4 He's from   5 It's from   6 She's from   7 He's from   8 She's from   9 She's from   10 It's from

4 ▶

> **Answers:** 1 This   2 Where   3 I'm   4 in   5 are   6 from   7 is   8 are   9 you   10 the   11 in   12 I'm

5 ▶

> **Answers:** 1 Yes, please.   2 Nice to meet you, too. 3 Pardon?   4 Good afternoon.   5 Thank you.

Notes for using the Common European Framework (CEF)

CEF References

1.1 Can do: check into a hotel

CEF A1 descriptor: can handle numbers, quantities, cost and time (CEF page 80)

1.2 Can do: greet someone at the airport

CEF A1 descriptor: can make an introduction and use basic greeting and leave-taking expressions (CEF page 76)

1.3 Can do: introduce someone; start a conversation

CEF A1 descriptor: can establish basic social contact by using the simplest everyday polite forms of: greetings and farewells; introductions; saying *please, thank you, sorry,* etc. (CEF page 122)

CEF quick brief

The Common European Framework (CEF) has been produced by the Council of Europe as a means of ensuring parity in terms of language teaching and language qualifications across Europe. It can be downloaded as a PDF file for free from www.coe.int from the section on Language Policy. There is a link from the *Total English* website – see below.

The CEF is a reference document for language teaching professionals and recommends that language learners use a Portfolio to document, reflect on and demonstrate their progress. *Total English* has a Portfolio which can be downloaded from www.longman.com/totalenglish. You may want to print one copy for each learner for the class when you first introduce the role of the Portfolio and the tasks for each unit. Suggested Portfolio tasks can be found at the end of every unit of the *Total English Starter Teacher's Resource Book.*

CEF Portfolio task

Download the Total English Portfolio free from www.longman.com/totalenglish.

Objective: to introduce students to the Portfolio and help them understand how they will use it.

1 ▶ Before the class, print one copy of the Portfolio for each student.

2 ▶ In class, distribute the Portfolios and explain briefly the role of the three sections (Language Passport, Biography and Dossier). You may want to do this in the sts' first language.

3 ▶ Ask sts to write their name and other details on page 1, and to fill in their Personal Details in the Language Passport on page 4. As the same Portfolio template is used for higher levels as well, some of the sections, e.g. 'Your exams and certificates' (in English) may not be appropriate for students at this level, who may have had little or no instruction in English.

2 My life

Overview

Summary

Lesson 1: Sts listen to Sabrina talk about her family, then talk about their own families.

Lesson 2: Sts listen to people asking for and giving personal details, then practise exchanging information.

Lesson 3: Sts read information from a website which gives personal profiles. They discuss personal details, email addresses and jobs and then write a personal profile about themselves.

Communication: Sts discuss their favourite things: restaurants, singers, CDs, books, films, actors and websites.

Film bank: Favourites

An extract featuring three different speakers who each talk a little about their favourite city, actor, book and TV programme.

This short film can be used at the end of the unit.

For ways to use this short film in class, see Students' Book page 117 and Teacher's Resource Book pages 133 and 142.

Lead-in

OPTIONAL WARMER

This activity reviews the alphabet and introduces the topic of *family*. Books closed. Play hangman, using the word *family*. If only a few sts participate, call on other sts and ignore any other suggestions. Sts tend to confuse or mispronounce letters. Always write the letter that has been suggested on the board to show sts what they have actually said.

False beginners Once the word *family* is revealed, elicit related words and write them on the board. Model pronunciation and ask sts to repeat after you. Ask sts to copy all the items onto a blank page in their vocabulary folder, entitling it *Family*. Suggest writing male and female relations in different colours.

1a ▶ Point sts to photo A and say: *Karen and Luke are mother and son.* Ask sts to fill in the other words from the box.

Answers: 1 <u>mother</u>, son   2 <u>father</u>, <u>daughter</u>   3 sister, brother   4 <u>father</u>, son   5 wife, <u>husband</u>   6 mother, daughter

---

b ▶ Play recording 2.1 for sts to check their answers (see above). With sts standing up, play the recording item by item and ask them to repeat as a class, bending their knees on the stressed syllables. Demonstrate and 'conduct' as they do it. Listen out for *th* and silent *gh*, and correct pronunciation as necessary.

▶ False beginners may say things like *Luke is Karen's son.* Don't write it on the board at this stage.

2a ▶ Do this as a competitive game. Give sts a maximum of two minutes.

Answers: 1 <u>mo</u>bile phone   2 <u>phone</u>   3 phone <u>number</u>   4 email <u>add</u>ress   5 com<u>pu</u>ter   6 <u>web</u>site   7 <u>photo</u>   8 <u>pass</u>port   9 <u>first</u> name   10 <u>sur</u>name   11 <u>add</u>ress

---

b ▶ Ask sts to listen and repeat (see above for answers). Play recording 2.2 item by item. Use movement/gestures to emphasise word stress. Watch compound stress (the primary stress of the second part/word is reduced to secondary stress). Point out that *mobile phone*, *phone number* and *first name* are compounds, although written in two words.

3 ▶ Five-minute activity: using the pictures from the book or other similar pictures, ask sts, in pairs or small groups, to ask each other *What's this?* Circulate, listen and correct pronunciation.

2.1 My family

In this lesson sts listen to Sabrina talking about her family, then talk about their own families. For the optional extension activity in the speaking section, ask sts to bring photos of family and friends. Bring some photos of famous families, e.g. the Royal family, for those who forget. Grammar: *Who ...?; my.*

OPTIONAL WARMER

This activity reviews numbers and can be used to set up learning partnerships. Write figures 0–9 on the board and elicit the numbers. Then ask sts to write down three numbers. Ask three sts to come to the front of the class and say their numbers as if they were hotel room numbers. Line them up in numerical order and ask the rest of the class to give their numbers and find their place in the line. Split the line into pairs or threes and suggest that sts form a learning partnership or group, i.e. they ring or email each other to keep updated if someone misses class, or they could arrange to study together.

Listening

1a/b ▶ Ask sts to look at the photos and work out who is who, then check as they listen. Play recording 2.3.

> **Answers:** a Sofia   b Marek   c Carl   d Anna
> e Tom   f Sarah   g James

c ▶ Ask sts to look at the numbers and try to match ages to people before they listen to check. Write the numbers on the board, point at them and ask sts to give you the matching names. Confirm the answer by saying a full sentence, e.g. *Sabrina's 37 years old.* At this stage, don't ask sts to repeat these sentences.

> **Answers:** Tom 3   Anna 32   Marek 60   Sofia 57
> James 40   Sabrina 37   Sarah 1   Carl 26

Vocabulary

> **OPTIONAL VOCABULARY LEAD-IN**
>
> Books closed. Ask sts what a *teenager* is, and specifically what the age range is for a teenager (as sts may be unaware of where the 'teen' comes from, opinions may vary). Ask the class to collaborate to give you the numbers from 10 to 20. Real beginners will need help but are likely to know at least some of the numbers. Let them experiment putting them together from what they already know. Write numbers 10–20 out on the board/an OHT. Underline *teen*.

2a ▶ Books closed. Ask sts to listen and repeat. Play recording 2.4. Check that they get the word stress right, underline with gesture or movement.

Tip Successful language teaching employs movement and rhythm.

b ▶ Books closed. Wipe the board/switch off the OHP and ask sts, in pairs, to count to 20, taking turns. Circulate, listen and correct. Then ask sts to write out the numbers from 10 to 20. Sts check spelling against the book/OHT.

3a ▶ Books still closed. Write *20, 30, 40, 50, 60, 70, 80, 90* in a column on the board.

▶ Real beginners Model pronunciation. Write numbers as words against the figures. Add a column with 2–9, with 2 aligned next to 20, 3 next to 30, etc. and a column with 12–19 and ask sts to spell the numbers for you as you write them. Point out *5/five* and *15/fifteen* vs *50/fifty*, and *40/forty* vs *4/four* and *14/fourteen*.

▶ Books open. Ask sts to read as they listen and repeat. Play recording 2.5 item by item. Draw sts' attention to the hyphens.

▶ False beginners Elicit how to say the numbers. Correct pronunciation and word stress.

b ▶ Sts 'test' each other.

c ▶ Ask sts: *How old is Carl?* etc. They will probably give you just the number. Introduce *He's/She's … years old.* Draw sts' attention to the How to … box, and continue asking about the people's ages.

> **OPTIONAL EXTENSION**
>
> Ask a student: *How old are you?* and write the question on the board. Get sts to stand in a circle and throw a ball between them, asking each other how old they are (see Introduction, page 11). (*Alternative:* if exchanging this sort of personal information is not appropriate for the mix of sts in your class, ask them to be a character from Ex. 1.)

Grammar

4a ▶ Ask sts to complete the Active grammar box individually. Go over the answers, pointing out the usage of contractions vs full forms. Model the /z/ sound and ask a few sts to repeat (further practice of this follows in Ex. 6).

> **Answers:** he   She

5 ▶ Ask sts to read the dialogues aloud in pairs twice, changing roles. Ask them to convey through tone/intonation how the people feel (scared, surprised, etc.). Circulate and correct as necessary (especially /z/).

> **Answers:** 1 A: he B: my   2 A: Who's B: She's
> 3 A: he B: He's my   4 A: Who's B: He's my

6a/b ▶ Ask sts to write answers individually, then compare with a partner and read the questions and answers in b aloud. Circulate and check spelling.

▶ False beginners Ask sts to close their books and explain that you are going to do a little quiz with them, asking the questions as in Ex. 6b. To make it more difficult, you can change the perspective, e.g. you are Carl and ask: *Who's my sister?*

> **Answers a:** 1 Carl is my brother.   2 Anna is my sister.   3 Marek is my father.   4 Sofia is my mother.   5 Sarah is my daughter.   6 Tom is my son.   7 James is my husband.

> **Answers b:** 1 Who's Marek?   2 Who's Carl?
> 3 Who's Sofia?   4 Who's Anna?   5 Who's Tom?
> 6 Who's James?   7 Who's Sarah?

Pronunciation

7a/b ▶ Ask sts to read and circle the number they hear as they listen. Play recording 2.6. For each sentence in turn, call on individual sts to read out the sentences and write the number they say on the board. Confirm that the number they said is what they wanted to say. Correct if necessary.

▶ Ask: *Which of these are teenagers?* Underline the relevant numbers and write them out as words. Ask sts to get up and demonstrate stress to contrast, e.g. 16 and 60 by bending your knees on the stressed syllable. Ask sts to repeat. (*Quick follow-on:* Ask sts to play bingo in small groups, only using numbers 13–19 and 30–90. Alternatively, ask sts to dictate numbers to the class which they note down first.)

Speaking

8a/b ▶ Ask sts to write a list of names. Then, in pairs, they ask and answer.

> **OPTIONAL EXTENSION**
>
> Sts need photos of family members for this exercise. Ask them to show their partners their photos and to ask/talk about the people in the pictures. Circulate and correct as necessary. This exercise may generate additional vocabulary which you will need to provide. Write new words on the board and go over them with the class after this activity. For those who forget to bring a photo, provide photos of famous families to talk about.

Lifelong learning

Authentic communication between sts generally takes place before or after class. Use their natural curiosity about each other to create authentic 'small talk' situations in class. The optional extension activities throughout this Teacher's Resource Book provide ideas for this. Also, picking up on a student conversation in English is a good way to effect the transition between break and class time and encourages sts to talk about themselves in English. In these small talk situations you may need to go beyond the grammar and vocabulary you have covered in class. Encourage sts to experiment and help them so that what they add in is in the range of their language abilities (a method called *scaffolding*). Students will enjoy real communication in English, and this prepares them for using English in the real world.

> **OPTIONAL WRAP-UP**
>
> Books closed. Brainstorm all family-related vocabulary with the class and extend this, e.g. by adding terms like *niece, nephew*. Write them on the board. You could ask sts to copy them onto the family page in their vocabulary folders (colour-coded for male and female) and to write *He's my .../She's my .... He/She is ... years old* at the bottom.

2.2 What's your phone number?

In this lesson sts listen to various dialogues that ask for and give personal details, and practise exchanging information. To create a semi-authentic situation in which sts are likely to give personal information, you could prepare forms (e.g. hotel forms) for sts to fill in for Ex. 4. Grammar: *What's your ...?*

> **OPTIONAL WARMER**
>
> This activity reviews family vocabulary and extends listening skills. Prepare a short text about yourself and your family. Sts are always curious to know who their teacher is. Use short sentences, but include phrases like *lives in* and *has* over and above what sts have learnt; possibly even *like* + sports, e.g. *like skiing*, etc., with 'international' words. Use repetition. Explain that you are going to tell sts about your family, and ask them to draw an illustrated family tree as you speak. Ask sts to compare notes and then have two or three sts draw their results on the board. Elicit or repeat what you've told them, pointing at the relevant parts of the family tree.

Listening

1a/b ▶ Ask sts to listen and mark the addresses they hear. Play recording 2.7. Ask them to repeat the addresses. Listen for word stress in items 3 and 5 (*-ty* vs *-teen*).

> **Answers:** 1a 2b 3b 4a 5b

2a/b ▶ Ask sts to look at the list of information about Ben and elicit words for the sort of information to expect, e.g. *surname, country, address*. Then play recording 2.8 (twice if necessary). Call on individual sts and write the answers they give on the board.

> **Answers:** a Gibson b Australia c 29 d 17, Road e 0208 391 224 f 078 724 91

Vocabulary

> **OPTIONAL VOCABULARY LEAD-IN**
>
> Ask sts what sort of situation they think recording 2.8 was, and how they liked the music. Draw happy and unhappy faces on the board and elicit relevant adjectives.

3a ▶ Model pronunciation of the five adjectives. Explain that they refer to what the people would like to express, not how they feel. Ask sts to read out and mime the words to give the answers.

> **Answers:** 1 It's bad. 2 It's OK. 3 It's good. 4 It's great. 5 It's awful.

b ▶ Explain that sts are going to listen to the judges' comments. Ask them to note them down as they listen. Play recording 2.9.

> **Answers:** Ben: He's awful. Terri: She's good. Vittoria: She's OK. Hans: He's great. Sanjay: He's bad.

c ▶ Play the recording again for sts to note down what they think. In pairs, ask sts to compare their ideas, using the sample dialogue as a guide. Have a vote on who sts think is best/worst.

d ▶ Brainstorm a few names before sts comment on them in pairs. You could bring in a few samples to listen to and ask sts to comment on them.

Grammar

> **OPTIONAL GRAMMAR LEAD-IN**
>
> Replay recording 2.8 and ask sts to note down the questions the judges ask Ben.

4a/b ▶ Ask sts to complete the table individually. Go over the answers by asking one student to read out the full question and another student to find the matching picture in b. Remind sts that phone numbers are given in individual digits (except double numbers), and in blocks of three or four, see Reference page 17.

> **Answers a:** name   your   phone   number

> **Answers b:** 1 What's your name?   2 What's your mobile phone number?   3 What's your address? 4 What's your phone number?

5a/b ▶ Ask sts to cover the Active grammar box and write down the questions from memory, then check against the box. Then ask sts to read the dialogues with a partner twice, changing roles. Circulate.

> **Answers:** 1 What's your phone number?   2 What's your address?   3 What's your mobile phone number?   4 What's your name?

Speaking

6a ▶ Ask sts to listen and note down the information. Play recording 2.10. Go over the answers, asking sts to spell the items for you, and write them on the board. Elicit what questions were asked in the recording. Refer sts back to the Active grammar box.

> **Answers:** 1 Simon Ambrose.   2 82 via Speranza, Rome.

b ▶ Ask sts to look at the How to ... box and invite two sts to read the dialogue.

7a/b ▶ Put sts into groups of four and ask them to decide who is who. They then exchange information. Circulate, listen and correct.

> **OPTIONAL WRAP-UP**
>
> Ask sts, in small groups, to brainstorm all the questions they have learnt so far. Pool information as a class and write the questions on the board. These should include *What's your name/address/ phone number? Where are you from? How old are you? Who's he/she?* Sts may suggest *Who are you? What's your job?* Elicit *Yes/No* questions by writing on the board: *... from Italy? Yes, I am.*
>
> Sts could write these down on a *Questions* page for their vocabulary folders.
>
> If time permits, ask them to interview a partner, using all the questions – if sts are comfortable with exchanging personal information.
>
> If you don't do the wrap-up at the end of the lesson, you can use it as a warmer for the next lesson.

2.3 Email friends

In this lesson sts read information from a website, giving brief personal profiles. They discuss personal details, email addresses and jobs and write a personal profile about themselves. Grammar: *his/her*.

> **OPTIONAL WARMER**
>
> Books closed. Prepare simple role cards, one per student, with a name, country of origin and telephone number. Use characters from the book and invent additional characters as required. Bring in music to play. Play 'cocktail party' (see Introduction, page 11: sts walk around as you play some music). When you stop the music, they talk to the person nearest to them, asking them about their identity and answering their questions.

Reading and listening

> **OPTIONAL LEAD-IN**
>
> Explain that sts are going to look at a website called *Email friends*. Ask them what they expect to find. Elicit a few ideas, but don't comment.

1a ▶ Scanning activity: read out the question. Then ask sts to open their books and give them 30 seconds to find the answers. Ask sts to shout out their answers.

> **Answers:** a Germany   b Canada   c Japan

b ▶ Ask sts to read and complete the sentences as they listen. Explain that they are going to listen to two people talking about the website. Play recording 2.11. Go over the answers as a class and write them on the board. Model and practise pronunciation of new words (jobs) and ask various sts to spell them.

Answers: a teacher   b accountant   c student

2a ▶ Write Frieda's email address on the board and ask various sts to say it. Circle the @ and write *at*, and the dot and write *dot*. Draw sts' attention to the How to … box.

▶ Dictate your email address to the sts, then write it on the board for them to check.

b ▶ Ask sts to exchange email addresses amongst each other. To make this authentic, explain that sts will be given email homework (see Ex. 10).

Tip It is useful to have email contact with your sts. Create a separate address if you don't want to use your personal one. You could suggest that sts do this as well, if they prefer. You could create a mailing list and write to your sts once a week. A sentence or two will do. It will help build sts' confidence. As a first email, you could write *Hi! This is how you start and end an email. Best wishes*.

3 ▶ Write *She's…* and *He's…* on the board. Ask sts to look at the website for a minute, then to close their books. Ask them to note down what they remember about the three people. Put sts in groups of three to exchange information. Circulate and monitor. Sts stay in these groups for the next exercise.

Vocabulary

4a ▶ In their groups of three, ask sts to match the pictures to the jobs. Allow for more than one item per job if sts don't come to an agreement. As they won't know the words, ask them to talk about *pictures 1–10*.

Answers: 1 doctor   2 artist   3 teacher   4 student 5 actor   6 police officer   7 engineer   8 accountant 9 sales assistant   10 manager

b ▶ Ask sts to listen and check their answers (see above). Play recording 2.12. Sts may ask what the items are in English. Elicit vocabulary they know and provide the rest. Leave this vocabulary exercise out if no one asks about the words or begins looking them up in a dictionary.

▶ Ask sts to listen again and underline the stressed syllables. Play the recording item by item and ask the class to repeat, emphasising the stressed syllable with a gesture or movement. Model and 'conduct' this.

Grammar 1

5 Ask sts to look at the Active grammar box and elicit the rule. Ask sts to complete the gaps.

Answers: an   a

6a ▶ Ask sts to listen and complete the sentences. Play recording 2.13. Check the answers together and write them on the board.

▶ Play the recording again, item by item, and ask sts to repeat.

Answers: 1 a teacher   2 actor   3 a student 4 an engineer

b ▶ Sts should write the items from Ex. 4a into the table individually, then check with a partner. Ask sts to say the words to check whether the article they have chosen 'sounds right'.

Answers: a: doctor   teacher   student   manager sales assistant   police officer   doctor; an: accountant   engineer   artist

c ▶ Ask sts to make notes before they talk to their partner.

Grammar 2

7 ▶ Ask sts to fill the gaps individually, then check with a partner. Practise pronunciation of *his* vs *he's*. As you go over the answers, ask sts to spell the answer for you. Correct/model pronunciation where necessary.

Answers: His   his   He's   Her   her   She's

8 ▶ With slower learners, ask sts to do 1–6 first and go over the answers and then do 6–12. In other classes, sts will manage to do 1–12 straight through. Ask them to fill in the answers individually and ask pairs of sts to read couplets. Correct any mispronunciation, particularly of *his/he's*.

Answers: 1 his   2 His   3 He's   4 he   5 He's   6 his 7 she   8 She's   9 She's   10 her   11 She's   12 her

Speaking

9 ▶ Refer sts to the Active grammar box for the questions they need to use. Write *his* with a male symbol and *her* with a female symbol on the board for everyone to see. As sts work in pairs, circulate and support. If you feel sts need further guided practice, ask them to change roles and do the exercise again. Otherwise go to Ex. 10.

Writing

Tip Writing helps sts build their language, even if what they need primarily is speaking skills. It is a good idea to do some writing in class, but the bulk of it can often be done at home.

10a ▶ Ask sts to write a short profile about themselves, as in the example. False beginners may be able to give details (job, family, age, country of origin, address, telephone number, email address). As sts write, circulate, help and correct. Ask them to write on a separate piece of paper. Collect and redistribute them.

b ▶ Ask sts to read through the profile and then present the other person to the class without mentioning his or her name. The rest of the class guess who it is. Gently correct the use of *his* and *her*.

▶ If you do not want to spend class time on Ex. 10, do the preparation and the follow-up in class. Ask sts to send their profiles to their partners by email, or to exchange them at the beginning of the next lesson, and to prepare a little talk introducing their partner to the class.

2 Communication: My favourite singer is …

In this lesson sts discuss their favourite restaurant/singer/CD/book/film, etc. and review the unit's language.

> **OPTIONAL WARMER**
>
> This activates and teaches relevant vocabulary and introduces the topic. Draw five faces (from enthusiastic to very negative) on the board and write the names of singers/films/books or similar items against them according to what you think about them. Elicit sentences from sts that convey this (*X is great/good/OK/awful*, etc.). Write the words on the board.
>
> Pick the item you wrote against the enthusiastic happy faces and say: *X is my favourite (singer/ actor, etc.). I like him/her/it best.*

1a ▶ You could put the words/pictures on cards and do this as a pair finding game (see Introduction, page 11). Pairs then match the rest of the pictures and words.

> **Answers:** 1 singer   2 restaurant   3 book   4 actor
> 5 website   6 city   7 CD   8 film

b ▶ Nominate two sts to demonstrate the question and answer. Model pronunciation if necessary. Then sts ask and answer in pairs.

2a ▶ Ask sts in groups of three to find three to five examples for each category.

b ▶ Put sts from different groups together in pairs and ask them to test each other. Before they begin, ask two sts to read the example. Elicit the difference between *Who's* and *What's* to remind sts.

3 ▶ **Real beginners** Ask sts to look at the table and write questions.

▶ **False beginners** Books closed. Use the words in the table to make questions for a dictation. Model question intonation. Ask sts to check their spelling against the book and to write a few more questions. Elicit ideas. Ask the class to repeat. 'Conduct' and correct pronunciation/intonation.

> **Answers:** What's your favourite restaurant?   What's your favourite website?   Who's your favourite actor? What's your favourite CD?   What's your favourite city?   Who's your favourite singer?   What's your favourite film?   What's your favourite book?

4 ▶ Ask sts to note down their own favourites first. If they find it difficult to decide, say/explain *at the moment*. Then ask them to interview each other, using the questions from b.

5a/b ▶ Ask sts to interview three more people. In a small group, elicit the results with the whole group and put together class statistics. This may result in the class deciding to go to a concert or film.

> **OPTIONAL WRAP-UP/UNIT REVIEW**
>
> Prepare a set of cards with matching questions and answers from the unit. Ideally, these should be on A4 paper with large print. Give one to each student. Sts mingle, read out their questions/answers to each other until they find the matching answer and then stand next to their partner. Pairs then read out their questions and answers and pin them up on the board. Ask sts whether they would like to add anything. If so, write it on the board. Sts could copy them onto a blank page for their vocabulary folders, with the title *Asking for and giving personal information*.

Review and practice

1 ▶

> Answers: 1 Julia's my   2 Adele's my   3 Karl's my
> 4 Karl's my   5 David's my   6 Adele's my   7 Julia's my
> 8 David's my

2 ▶

> Answers: 1 Who's Julia?   2 Who's Adele?   3 Who's Karl?
> 4 Who's Karl?   5 Who's David?   6 Who's Adele?
> 7 Who's Julia?   8 Who's David?

3 ▶

> Answers: 1 What's your address?   2 What's your phone
> number?   3 What's your mobile phone number?
> 4 How old are you?   5 Where are you from?   6 How do
> you spell that, please?

4 ▶

> Answers: 1 What's your name?   2 How do you spell
> that, please?   3 How old are you?   4 Where are you
> from?   5 What's your address?   6 What's your phone
> number?

5 ▶

> Answers: 1 What's her first name?   2 How old is she?
> 3 What's her job?   4 Where is she from?   5 What's his
> first name?   6 How old is he?   7 What's his job?
> 8 Where is he from?

6 ▶

> Answers: 1 twelve   2 doctor   3 address   4 accountant
> 5 singer   6 phone number

Notes for using the Common European Framework (CEF)

CEF References

2.1 Can do: give basic information about your family

CEF A1 descriptor: can reply in an interview to simple direct questions spoken very slowly and clearly in direct, non-idiomatic speech about personal details (CEF page 82)

2.2 Can do: ask for and give personal details

CEF A1 descriptor: can ask and answer questions about themselves and other people, where they live, people they know, things they have (CEF page 81)

2.3 Can do: give information about other people; write a short personal profile

CEF A1 descriptor: can ask for or pass on personal details in written form (CEF page 83)

CEF quick brief

One feature of the CEF is its focus not on grammatical structures, but on the real life uses a learner can make of their language in order to achieve real life goals. Adopting what it calls 'an action-oriented approach' (CEF page 9), the CEF lists a number of *Can do* statements, which cover a range of practical applications across the four skills, from writing postcards to asking for things.

The final column of each unit of the *Total English Starter Teacher's Resource Book* links the CEF's *Can do* statements to the content of each unit of the Student's Book. For example, on page 25, sts are asked to write a short personal profile of someone. This relates to the following CEF descriptor, worded as a *Can do* statement:

'can write simple phrases and sentences about themselves and imaginary people, where they live and what they do' (CEF page 62)

The Teacher's Resource Book features three such links from each unit, although these are intended as a sample rather than an exhaustive list. In this way, you, as the teacher, can see how the *Total English* syllabus is connected to the CEF.

CEF Portfolio task

Download the Total English Portfolio free from www.longman.com/totalenglish.

Objectives: to familiarise students with the procedure of updating their Language Biography; to introduce the role of the dossier.

1 ▶ Refer sts to the Update grid on page 3.

2 ▶ Explain that the portfolio is a kind of diary which they can update as often as they like. Point out the Guidelines for updating your portfolio, and ask which section should be added to most often (the Language Biography). You may wish to make a recommendation appropriate to your teaching situation, e.g. that sts update it every time they finish a unit of the Students' Book, or that they do it either for homework or in class once a fortnight.

3 ▶ Encourage sts to use both columns (the *I need more help with this* as well as the *I can do this*, in order for the activity to be meaningful.

4 ▶ For each student, select one piece of work you feel they have completed well and recommend that it be logged as their first contribution to the dossier.

5 ▶ Explain the role of the dossier and tell sts that they should aim to add to it regularly, and document the process on page 18 of the Portfolio.

Overview

Lead-in	**Vocabulary:** tourist sights, places in town
3.1	**Grammar:** *we're/they're*; affirmative of *to be*; *our/their*
	Vocabulary: basic adjectives
	Can do: write a simple holiday email
3.2	**Grammar:** plural nouns; negative of *to be*
	Vocabulary: holiday things
	Can do: say what's in your suitcase
3.3	**Grammar:** *Yes/No* questions with *to be*
	Vocabulary: days of the week; *here*, *there*; prepositions
	Can do: ask for tourist information
Com. Focus	See you on Friday – an everyday telephone conversation

Summary

Lesson 1: Sts talk and write an email about a holiday.

Lesson 2: Sts talk about what they pack for a holiday, expanding their holiday-related vocabulary.

Lesson 3: Sts read leaflets and ask for and give information about tourist attractions.

Communication: Sts have a simple telephone conversation.

Film bank: Across Canada

An extract which details a five-day journey across Canada, from Peggy's Cove in Nova Scotia to Vancouver on the west coast.

Possible places to use this short film are:

▶ after 3.2

▶ after 3.3

▶ at the end of the unit

For ways to use this short film in class, see Students' Book page 118 and Teacher's Resource Book pages 134 and 143.

Lead-in

OPTIONAL WARMER

This activity introduces and personalises the topic. Books closed. Pretend you are, or dress up as, a tourist (e.g. with map, camera, sunglasses) and ask sts: *What am I?* Elicit *tourist*. Write *sightseeing* on the board and ask: *In your town, what must a tourist see?* Brainstorm tourist sights in the area. Accept suggestions in L1 and provide/elicit language. Introduce vocabulary from Exs. 1 and 2 if an opportunity presents itself. Write all suggestions on the board or on an OHT and model pronunciation.

1a ▶ Point to the photos and ask *What are these?* Elicit answers from the class, referring sts to the box if necessary. Model and correct pronunciation.

Answers: A: a castle B: a cathedral
C: a museum D: a palace

b ▶ To make this more memorable, hand out small cards to groups of four. Ask sts to draw sketches of the items on one side of a card, and write the word on the other side, checking against a dictionary if necessary. They should draw a set of cards between them. Prepare a 'word box' for each group to collect their cards in. Ask them to write their names on their box. If possible, keep them in the classroom to use for vocabulary practice and revision activities.

c ▶ **Real beginners** Ask sts to listen, read the words in boxes 1a and b and underline the stressed syllables. Play recording 3.1.

▶ To go over the answers, ask a student to give you the stressed syllable and repeat the word, then get the whole class to repeat. 'Conduct'. It may be necessary to play the recording again, item by item. Go through any additional vocabulary on the board from the warmer activity. Model pronunciation and ask the class to repeat. Underline the stressed syllables.

▶ **False beginners** Ask sts to close their books and write down the words they are going to hear. Play recording 3.1. Then have them check their spelling against the boxes in Exs. 1a and b and underline the stressed syllables.

Answers: a <u>cas</u>tle   a ca<u>thed</u>ral   a <u>pal</u>ace
a mu<u>se</u>um   a <u>gall</u>ery   a de<u>part</u>ment <u>store</u>
a <u>mar</u>ket   a <u>moun</u>tain   a <u>lake</u>

2a ▶ Elicit which palaces sts can think of. They are likely to come up with *Buckingham Palace*. Write this on the board and point out that *Palace*, as part of a name, is capitalised. Ask sts to look at number 3 and to write the answer, then to find the other answers. Go over the answers as a class.

Answers: 1 Castle   2 Museum   3 Palace
4 market   5 department store   6 Mountain
7 Lake   8 Gallery

b ▶ To introduce this exercise, look at the ideas you collected in the warmer activity and add places/find examples for them. Then ask sts to brainstorm further ideas and write them on the board.

OPTIONAL EXTENSION

Look at the ideas on the board, and write a *?* against the ones you don't know and a *!* against the ones you know. Say: *I know X in Y* and write this on the board. Ask sts to tell their partners which ones they know. Circulate and monitor.

3 ▶ Go back to the places you've collected on the board. This time, label them with happy faces or + symbols, making very clear which one is your favourite. Say: *X in Y is my favourite tourist attraction (in Mexico/ England, etc.).* Then ask a student: *What's your favourite tourist attraction?* Repeat around the class.

3.1 We're in Istanbul

In this lesson sts talk about and write an email about a holiday. For further practice after Ex. 1, ask sts to bring in postcards of sights they know. Also bring a few yourself in case sts forget. Grammar: the verb *to be* with *we* and *they*; *our* and *their*.

> **OPTIONAL WARMER**
>
> If sts made word boxes in the Lead-in (see Ex. 1b), ask them to work in the same groups. Give each group their box. Ask sts to practise the words from the boxes and to talk about their favourite lake/ mountain/palace, etc. Ask them to write a sample sentence on the back of each card. Alternatively, write the new vocabulary from the Lead-in on the board and ask sts, in groups, to talk about their favourite places.

> **OPTIONAL EXTENSION**
>
> If you develop word boxes, encourage the groups to add to their box each lesson, by writing out cards of important verbs or phrases. Practise using the cards.

Vocabulary

1a ▶ **Real beginners** In (their word box) groups, ask sts to match the places and sights. They could add any new words (e.g. *bridge, tower*) to their word box.

> **Answers:** 1 Maiden's Tower in Istanbul.　2 Willy Brandt House in Berlin.　3 The House of the People in Bucharest.　4 The Burgtheatre in Vienna. 5 Charles Bridge in Prague.　6 Spaghetti Junction in Birmingham.

b ▶ Ask sts to decide in their groups which adjectives apply (allow more than one answer if sts can explain, e.g. *the Burgtheatre (as a building) is old. The 'theatre' is modern.).* Circulate and answer vocabulary questions/ provide language. Pool ideas.

> **Answers:** 1 Maiden's Tower is small.　2 Willy Brandt House is modern.　3 The House of the People is big.　4 The Burgtheatre is old.　5 Charles Bridge is beautiful.　6 Spaghetti Junction is ugly.

1a/b ▶ **False beginners** Sts may be able to go through this quickly. You could even ask them to look at a and b for a minute and then ask them to close their books and tell you about the pictures.

> **OPTIONAL EXTENSION**
>
> Using the picture postcards sts have brought (or the ones you provide – everybody should have at least three), ask sts to look at their pictures and note down a few ideas. Then ask them to stand in two concentric circles, the inner circle facing outwards, the outer circle facing inwards, so that everybody has a partner to talk to. Sts show each other their postcards and explain what they are. After two minutes, ask one circle of sts to move on to the next partner.

2 ▶ You could extend the postcard theme by asking sts to think of something interesting to say about the sights on their postcards. Alternatively, ask sts to choose places they know and talk about them.

Reading

> **OPTIONAL READING LEAD-IN**
>
> This activates sts' ideas about holiday emails and elicits relevant language. Elicit ideas about what sts say in a letter or postcard. Make notes on the board. Ask: *Do you write postcards when you are on holiday? Do you write emails when you are on holiday?*

3a ▶ Ask sts to read the email. Ask them to check whether Rebecca writes about the same things they write about (compare with the notes on the board). Ask: *Who is in the photo in the email?*

> **Answers:** Magda and Zarek are in the photo.

b ▶ Give sts three minutes to find the answers. Check them by asking individual sts to read the relevant sentence in the email.

> **Answers:** 1 T　2 F　3 F　4 F　5 T

▶ Go through email terminology with sts (*attachment, subject line, to, from, cc, bcc*) and ask them to read the email addresses aloud.

c ▶ Elicit one or two adjectives to make sure everybody knows what an adjective is. Go through the adjectives in turn. Explain that there is a difference between *We are fine* and *to be good*; and between *great* and *big*. Explain *How are you?*

> **Answers:** fine　great　big　beautiful

Grammar 1

4 ▶ Ask sts to fill in the Active grammar box individually. Check the answers and write them on the board. Remind sts when to use full forms and when to use short forms.

> **Answers:** 're (are) – for both gaps

5 ▶ Ask sts to fill in the words individually. Ask them to close their books and dictate the correct sentences to them. As you dictate the sentences, write the answer for each gap on the board. Ask sts to check their answers in the book first and then their spelling.

> **Answers:** 1 're   2 're   3 're   4 's   5 's   6 'm   7 're   8 's

Grammar 2

6 ▶ Ask sts to find the words they need to complete the Active grammar box in Rebecca's email (Ex. 3) and shout out the answers. Write the answers on the board. Model pronunciation/intonation. Ask sts to repeat the sentences. 'Conduct' them.

> **Answers:** our   Their

7 ▶ Ask sts to work individually. Go over the answers, asking sts to give full sentences. Correct intonation as necessary.

> **Answers:** Their   2 Our   3 Their   4 Their   5 Our   6 Our

8 ▶ Ask a student to read the example and make sure sts understand the idea. Ask them to circle the correct word, then go over the answers asking sts to give you full sentences. Point out that some of them are questions. Correct intonation (model if necessary). Ask sts what rule they can see here. Elicit that possessive adjectives are used with a noun, like other adjectives.

Language note Sts may try to find a difference in pronunciation between *they're* and *their*. Explain that there is no difference – see Pronunciation warmer.

> **Answers:** 1 our   2 They're   3 We're   4 We're   5 Their   6 They're   7 our   8 They're

Pronunciation

> **OPTIONAL PRONUNCIATION LEAD-IN**
>
> Books closed. Explain that you are going to read the sentences from Ex. 8 and that sts need to decide whether they hear *they're* or *their* (no pronunciation difference). Sts must think about the meaning of the sentence to decide which word they hear. Read the sentences, then go over the answers carefully.

9a ▶ Explain that sts are going to do a dictation. Play recording 3.2 item by item. As you play the recording, write the sentences on the board or an OHT, leaving a gap for *their/they're*. Ask sts to check their spelling against the board/OHT. Then call on individual sts to give you *their* or *they're*, and write the answers on the board/OHT.

> **Answers:** 1 They're from Spain.   2 Their mother is Tina.   3 Their hotel is in Vienna.   4 They're students.   5 They're in Istanbul.   6 Where is their camera?

b ▶ Ask individual sts to read the full sentences from the board/OHT. Correct/model pronunciation and intonation. Ask the whole class to repeat and 'conduct' intonation.

Writing

10a ▶ Ask sts to agree where they would like to go, and to write an email from there together. Ask them to copy the sentences, using their individual ideas.

▶ **False beginners** Encourage sts to go beyond the given ideas, e.g. by describing the tourist attraction in their picture. Circulate and support.

b ▶ Refer sts to the Writing bank at the back of the book. Ask them to exchange email addresses with their partners and to write them a holiday email.

3.2 What's in your suitcase?

In this lesson sts expand their holiday-related vocabulary and talk about what they pack for a holiday. Grammar: negative of *to be*; plural nouns.

> **OPTIONAL WARMER**
>
> Draw a suitcase on the board and ask: *What's in your suitcase?* Brainstorm basic vocabulary, eliciting items from the lesson, and write all the items on the board. Clarify their meaning and model pronunciation.

Vocabulary

1a ▶ Ask sts to look at the pictures, then ask about each item: *What's number 1?* etc. Encourage sts to shout out their answers. Add any items not covered in the brainstorming to those on the board. Put sts in groups to add the new words to their word boxes or vocabulary folders.

> **Answers:** 1 a suitcase   2 a map   3 a top   4 a camera   5 a pair of shoes   6 a book   7 a pair of trousers   8 a skirt   9 a backpack   10 an MP3 player

b ▶ Ask sts to listen and underline the stressed syllables (see above). Play recording 3.3. Ask sts to stand, play the recording again, item by item, and get sts to repeat, underlining word stress through movement. 'Conduct'. Watch unstressed *of* /əv/.

Listening

2 ▶ Ask sts to listen and identify which conversation matches which suitcase. Play recording 3.4. Elicit answers.

> Answers: 1C 2A 3B

Grammar 1

3a ▶ Write out the Active grammar box on the board, leaving the plural *s* off the nouns in the right-hand column. Play the 3rd conversation in recording 3.4 again, then point to *one book* and ask: *one book?* Elicit *two books*. Complete the gap and add the *s* to *book*. Repeat for the other items.

> Answers: two three shoes

b ▶ Ask sts to listen to the three dialogues and continue the list of items. Play recording 3.4, twice if necessary.

c ▶ Ask sts to compare their lists with their partner's. Then play the recording again for sts to check their answers.

> Answers: Dialogue 1: a map a camera two books
> a top two pairs of trousers a pair of shoes
> Dialogue 2: two cameras an MP3 player a pair of
> shoes two skirts three tops three books
> a backpack
> Dialogue 3: a camera two maps two books
> three tops an MP3 player a pair of trousers
> a skirt five pairs of shoes

Pronunciation

> **OPTIONAL PRONUNCIATION LEAD-IN**
>
> This introduces relevant phonetic symbols and sounds. Books closed. Write *palace*, *museum* and *market* on the board. Ask sts to make these plural. Write the plurals and model pronunciation. Write the corresponding phonetic symbols under the words. Make sure you demonstrate the difference between /z/ and /s/.

4a ▶ Ask sts to open their books and look at the list of words. Explain that they are going to listen to these words and then decide which word has which pronunciation. Play recording 3.5. Elicit the answers by asking sts to tell you whether it is like *markets*, *museums* or *palaces*.

> Answers: a /ɪz/ b /s/ c /s/ d /z/ e /z/
> f /s/ g /z/ h /s/

b ▶ With a small class, ask individual sts to repeat. With a large class, ask sts to repeat as a class and ask one or two sts to repeat individual words. Play the recording item by item. If sts find it difficult to imitate the recording, model the pronunciation.

▶ Ask sts to work out a rule. They will probably find a rule for /ɪz/. Explain the difference between /s/ and /z/ as voiced and unvoiced and explain that you use /s/ after unvoiced sounds (/p/, /t/, /k/) because it is easier to pronounce it that way.

Lifelong learning

Write *camera, Japan* and *trousers* on the board. Ask a few sts to say them. Show how the stress is in different places in different words and how some written vowels are not pronounced at all, e.g. *camera* has two syllables in English. Underline the stressed syllables. Circle unstressed vowels and remind sts of the schwa /ə/ sound. Ask sts to read the Lifelong learning box.

Speaking

5a ▶ Put sts in pairs. Ask them to look at the pictures on page 32 and describe one of the suitcases to their partner until he/she guesses correctly. They change roles. Circulate and correct pronunciation.

▶ **False beginners** With stronger sts, you could go straight to 5b.

b ▶ Ask sts to work together to remember the items.

c ▶ Play a game of 'I pack my suitcase' – a memory and vocabulary game. One student begins by saying: *I pack my suitcase. Two skirts.* The next student repeats what the first one said and adds an item, the third repeats everything and adds an item, etc. Go round the class until someone makes a mistake in the order or number of items, or can't think of anything to add. Nouns can't be reused and sts must give the quantity of each item.

Listening

6a ▶ Books closed. Ask sts: *Who asks you 'What's in your suitcase?'* Elicit/teach *airport, customs.* Ask sts to listen and note down the woman's name and what's in her suitcase. Play recording 3.6. Ask sts to compare answers with a partner. Play the recording again if necessary. Elicit the answers. Watch pronunciation of *Miss* /s/ vs *Mrs* /ɪz/. Accept and write on the board all answers sts suggest for question 2. If sts give you items that are mentioned but aren't actually in the suitcase, replay the recording.

> Answers: 1 Her name is Mrs Jane Miles. 2 An MP3 player and two maps.

b ▶ Ask sts to listen again and complete the phrases. Ask sts to say Jane's sentences, exaggerating the intonation to sound offended or angry.

Answers: I   It   They

Grammar 2

> **OPTIONAL GRAMMAR LEAD-IN**
>
> Pick up a book from a student's desk and say: *Oh, a camera.* If none of the sts corrects you, correct yourself and say: *It isn't a camera. It's a book,* exaggerating the pronunciation. Encourage a few sts to get up and do the same. This should be a fun activity.

7 ▶ Ask sts to complete the Active grammar box and go over the answers. Read out the sample sentences from the Active grammar box.

Answers: aren't   isn't   aren't   aren't

8a ▶ **Real beginners** Ask sts to do a first, then check the answers. Then ask them to do b with a partner. Check the answers as a class.

▶ **False beginners** Sts could go straight on with b after a.

Answers: 1 aren't   2 'm not   3 isn't   4 isn't
5 aren't   6 isn't

b ▶ Ask two sts to read the dialogues out loud. Watch intonation (contrastive stress) and correct as necessary. Ask sts to practise the dialogues with their partners. Circulate and correct intonation.

Answers: I'm not   aren't   isn't   'm not   isn't

9a ▶ Ask sts to look at the table and elicit what questions they need to ask. Have sts ask you the questions. Give answers and ask sts to note them down.

▶ **Real beginners** Write the questions on the board.

b ▶ Ask sts in pairs to write sentences as suggested. Elicit more examples, e.g. *My teacher and I are from this city. My partner isn't from this city.* Circulate. Ask pairs to present their sentences to the class.

Speaking

10 ▶ Ask sts to write and then practise a dialogue with their partner and ask a few pairs to act out their dialogues for the class.

> **OPTIONAL WRAP-UP**
>
> Ask sts in groups to brainstorm items they would pack into their suitcase and add cards to their word boxes and/or write a page for their vocabulary folders.

3.3 Tourist information

In this lesson sts read leaflets and ask for and give information about tourist attractions. Grammar: *Yes/No* questions with *to be.*

> **OPTIONAL WARMER**
>
> Introduce the topic by writing the name of a local tourist attraction and tourist information office on the board. Ask sts: *What can the tourist information office tell you?* Elicit ideas. Ideally, build up a short text, similar to the ones in Ex. 2.

Vocabulary

1a ▶ **Real beginners** Ask sts to read the days as they listen. Play recording 3.7. Play the recording again, item by item, and ask sts to repeat.

▶ **False beginners** Books closed. Use recording 3.7 as a dictation. Ask sts to check their spelling against the book. Then ask individual sts to read the days and have the class repeat. Correct/model pronunciation.

b ▶ Ask sts to stand in a circle. Say: *Monday,* throw the ball to a student and ask him/her *to say Tuesday,* etc. Go through the week a few times, correcting as necessary. Then ask sts to write down the days of the week from memory. Ask individual sts to say and spell a day each and write them on the board. Point out the capital letters.

Reading

2a ▶ Listen in as sts read the information to each other, then get a few sts to say the addresses, etc. Correct as necessary. Ask what *postcode* is – sts may be surprised to find that it does not precede the name of the town, and that it is a combination of letters and numbers.

b ▶ Ask sts to find the underlined words (*open, closed, entrance, top, free, near*) and see if they can work out their meaning from the context. Pool ideas and clarify meanings.

c ▶ Ask sts to cover the text, read each statement and decide on the right answer from memory. Then give them two minutes to check their ideas against the texts. Go over the answers.

Answers: 1 isn't   2 isn't   3 is   4 is   5 isn't
6 isn't

Listening

3a ▶ Ask sts to look at the texts again and give them one minute to memorise the most important information. Then ask them to close their books. Play recording 3.8 and ask sts to make notes. To check the answers, ask relevant comprehension questions first, e.g. *Is number 1 open on Mondays? Is number 2 in London?* Then ask sts which dialogue fits which place. Elicit suggestions.

▶ Ask sts to go back to the text to check their ideas. Pool information.

> **Answers:** 1 Hampton Court Palace   2 The British Museum   3 The Whitechapel Art Gallery

b ▶ Demonstrate the difference between *here* and *there* by talking about things in the classroom, e.g. *My book is here. Her book is there.* Write *here* and *there* on the board and ask sts to practise this with a partner. Then ask sts to look at the How to … box. Demonstrate that you say *Here's …* as you hand something to someone.

▶ Ask sts to listen to the dialogues again and complete the gaps. Play recording 3.8 again. Check the answers by replaying it and asking sts to put their hands up when they hear one of the words.

> **Answers:** 1 here   2 here   3 Here's, here, there   4 here   5 Here's, here, there

> **OPTIONAL EXTENSION**
>
> Ask sts to draw a map of where they live. Teach *I live in X street. It's near … .* In pairs, sts explain to each other where they live and what landmarks there are. With real beginners, demonstrate this by drawing a map of where you live on the board and explaining where you live.

Grammar

4a ▶ Prepare cards or sheets of A4 paper with the words in the example. Ask six sts to come to the front of the class and give them each a card. Ask them to make a positive statement by standing in the correct order. Now ask them to move around to make a question for which the answer is *Yes* or *No*. Write the statement and question on the board.

b ▶ Ask sts in pairs to read the dialogues in the tapescript. Then ask them to underline all the questions and the corresponding short answers.

▶ Books closed. Read out the questions from the dialogues and ask sts to give the answers. Make up more questions and call on individual sts so that everyone gives an answer.

c ▶ Ask sts to work individually. Ask two sts to read the questions and answers as mini-dialogues to the class and write the answers on the board as they do so. Point out that they shouldn't just say *Yes* or *No* because that sounds rude.

> **Answers:** Am   Are   Is   Are   Are

Language note Politeness is an important point to cover when teaching English (cf. Lesson 1.3). Emphasise this through, e.g. the repeated use of *please* and *thank you*.

5a/b ▶ **Real beginners** Ask sts to complete a and go over the answers, then do b in pairs. Then ask them to practise saying the questions and answers.

▶ **False beginners** Ask sts to do both a and b before you go over the answers.

> **Answers a:** 1 am   2 Is, isn't   3 Is, is   4 Are, are   5 they, aren't   6 Is, is   7 Are, aren't   8 Are, am

> **Answers b:** 1 a Is it open today?   b Yes, it is.   2a Are you from Italy?   b No, I'm not.   3a Is she from the UK?   b Yes, she is.   4a Is it a museum?   b No, it isn't.   5a Is the shop open?   b Yes, it is.   6a Are you an actor?   b No, I'm not.

Reading and speaking

6 ▶ Put sts in pairs and ask them to decide who is A and who is B, then tell sts B to find their information. Explain that they have some information, and that the other student is going to ask them questions about it. Give sts a minute to read their texts. Circulate and support. Make notes for a correction spot at the end.

> **OPTIONAL WRAP-UP**
>
> If sts are developing word boxes, they could add important words, or they could write a new page for their vocabulary folders. Play a game: Sts take turns drawing cards from the word box. Sts show their card to the others in their group and ask: *Is this X (using a wrong word)?* The other sts answer *No, it isn't.* The more questions a student manages to ask about an item, the more points he/she scores. The final question (i.e. when the student runs out of ideas) is the one the others can truthfully answer with *Yes, it is.*

3 Communication: See you on Friday

In this lesson sts have a simple telephone conversation, recycling the unit's language and adding *very* as an intensifier.

> **OPTIONAL WARMER**
>
> This activity introduces vocabulary building strategies for learning opposites and helps make sts aware of shades of meaning. Put the adjectives from Ex. 1a on cards so that you have one for each student (add some if necessary). Give each student a card and ask them to find their opposite. Explain that for some there is more than one possibility. Sts then present and mime/demonstrate their pair of adjectives to the class. Discuss *old – new* vs *old – modern*. Elicit *young* as another alternative, possibly *old-fashioned*. Sts may decide to present a continuum *awful – bad – good – great*. Write the words on the board in pairs of opposites.

1a ▶ See optional warmer activity. Ask sts to copy the words from the board onto a new page for their vocabulary folders in pairs of opposites and check meanings if necessary.

b ▶ Ask sts to find all the nouns in the box, then ask them what word class the words on the board are. Ask them to write *Adjectives* at the top of their new vocabulary page.

> **Answers:** Nouns: skirt suitcase book food backpack camera map; Adjectives: small old bad beautiful ugly hot cold good nice modern big awful great new fine

c ▶ Elicit the answer (*very* is used with adjectives) and ask sts for more examples, e.g. *My teacher is very nice*.

2 ▶ Books closed. Write questions 1–6 on the board and ask sts to listen for the answers. Play recording 3.9. Ask sts to check their answers with a partner, then against the text. Play the recording again and ask sts to mouth the text as they listen and read.

> **Answers:** 1 She's in Morocco.   2 No, she isn't.
> 3 Yes, it is.   4 Yes, it is.   5 No, it isn't.   6 Yes, it is.

3a ▶ Ask sts to read the dialogue with a partner twice, changing roles.

b ▶ Write the skeleton dialogue on the board or on an OHT so as not to tempt sts to look at the dialogue. Ask them to close their books as they practise the dialogue.

4a/b ▶ Ask sts to inclatude more detail if they wish. Invite one or two pairs to act out their dialogue for the class.

▶ End the class by explaining the use of *See you on Friday* and say *See you tomorrow* (or whenever your next class happens to be).

Review and practice

1 ▶

> **Answers:** 1 are my friends   2 are from Manchester
> 3 Their favourite car   4 're in our room
> 5 're   6 our favourite

2 ▶

> **Answers:** 1 our   2 They're   3 they're   4 We're   5 Our
> 6 Their   7 we're   8 they're

3 ▶

> **Answers:** 1 'm   2 isn't   3 aren't   4 She   5 aren't   6 I
> 7 aren't   8 isn't   9 You   10 not

4 ▶

> **Answers:** 1 Are we near the gallery?   2 Is the museum open?   3 Are they from Italy?   4 Is she your friend?
> 5 Is the lake near here?   6 Are the department stores open today?   7 Are we in the York Hotel?

5 ▶

> **Answers:** 1 Yes, we are.   2 No, it isn't.   3 Yes, they are.
> 4 No, she isn't.   5 Yes, it is.   6 No, they aren't.
> 7 Yes, we are.

6 ▶

> **Answers:** 1 MP3 player/suitcase   2 big/small
> 3 Wednesday/Thursday   4 museum/gallery
> 5 cathedral/palace

Notes for using the Common European Framework (CEF)

CEF References

3.1 Can do: write a simple holiday email

CEF A1 descriptor: can write a short simple postcard (CEF page 83)

3.2 Can do: say what's in your suitcase

CEF A1 descriptor: can ask and answer questions about themselves and other people, where they live, people they know, things they have (CEF page 81)

3.3 Can do: ask for tourist information

CEF A1 descriptor: can ask and answer simple questions, initiate and respond to simple statements in areas of immediate need or on very familiar topics (CEF page 81)

CEF quick brief

The CEF dispenses with the labels traditionally used to describe levels of language proficiency like *Beginner*, *Upper-Intermediate* and so on in favour of simple, alphanumeric names: A1, A2, B1, B2, C1 and C2, which can be used as an objective description of a learner's level in any language, not just English. All of *Total English Starter*, as well as parts of *Total English Elementary* are at A1, the lowest of the six levels. It is not expected that when learners reach the end of the *Total English Starter* course they will have 'completed' A1 and be ready to start A2, but that they will be *closer* to the end of A1 and the start of A2. As such, the A1 descriptors (*Can do* statements) need to be interpreted at Starter level.

CEF Portfolio task

Download the Total English Portfolio free from www.longman.com/totalenglish.

Objective: to explain how the grid with the *Can do* statements works, especially the right-hand column, which links the *Can do* statement to a specific activity on a specific and given page in the Students' Book.

1 ▶ Show the sts the activity in the Students' Book referred to in the Portfolio's '*Total English* Book/page reference' column in order to refresh their memory.

2 ▶ Make sure sts restrict themselves to the descriptors specific to the unit in question, and explain that these are spread out over the five sections, and that there will normally be one or two references to any unit in any section.

3 ▶ Unit 2, for example, is referenced by the following *Can do* statements: (in the Listening section): statements 2 and 3; (in the Reading section): statement 2; (in the Spoken interaction section): statements 2 and 3; (in the Spoken production section): none; (in the Writing section): statements 3 and 4.

4 In town

Overview

Lead-in	**Vocabulary:** places in town
4.1	**Grammar:** *Can I have ...?*
	Vocabulary: food and drink; prices
	Can do: order food in a café or coffee shop
4.2	**Grammar:** *this, that, these, those*
	Vocabulary: clothes, colours
	Can do: ask for and understand prices
4.3	**Grammar:** possessive *'s*
	Vocabulary: irregular plurals
	Can do: ask about things and make simple transactions
Com. Focus	Excuse me, where is the ...?

Summary

Lesson 1: Sts listen to and practise simple dialogues to order food and drinks.

Lesson 2: Sts talk about markets and learn about the Portobello market in London. They learn to describe clothes and ask about prices.

Lesson 3: Sts hear people buying tickets and other items and practise simple transactions.

Communication: Sts ask for and give information about where places are in a town.

Film bank: The flowers

An extract based in a florist and a café. A young man buys a large bunch of flowers for his mother's birthday and a small bunch for his new girlfriend. He goes to a café. His girlfriend turns up, followed shortly (and unexpectedly) by her father. The father is the florist, so feeling rather embarrassed, the young man gives the large bunch of flowers to his girlfriend.

Possible places to use this short film are:
▶ after 4.2

▶ at the end of the unit

For ways to use this short film in class, see Students' Book page 119 and Teacher's Resource Book pages 135 and 143.

Lead-in

1a ▶ Real beginners Ask sts to match the pictures and words. To expand vocabulary further, ask sts what else they can see in the pictures. Elicit/provide words and write them on the board.

Answers: A café   B cashpoint   C train station
D newsagent   E cinema   F car park   G bookshop
H bank   I chemist   J restaurant
K supermarket   L bus stop   M market

b ▶ Ask sts to look at the words in the box and just listen the first time. Play recording 4.1. Re-play the recording item by item and ask sts to underline the stressed syllables (see above for answers). Ask sts to repeat the words as a class and/or individually. Watch compound stress. Model and correct.

Language note A lot of these items are compound nouns. Explain that there is no rule for whether compound nouns are written as one or two words – they just have to be learnt one by one. Compound stress is important: primary stress on the first part, secondary on the second part of a compound noun, e.g. *newsagent, cashpoint, car park*.

1a ▶ False beginners Books closed. Elicit places in town, then ask sts to match the pictures and words. To expand vocabulary further, ask sts what the items in the pictures are and elicit further related words, e.g. what you can buy there. Write the new words on the board as word maps and ask sts to copy them. Alternatively, ask groups of sts to create word maps and put them on pieces of paper or OHTs. The results can be pooled, corrected and copied by everyone. See above for answers.

b ▶ Ask sts to look at the words in the box, then to close their books. Use recording 4.1 as a dictation, playing it item by item. Ask sts to write the words and underline the stressed syllables. They check their spelling against the book. Ask individual sts to give you the correct stress and pronunciation. Watch compound stress and correct as necessary – see Language note and answers above.

c ▶ All students Ask sts to cover the words in the box and, working in pairs, to name what they can see in the pictures.

2 ▶ Put sts in pairs. Encourage them to ask for and give reasons for their answers. Provide vocabulary as necessary, e.g. adjectives. Write additional words on the board, in pairs of opposites, e.g. *cheap – expensive, near – far* for sts to note down.

OPTIONAL WRAP-UP

Sts work in groups to add all the new words to their vocabulary folders or word boxes. For practice, ask sts to take turns pointing to a word or taking a card and giving as many related words as they can think of, e.g. *café – sandwich, coffee,* tea.

4.1 Can I have an espresso, please?

In this lesson sts listen to and practise simple dialogues to order food and drinks; Grammar: *Can I have ...?*

> ### OPTIONAL WARMER
>
> Brainstorm with the class what you can order in a café and write the words on the board as a word map around *café*. To elicit English words that are used internationally, mention *Starbucks*, *New York Bagels* or any other chains your sts are likely to know. Ask sts to copy the word map for their vocabulary folders. With false beginners, you could elicit how to order – *Can I have ..., please?*

Vocabulary

1a ▶ Ask sts to look at the pictures and match the words from the optional warmer and the box to the pictures. Talk about the differences between *instant* and *real* coffee and where each is served.

> **Answers:** 1 an instant coffee   2 a black filter coffee
> 3 a white coffee   4 an espresso   5 a cappuccino
> 6 an iced coffee

b ▶ Ask sts to listen and make notes. Play recording 4.2 and pool information.

> **Answers:** instant coffee – the UK   black coffee –
> the US   espresso – Spain   cappuccino – Italy
> iced coffee – Greece

c ▶ Provoke discussion by saying: *I think most people's favourite coffee in ... is instant coffee.* Write the sentence on the board as a model. Pool sts' ideas – opinions are likely to vary.

2a/b ▶ Clarify meanings of *very nice* and *awful* by drawing happy/unhappy faces and ask sts to write their sentences on a piece of paper. Sts work in pairs or, with a large class, in groups of four. If they work in groups, collect and redistribute the sheets of paper within the group. Ask sts to read the sentences on the piece of paper you've given them. The group guess who wrote them.

3a ▶ Ask sts to label the pictures and words in pairs. Don't go over the answers yet – see b.

> **Answers:** 1 an orange juice   2 a sandwich
> 3 a mineral water   4 a salad   5 a piece of cake
> 6 a cup of tea

b ▶ Explain that each of the pictures goes with one of the three dialogues sts are going to hear. Play recording 4.3. Ask sts to check their answers with a partner, then go over them as a class.

> **Answers:** A2   B1   C3

4a ▶ Ask sts to look at the words in the box and the items and guess or answer from memory. Play recording

4.3 again for them to fill in the gaps. Ask sts to go to the tapescript on page 146 to check their answers. Ask pairs of sts to read the dialogues to the class. Point out (and correct, if necessary) rising/falling intonation in phrases like *Certainly, Sure, Anything else?* etc. Note that *Can I have ..., please?* has no rising intonation because it is a request, not a real question.

> **Answers:** 1 chicken   2 large   3 ham   4 small
> 5 chocolate

b ▶ With real beginners or slower learners, ask sts to read the tapescript on page 146 in pairs before they practise ordering food. Remind sts to use polite forms (as in the dialogues in the book). Circulate and correct as necessary. Watch intonation.

Language note At beginners' level, sts inevitably focus on getting the message across, i.e. on the transactional aspect of communication. There are a few simple phrases which make communication polite and friendly – which is the interactional aspect of communication, e.g. *sorry, yes, please, no, thank you, excuse me, certainly* (c.f. these dialogues and Lesson 1.3). Practise these with sts right from the start and remind them again and again. Otherwise they are likely to come across as unfriendly or rude. Put these phrases on cards (laminate them for long-term use if you can), and whenever sts do role play, hand them out and ask sts to use as many of them as appropriate.

Grammar

5 ▶ Ask sts to match the parts of the questions (the focus here is on singular vs plural; *a* vs *an*). Check the answers. Explain that this is the question form, but that it is a request rather than a genuine question.

> **Answers:** Can I have a cheese sandwich, please?
> Can I have an iced coffee, please?   Can I have two
> orange juices, please?

6a ▶ Ask sts to fill in the gaps individually, then compare with a partner. Check the answers by asking three sts to read the conversation to the class.

> **Answers:** 1 Can I have an   2 else   3 Can I have a
> 4 Can I have a   5 Anything   6 thank you

b ▶ Put sts into groups of three and ask them to read the conversation in a.

> ### OPTIONAL EXTENSION
>
> Ask sts to add food and drink cards to their word boxes. They can practise in groups, by putting the food and drink cards in a pile, drawing cards in turn and ordering what's on the card. The student sitting opposite answers.

Pronunciation

7 ▶ This exercise focuses on linking words by joining the final consonant of a word directly to the vowel of the following word. Ask sts to listen and repeat (with their books closed and without thinking about the individual words). Play recording 4.4. Then ask them to look at their books. Point out that the phonetic script gives sound groups, not separate words. Ask a few sts to say the sentence, then introduce some variation, but ensure each individual student says a sentence. Listen for and correct how they link words.

Vocabulary

> **OPTIONAL VOCABULARY LEAD-IN**
>
> Play a game to review numbers. Sts stand in a circle. Say: *Seven times seven,* and throw the ball to a student. He/She answers and asks the next question, etc. Introduce *plus, minus, times, divided by* and *equals,* and ask sts to form their next question using the answer to the last one, e.g. *seven times seven equals 49, 49 minus 23 equals 26,* etc. Alternatively, have a game of bingo.

8a ▶ Ask sts to complete the table.

Language note Point out that the currency symbol comes first, before the figures, for written prices (except a fraction of the currency unit – *p, c,* etc.), but that the currency is often not spoken, e.g. *one fifty.*

> **Answers:** nine fifty tweny ninety

b ▶ Ask sts to circle the prices as they listen. Check the answers. In a real beginners' class, go through all the prices, asking individual sts to read them aloud.

> **Answers:** 1b 2b 3a 4a 5c

c ▶ As sts practise saying and writing the prices in pairs, listen in and correct. You may find that false beginners can miss out this part of the exercise.

Speaking

Both Exs. 9 and 10 are dialogues/role plays ordering food. Ex. 9 should be slightly more language and accuracy oriented. False beginners may be able to go straight to Ex. 10 after looking at the How to ... box.

9a ▶ Ask two sts to read the How to ... box to the class as a (skeleton) dialogue. Ask sts to have another look at the phrases, then to close their books. You could use a pair finding activity with cards, e.g. *cheese – sandwich, chocolate – cake, black – coffee, a cup of – tea, orange – juice,* etc. Shuffle the cards, give one to each student and ask them to find a matching partner. Ask them to write a dialogue with their new partner. When they have finished, ask them to check their dialogue using the How to ... box.

b ▶ Ask a few pairs to perform their dialogues to the class. Real beginners may be more comfortable reading out their dialogues.

10 ▶ Rearrange the pairs, using the cards again, and ask sts to do a role play using the menu. Alternatively, bring authentic menus or ask sts to write their own menu, which they can then add to their vocabulary folders.

> **OPTIONAL WRAP-UP**
>
> Ask sts to add the dialogue from Ex. 9 and/or their menu from Ex. 10 to their vocabulary folders.

4.2 Portobello market

In this lesson sts talk about markets and learn about the Portobello market in London. They learn to describe clothes and ask about prices. To make Ex. 1b more lively, put the questions and answers on cards as a pair finding game. Grammar: *this, that, these, those.*

Reading

1a ▶ You could introduce the topic by bringing in the Beatles' *Ob-La-Di,Ob-La-Da* and playing the first verse and chorus. Ask sts: *Where does Desmond work?* Play the first part of the song again, if necessary. The answer is, of course, *market place.* Ask sts what sorts of market they know, and what you can buy there. Brainstorm ideas as a class or in groups. Pool ideas and write new words on the board. Play the complete song to round this off, but don't go into any textual detail.

b ▶ Books closed. You could put the questions and answers from the text on cards and use these as a pair finding game. Once sts have found their partner, ask pairs to read their question and answer to the class. Then ask the class what they think this is about. If someone has been to Portobello market or a similar market, ask them to describe it a little further. Alternatively, sts read the text in pairs and match the questions and answers.

> **Answers:** 1 Where is the market?　2 What is it? 3 Is it big?　4 When is it open?　5 Is it free? 6 What is on sale in the market?

c ▶ Ask sts to read the text (again) and answer the true/false questions with their partner. Go over the answers. Check that sts understand *on sale* and *popular,* and that they don't confuse *West London* with *west of London.*

> **Answers:** 1 T　2 T　3 F　4 F

2a ▶ Ask sts to think of a special market or shop they have been to and to write a similar text about their market, using the questions as a guide. Circulate and help with vocabulary.

b ▶ Put sts in pairs and ask them to interview each other about their texts. Ask them not to tell their partner exactly what they wrote about – sts should try to find out by asking questions.

Vocabulary

3a/b ▶ **Real beginners** Ask sts to match the colours and items of clothing as they listen. Play recording 4.6. Check the answers.

▶ Point to each of the pictures in turn and ask: *What is this?* Elicit answers, watch and correct the use of the indefinite article and pronunciation.

▶ **False beginners** Ask sts to close their books and write down what they hear. Play recording 4.6 item by item, as a dictation. Ask sts to check their answers against the words and pictures in the exercise.

Answers: 1 i   2 a   3 f   4 c   5 h   6 d   7 g   8 b   9 e

c ▶ In pairs, ask sts to write a description of one or two sts in the class. It should be very detailed and begin with small, insignificant things. This will involve a detailed look at vocabulary. Circulate and provide vocabulary as necessary.

▶ Ask sts in turn to read out their description item by item until the class guesses who they are talking about. Write any new words on the board.

Listening and speaking

4 ▶ Ask sts to read the How to … box. Then hold your book up, point to the red hat and ask a student: *How much is it?* If necessary, demonstrate a few more examples, then ask sts to practise in pairs.

5a ▶ Explain that sts are going to listen to a dialogue. Ask them to focus on the prices and to correct the mistakes in the picture. Play recording 4.7. Go over the answers.

Answers: a £3.50   b £12.85   c £17.99   d £8.45
e £9.00

b ▶ Ask sts to look at the questions and to try and reconstruct them from memory, then play recording 4.7 again. Direct sts to the tapescript on page 146 and go over the answers together. Model pronunciation, contrasting *this* and *these*. Explain that the Active grammar box will clarify the meaning of these words.

Answers: 1 this   2 these   3 that   4 these

Grammar

6 ▶ Ask sts to look at the questions in Ex. 5b and the Active grammar box and to discuss with a partner what *this, that, these* and *those* mean and where they should go in the box. Check the answers and make sure sts understand the difference between *this/these* and *that/those*. To clarify, talk about items in the classroom and things you can see from the window.

Answers: this   that   these   those

7 ▶ Ask sts to complete the sentences with *this, that, these* and *those*. Check the answers and elicit explanations for the correct answers.

Answers: 1 those   2 those   3 these   4 these
5 this   6 that

Speaking

8 ▶ **Real beginners** Before starting this exercise, ask sts to copy the How to … box and expand it if they wish.

▶ **All students** Put sts in pairs and allocate roles (A and B). Ask sts A to choose prices for the items and sts B to think about the questions to ask. Real beginners can use their How to … boxes for reference. After five minutes, ask sts to swap roles. Circulate and monitor as sts practise asking about and giving prices.

Writing

9 ▶ You could set this for homework/self-study. Ask sts to write a text about a market or shop. Ask them to write about the things on sale – what they are like, the prices, and about the people, etc. Ask them to try to use 15 different adjectives in their text.

> **OPTIONAL WRAP-UP**
>
> Ask sts to add colours (using coloured pens) and clothing to their word box. Play 'market' using the cards: groups create their goods by combining adjectives and nouns from their word box and display them 'for sale'. Two sts from each group 'sell', the others walk around the room and 'buy'.

4.3 Around town

In this lesson sts hear people buying tickets and other items and practise simple transactions. Grammar: possessive *'s*.

> **OPTIONAL WARMER**
>
> This activity introduces the topic and reviews vocabulary. Bring in a few used theatre/cinema/train tickets, receipts and plastic bags. Distribute them to groups of three sts and ask them to note down what places the items are from. Sts will probably have some things on them themselves to add and identify where they are from. Pool vocabulary and write new words on the board.

Vocabulary

1a ▶ Ask sts what they can see in the pictures: *Where are these people?* Elicit ideas.

Answers: Photo A = supermarket   Photo B = chemist   Photo C = station   Photo D = cinema

b ▶ Give sts a minute to match a description to each picture. Check answers as a class by asking sts to read the descriptions. Make sure you correct pronunciation, especially of *women* in 3.

Answers: 1c   2b   3d   4a

2a ▶ Real and false beginners alike will be able to guess the singular forms, and the irregular plural *women* has come up in Ex. 1b. Ask sts in pairs to discuss and complete the chart. As they do so, copy the chart on the board. To go over the answers, ask sts to spell them for you and add them to the chart on the board. Model and practise pronunciation as a class and individually. Circle relevant sections of the words to indicate what changes. Point out that *baby – babies* is a change you cannot hear.

> **Answers:** man   woman   child   baby

b ▶ Wipe the board and ask sts to go to page 109. Give them a minute to note down what they can see in the photos. Ask: *What's in photo A?* Elicit the answer and ask a student to spell it for you. Write it on the board. Do the same for photos B–F. Ask sts to explain the irregular plurals. (*Quick follow-on*: Look at Reference page 47 and go through the categories of irregular plurals. Practise and correct pronunciation.)

> **Answers:** A two men   B two men and a woman
> C a man, a woman and two children   D two women
> and two babies   E two men and two women
> F a woman, a child and a man

Reading and listening

3a ▶ Books closed. Ask sts to remind you where each photo is. Play recording 4.8. Elicit ideas for which conversation takes place where, then ask sts to go to the book and match the pictures to the dialogues.

> **Answers:** 1 c   2 b   3 d   4 a

b ▶ Give sts a minute to look at the dialogues and fill in the gaps from memory, then ask them to check their answers by listening again. Re-play recording 4.8. Go over the answers.

> **Answers:** 1 tickets   2 Here   3 forty-eight   4 please
> 5 have   6 Can   7 you   8 number

4a/b ▶ Ask pairs of sts to read the dialogues to the class, then get sts to practise them in pairs. You can encourage false beginners to modify the dialogues straight away.

Language note Point out to sts that in dialogue 4, the price is given as *x pounds and x pence*. Elicit that this structure is used when there is less than 10 pence in the pence part of the price. Sts could add this to the prices table in Ex. 8a on page 41.

5a ▶ Books closed. Read out the phrases from the How to … box and elicit words for the gaps. Then ask sts to write in the words. You could suggest that they copy out the How to … box for their vocabulary folders and add other places and phrases.

> **Answers:** return   packet   that's   here   you   your

b ▶ Put sts in pairs and ask them to write a dialogue. Explain that they will perform in front of the class, so they should use receipts, credit cards, bags, etc. to make it more real. Explain that the jury (i.e. the class) will give each pair points for realism, fun and originality. Circulate and support. You may want to allocate places in town to groups so that you cover a range of different situations.

c ▶ As pairs of sts perform their dialogues, ask everybody to give them points on a scale of 1–10 for realism, fun and originality. Sts shouldn't sit and read dialogues, but try to act them out. In these situations, the customer is likely to be standing up. Note down scores. Bring in a small prize for the winners.

Grammar

6a ▶ Ask a few sts to pick up an item from their desk and come up to the front of the class. Ask each of them in turn: *Is this your book/bag/pen …?* Then turn to the class and explain: *This is Peter's book,* etc. Ask them to swap their items. Ask the class: *Is this Heike's book?* The class should correct: *No, it's Peter's book.*

> **Answers:** 1 Jack   2 Shula   3 Mike   4 Shula
> 5 Mike

b ▶ Ask a student to read the first two sentences in the Active grammar box to the class. With real beginners, ask a student to explain why one sentence has *They're* and the other *It's*. Then ask sts to fill in the Active grammar box. Elicit/explain that the apostrophe in contractions stands for one or more letters you leave out, but that possessive *'s* is not a contracted form. It simply requires the apostrophe to distinguish it from plural *s*.

Language note It is an increasingly common spelling mistake in the UK to use apostrophes in noun plurals.

> **Answers:** Mike's   Shula's   Mike's

7 ▶ Possessive *'s* is not a particularly complicated structure, but the apostrophe is very important. That is why the structure requires writing practice. Ask sts to write the sentences. To go over the answers, ask a student to write *names + 's* on the board. (*Quick follow-on*: Dictate a few sentences like the ones in Review and practice Ex. 4 to the sts and check that they understand the difference between the *'s* constructions.)

> **Answers:** 1 It's Kevin's passport.   2 They're Rosie's
> shoes.   3 This is Takumi's email address.
> 4 What is Adele's address?   5 Are you Teresa's
> brother?   6 That is Janek's suitcase.

Speaking

8a/b ▶ Pick up a few items from sts' desks and ask the class: *Is this X's pen/book/bag, etc.?* Collect an item from each student. Put everything on a table in the middle of the classroom and assemble sts around it. Encourage sts to pick up items and ask: *Is this X's …?* Then get sts to point at items from a distance and ask questions about them.

> **OPTIONAL WRAP-UP**
>
> Use the collection of items as a market stall. Elicit that before you buy something, you usually ask the price. Demonstrate a dialogue combining language from lessons 4.2 and 4.3, e.g. *How much …?/Can I have … + demonstrative pronoun.* Sts then 'buy' their item from you.

4 Communication:
Excuse me, where is the ...?

In this lesson sts ask for and give information about where places are in a town.

OPTIONAL WARMER

Prepare a word square with places in town or a simple worksheet of places in town with jumbled up letters – one photocopy per student. Ask sts to find the words as quickly as possible and to shout *Bingo!* when they have finished. Check the answers.

1a ▶ Make sure sts understand the difference between *near* and *next to*. Explain *near* by talking about towns and get sts to practise a few sentences using *near*. Clarify the meaning of the prepositions by talking about where sts are sitting, *A is next to B,* etc. Draw diagrams on the board to illustrate them.

▶ Ask sts to match the sentences to the pictures. Check the answers. Then ask them, in pairs, to make up other general sentences, e.g. *the school is next to the library; X town is near Y town.*

> **Answers:** 1D 2B 3A 4C

b ▶ Ask sts to study the map for a moment before they listen. Explain that they are going to hear mini-dialogues which will tell them what some of the places labelled with letters are. Play recording 4.9. Check the answers together.

> **Answers:** gallery = f train station = n
> supermarket = i

2a ▶ Ask sts to look at the How to ... box. Ask two sts to read the 'positive' dialogue and two others to read the 'negative' dialogue to make sure everybody understands the How to ... box. Explain that *you're welcome* is a reaction to *thank you*, not a greeting of welcome.

▶ Demonstrate a question by asking: *Where's the market?* Elicit *It's on Mercer street.* Give sts a few minutes to ask and answer about the places given on the map. Circulate and monitor.

b ▶ Explain the information gap exercise. Ask sts not to look at each other's map, but to explain to each other where the places are. Ask them not to forget polite phrases. Circulate and correct as necessary. (*Quick follow-on for false beginners:* With books closed, ask sts whether people sometimes ask them in the street where something is in English. Elicit what people ask/what they answer and write ideas on the board. Use examples from your area to create mini-dialogues.)

OPTIONAL WRAP-UP

Ask sts to draw pictures demonstrating the prepositions on the board. Include *in*. Correct/ clarify as necessary, then ask sts to copy them into their vocabulary folders.

Review and practice

1 ▶

> **Answers:** 1 Can I have an 2 Can I have a 3 Can I have a 4 Can I have two 5 Can I have a 6 Can I have two

2 ▶

> **Answers:** 1 Good morning. Can I help you? 2 Yes, Can I have a chicken sandwich and an espresso, please? 3 Certainly. Anything else? 4 No, thank you. 5 Eat in or take away? 6 Take away. 7 That's 4.55, please.

3 ▶

> **Answers:** 1 that 2 these 3 this 4 those 5 that 6 those

4 ▶

> **Answers:** 1 This is Jamie's suitcase. 2 That's Dorota's baby. 3 They're Placido's daughters. 4 That's Jay's restaurant. 5 They're Michael's friends. 6 He's Lillian's brother. 7 They're Pat's children. 8 That's my Dad's café.

5 ▶

> **Answers:** Paul's bedroom Tom's bedroom Hilda's husband Hilda's dog

6 ▶

> **Answers:** 1 restaurant 2 cappuccino 3 trousers 4 people 5 train station 6 mineral water 7 orange 8 children 9 iced coffee 10 black bag

Notes for using the Common European Framework (CEF)

CEF References

4.1 Can do: order food in a café or coffee shop

CEF A1 descriptor: can ask people for things and give people things (CEF page 79)

4.2 Can do: ask for and understand prices

CEF A1 descriptor: can handle numbers, quantities, cost and time (CEF page 80)

4.3 Can do: ask about things and make simple transactions

CEF A1 descriptor: can ask and answer simple questions, initiate and respond to simple statements in areas of immediate need or on very familiar topics (CEF page 81)

CEF quick brief

The learner's Portfolio, like the CEF, contains *Can do* statements for learners to assess their own learning. Although they are worded simply in the Portfolio, many of them will still need a gloss in order for learners to complete the tasks. They are simplified statements about a skill relating to a specific page on the Students' Book, not verbatim quotations from the CEF. In Unit 4, for example, sts are asked on page 43 to ask for and give prices. This is referenced in the Spoken interaction section of the Portfolio as *I can ask for and understand prices*. This corresponds to the following descriptor from page 80 of the CEF: can handle numbers, quantities, cost and time. These descriptors are for the teacher's reference rather than the sts', and do not appear in the *Total English* Students' Book or the Portfolio.

CEF Portfolio task

Download the Total English Portfolio free from www.longman.com/totalenglish.

Objective: to show sts how their entries in their portfolio can influence the content of classes.

1▶ Set sts a deadline to complete their self-assessment for the *Can do* statements relating to Unit 4, and ask sts to bring their portfolio to a particular lesson.

2▶ During this lesson, conduct a poll to find out which of the *Can do* statements sts feel most able to do, and which they feel the least confident about.

3▶ Plan a subsequent class with the aim of developing the learners' competence in the area(s) for which they feel they still need more help.

4▶ Afterwards, give them the opportunity to revise their entries in their portfolio.

Overview

Lead-in	**Vocabulary:** *north, south,* etc., landscapes and places
5.1	**Grammar:** *there is/are*
	Vocabulary: *some, a lot of*
	Can do: give a simple description of a place
5.2	**Grammar:** *Is/Are there ...?; there isn't/ aren't; some, any*
	Vocabulary: nationalities
	Can do: ask about a new town and where important places are
5.3	**Grammar:** *can/can't*
	Vocabulary: telling the time
	Can do: talk about general abilities
Com. Focus	A Bed & Breakfast

Summary

Lesson 1: Sts learn about Cornwall and talk about their favourite holiday destinations.

Lesson 2: Sts describe and ask and answer about where places are in relation to each other.

Lesson 3: Sts work with a brochure for language and activity courses and talk about what hobbies and activities they can and can't do.

Communication: Sts learn about a typical B&B (Bed and Breakfast) and describe a room in one.

Film bank: Holiday places

An extract showing three separate holiday destinations. There is a short description of each place.

Possible places to use this short film are:
- ▶ after 5.2
- ▶ at the end of the unit

For ways to use this short film in class, see Students' Book page 120 and Teacher's Resource Book pages 136 and 144.

Lead-in

OPTIONAL WARMER

This activity reviews colours and countries and introduces the topic. Prepare some small flags in black and white beforehand. Books closed. Put sts into groups of three and give each group a set of flags. Ask them to decide what colour(s) should be in each flag, and what countries they belong to. You could extend this by asking them to draw flags, label the colours and write the country underneath. If you have sts from different countries in the class, ask them to present their flag and tell the class about it. Sts could add any new countries to the relevant page in their vocabulary folders.

1a ▶ Point to photo A and ask: *What country is this?* Elicit that Australia is a continent and a country. Read the words in the box to the sts and ask them to repeat. Then ask a student to do number 1. Write the sentence *Darwin is in the north of Australia* on the board. Ask sts to write the other sentences.

Answers: 1 Darwin = north 2 Perth = west
3 Brisbane = east 4 Adelaide = south
5 Alice Springs = centre

b ▶ Ask sts to listen and check. Play recording 5.1.

Language note Emphasise the structure of the sentence. Explain the difference between *south of* and *in the south of.* (*Birmingham is south of Manchester. London is in the south of England.*)

2 ▶ If sts come from different places, ask them where their home town is. Ask: *Where are you from (in ...)? Where is that?* Otherwise ask sts to think of the six most important/interesting/beautiful places and describe where they are. False beginners could add some extra information about each place.

3a/b ▶ Do this as a class. Ask sts to look at the pictures and match them to the type of landscape. Elicit answers. Ask them to match the words from the box to the pictures and elicit answers.

Answers a: city – D countryside – B coast – C

Answers b: city: buildings, roads countryside: trees, a river coast: the sea, a beach

c ▶ Play recording 5.2 for sts to check.

4a ▶ Put sts into groups of three and ask each group to produce a mind/word map on one of the types of landscape (ideally on A3, with thick felt tip pens). Make sure all three landscapes are covered. Groups then present their mind maps. Discuss, amend and correct them, and display them in the classroom, if possible. Ask sts to copy them for their vocabulary folders.

b ▶ **Real beginners** Ask: *What's in the photo?* Then put sts into pairs and ask them to talk about the photos.

▶ **False beginners** Write on the board *There are trees in the photo. There's a river in the photo.* Model pronunciation and ask sts to repeat. Then put sts into pairs and ask them to talk about the photos.

▶ **All students** Ask: *Which of these is a good place for a holiday?* Elicit ideas.

5.1 Cornwall

In this lesson sts learn about Cornwall and talk about their favourite holiday destinations. Grammar: *there is/are*.

Ask sts to get up and walk around the room to look at the flags and mind maps they produced in the Lead-in. If this is a separate session, make sure the materials are still there or bring them to class. Ask sts to choose three countries and think of three places in each of these countries: a city, a small place in the countryside and a place on the coast. With a small class, work with everyone. Divide a large class into groups. Ask sts to explain to the other sts where their chosen places are located and to say something about them. They should be hot tips for a good holiday! Encourage false beginners to give more details.

Reading

1a ▶ Ask sts what their favourite place for a holiday is. They can choose from the places that have just been presented in the optional warmer, or come up with a new idea.

b ▶ Give sts two minutes to read the text quickly to find the places and label the map. This is a scanning activity. Sts do not need to read the text in detail to complete the task.

> **Answers:** 1 Tintagel Castle   2 The Eden Project
> 3 Tate St. Ives   4 The Minack Theatre   5 Pendennis
> Castle

2a ▶ Ask sts to find the answers in the text, then to cover their text. In groups of three, get them to ask and answer the questions. They should only look back at the text if the group doesn't agree on the correct answer. Circulate, support and correct as necessary. Check answers as a class.

> **Answers:** 1 It's in the south-west of England.
> 2 They're in the north of Cornwall and the south of Cornwall.   3 It's a gallery.   4 It's a new tourist attraction.   5 It's in the west of Cornwall.

b ▶ Explain the task: sts will hear the same text, but when there is a beep, they should say the word that follows. Read the first part of the text and get sts to say *England*. Then ask sts to close their books. Play recording 5.3. This is a fast-moving exercise; encourage sts to react quickly. If they find responding to the recording difficult, read the text to them and pause in some places.

Speaking

OPTIONAL SPEAKING LEAD-IN

Ask sts to look at their *Places in town* page in their vocabulary folders and decide what adjectives could go with each place. Pool ideas and write a few on the board. Say: *I think (example) is important for a good holiday.*

3a ▶ Ask sts to look at the box and choose three things that they think are important for a good holiday, (plus one or two on the board from the optional warmer activity, if you did it).

b ▶ Read the How to … box to the sts and ask them to repeat *I think* (watch /θ/). Elicit a few sentences – with real beginners, one from each student – to check they can produce the structure and pronounce *I think* correctly.

c ▶ Before you put sts in pairs, ask them to number their ideas on a scale of 1 = very important to 5 = not so important. In pairs, they exchange ideas. Circulate and monitor. After three to four minutes, ask sts to try and agree on the three most important points. Give them another two minutes, then ask pairs to present their ideas to the class using *We think*.

Grammar

4a ▶ Ask sts to go back to the text and underline *there* and the word which follows it. Elicit what can follow *there*.

b ▶ Ask sts to complete the Active grammar box and to make a rule for *there's/there are*. Elicit answers. (*Quick follow-on:* Say one or two sentences about the class, e.g. *There are three students from Poland in this class. There's a doctor in this class.*, etc. and ask the class to decide whether the sentences are true or false.)

> **Answers:** is   are

5a ▶ Ask sts to complete the sentences individually, then compare with a partner. Go over the answers as a class.

> **Answers:** 1 There's   2 There's   3 There are
> 4 There are   5 There are   6 There's   7 There are
> 8 There's

b ▶ Ask a student to read the example. Give sts a few minutes to make more sentences with a partner. Elicit answers.

OPTIONAL EXTENSION

Ask sts to note down five different places in their home town (not five cathedrals, but, e.g. a museum, a market, a shopping centre, a church) and tell their partner where these are located. Circulate, support and correct as necessary.

Vocabulary

6a ▶ Read the sentences to the sts. Read them again, and after each sentence ask sts which picture matches.

> **Answers:** a2   b 3   c1

b ▶ Ask sts to mark sentence intonation and pronunciation as they listen and check their answers. Play recording 5.4. Ask individual sts to repeat the sentences. Correct pronunciation.

Language note *A lot of* is generally used in positive statements, and *many* in questions and negative statements. If sts find *a lot of* difficult at this level, they can use *many* instead.

7a ▶ Ask sts to write the sentences individually and then check with a partner. Go over the answers as a class.

> **Answers:** 1 There are some   2 There are a lot of
> 3 There's a/one   4 There's a/one   5 There are a lot
> of   6 There are some

b ▶ Read the sample sentence to the sts and elicit a rule for the position of the adjective (before the noun). Ask sts, in pairs, to decide which adjective fits which sentence, then ask pairs to read sentences to the class. (*Quick follow-on:* Ask sts to make the sentences true for their own town.)

> **Answers:** 1 There are some nice galleries in Newchester.   2 There are a lot of good restaurants in Newchester.   3 There's a beautiful river in Newchester.   4 There's a big lake in Newchester.
> 5 There are a lot of great shops in Newchester.
> 6 There are some modern cinemas in Newchester.

Writing

8 ▶ Put sts into groups of three and ask them to brainstorm ideas, then write sentences.

9a/b ▶ You could set this for homework or self-study. Look at the example and read the advice in the Writing bank, first as a class, then ask sts to work individually and write a text. Ask them to write it out neatly and to add pictures if they wish. In the next lesson, ask sts to display their texts.

> **OPTIONAL WRAP-UP**
>
> Ask sts to add new vocabulary to their vocabulary folders and/or their word boxes. If they have word boxes, ask them, in their groups, to go through the cards and divide the words into two groups: those they feel they know (to be recycled in three weeks' time – put them into a separate envelope) and those they feel they should practise every week.

5.2 In a new town

In this lesson sts describe and ask and answer about where places are in relation to each other. Grammar: *Is/Are there? there isn't/aren't; some, any.*

> **OPTIONAL WARMER**
>
> Revise key vocabulary from the previous lesson. Either write words on the board or put sts into their word box groups. Each student in turn chooses a word on the board, or picks a card from the box, says the word to the other sts and asks them to make a sentence each using it. Then the student who chose the word/card translates it.

Vocabulary

1a ▶ Ask sts to look at the pictures and ask them: *Where is the man in picture a?* Elicit *He's in the box.* Ask sts to work with a partner to match the other prepositions to the other pictures. Elicit the answers. Pay particular attention to *near*, *next to* and *opposite*, and make sure you clarify meanings/differences in meaning. Draw attention to the road in g so that sts understand *opposite*.

> **Answers:** a in   b on   c under   d next to   e in front of   f behind   g opposite   h near

b ▶ Elicit what shops/places there are on the on the map. Ask sts to use full sentences, e.g. *There's a cinema, the Rio Cinema.* Ask sts to complete the sentences individually, then check with a partner. Don't go over the answers yet – see c.

> **Answers:** 1 next to   2 in front of   3 opposite
> 4 behind   5 near

c ▶ Play recording 5.5 for sts to check their answers. Ask sts to memorise the map, then to close their books. Ask sts to note down as many sentences as they can describing the city centre. Ask individual sts to say a sentence each to describe the town on the map.

Listening

2a ▶ Ask sts what they think the places labelled a–e on the map could be. Play recording 5.6 and ask sts to complete the gaps as they listen. Go over the answers. Ask sts to try and tell you what exactly was said on the recording.

> **Answers:** a (a) café   b (an) Indian restaurant
> c (a) Chinese restaurant   d (a) bank   e (a) museum

b ▶ Ask sts to read the statements and guess whether they are true or false, then play the recording again. Check the answers as a class.

> **Answers:** 1 T   2 F There are restaurants *next* to the chemist and newsagent.   3 F *There is* a bank near the hotel.   4 F The *bank* is closed today.   5 T
> 6 F *There isn't* a gallery in the square.

3a ▶ Close your book and say with a grave face: *The lesson is over.* Wait to see how sts react, then mirror their reactions back to them in English. Ask: *Is this good or bad news?* Ask sts to open their books again and look at the How to … box. Demonstrate each of the reactions given.

b ▶ Explain that sts are going to hear and react to news which is either good or bad. Ask sts to work in pairs, taking it in turns to make sentences and react to the news. Point out to sts how important intonation is – both for giving news and for reacting. Circulate and monitor.

▶ **False beginners** Ask sts to use *I'm afraid* at the beginning of sentences which give bad news. Explain that this softens the statement a little and prepares the listener for bad news.

Grammar

OPTIONAL GRAMMAR LEAD-IN

In groups of three, ask sts to read the dialogue (recording 5.6, tapescript page 147). Encourage them to be as lively as possible. Circulate and monitor.

4 ▶ Give sts a minute to complete the Active grammar box, then elicit answers.

Answers: isn't   aren't   Is   aren't   are   aren't

5 ▶ Ask sts to write the sentences individually. As they write, remind them of the use of *any*. Ask individual sts to give their answers and write them on the board.

Answers: 1 There aren't any bus stops in the square. 2 There isn't a supermarket in the square.   3 There aren't any car parks in the square.   4 There isn't a market in the square.   5 There isn't a cinema in the square.   6 There aren't any galleries in the square.

6a ▶ Ask a student: *Where are you from?* Then ask: *Are there any good cinemas in X?* Ask one or two more sts. Then put sts into groups of three and ask them to write questions. Encourage them to add other questions of their own and support as necessary.

Answers: 1 Are there any good cinemas in your home town?   2 Is there a big museum in your home town?   3 Are there any nice departments stores in your home town?   4 Is there a palace in your home town?   5 Are there any modern supermarkets in your home town?   6 Are there any popular galleries in your home town?

b ▶ Put sts from different groups into pairs and ask them to interview each other about the place they are from. Ask sts to take notes about what their partner tells them.

▶ For homework or self-study, ask sts to write a text about the place their partner comes from. In the next lesson, ask partners to exchange texts and discuss/correct them together.

Vocabulary

7a ▶ Re-use the flags from the optional warmer activity in the Lead-in if you did it. Ask sts to find the flags that match the sentences. Alternatively, ask sts if they know the country names. As you go over the answers, check and correct pronunciation. Model it if necessary.

Answers: 1 French/France   2 Italian/Italy 3 English/England   4 Indian/India   5 Chinese/China

b/c ▶ Ask sts to match the restaurant names and nationalities and to listen to the recording to check their answers. Play recording 5.7. Note that sts will hear different non-native accents.

▶ Elicit further ideas by asking sts what restaurants they know. Write all nationalities that are mentioned on the board. Go through all suggestions, elicit the matching countries and write them on the board, too. Explain that these are nationalities, adjectives and languages. Point out the capital letters.

Answers: Chez Pierre is a French restaurant. King Henry's is an English restaurant.   La Spiga is an Italian restaurant.   Wong Li is a Chinese restaurant.   The Taj Mahal is an Indian restaurant.

8a ▶ Put sts into groups of three and ask them to complete the table and then brainstorm further countries and nationalities. After a few minutes, pool ideas and add any new words to those on the board.

Answers: Scottish   Ireland   Welsh

b ▶ In groups or pairs, get sts to discuss their favourite things. Ask sts to first exchange ideas and then to find their favourites as a group, e.g. *Our favourite restaurant is Chinese.*

Speaking

9 ▶ **Real beginners** Divide sts into two groups, A and B. Ask sts to turn to the relevant pages. Working in pairs or small groups of all As or Bs, sts prepare for the activity by describing what's where on the map or writing out questions together. Then they work as an A and B pair to ask for and give information.

False beginners Put sts into pairs, A and B. Give sts a few minutes to prepare for the task individually. They then work with their partner to ask for and give information.

5.3 Can she cook?

In this lesson sts work with a brochure for language and activity courses and talk about what hobbies and activities they can and can't do. Grammar: *can/can't.*

Vocabulary

1a ▶ Ask sts to look at the brochure and elicit what sort of brochure it is, and what it advertises. What is the idea of *Language Plus*? Draw sts' attention to the symbols and ask them to match them to the words in the box.

Answers: Course 171: play golf   Course 172: cook Course 173: play the piano   Course 174: swim Course 175: drive   Course 176: dance Course 177: sing   Course 178: use a computer

b ▶ Ask sts to cover the word box and practise in pairs. Circulate and monitor. If sts use the *-ing* form, don't comment at this stage.

Listening

2a ▶ Explain that sts are going to listen to a dialogue between two people about this brochure. Ask them to look at the information first and then listen. Play recording 5.8. Ask sts: *Who is the course for?* Then elicit information about Vanda.

> **Answers:** Name: Vanda   Relationship to James: cousin   From: Germany   English level: A1

b ▶ Ask sts what information Patricia and James need in order to choose a course for Vanda (what she can/can't do, what she likes/dislikes). Ask them to look at the list of activities. Go through them and ask sts to mime them to clarify meaning. Then get them to listen and find out whether or not Vanda can do these things. Play recording 5.9.

> **Answers:** 1 drive: Yes   2 swim: No   3 play golf: No   4 cook: No   5 use a computer: Yes   6 dance: Yes   7 sing: Yes   8 play the piano: No

c ▶ Ask sts to compare their answers with a partner, then to listen and check their answers. Play recording 5.9 again.

> **Answers:** Course 177

d ▶ Ask: *Which course is good for you?* Say: *I think course (171) is good for me. I can't (play golf)*. Write a sample sentence like this on the board. Call on individual sts to give similar statements.

3 ▶ Ask: *What is the first thing James and Patricia do?* (They greet each other.) If sts don't remember, draw their attention to the How to ... box. Ask two sts to read the How to ... box as a mini-dialogue. Explain that *How are you?* doesn't require a detailed answer. Ask sts to get up and walk around the classroom. Play some music. Whenever you stop the music, sts stop and greet the person they are standing next to.

Grammar

4 ▶ Ask sts to complete the Active grammar box. Ask them to think of a formula for these sentences (pronoun + *can* + verb).

> **Answers:** can't   Can

5a ▶ Ask sts to write the sentences individually. Check that they understand the tick and cross as symbols for positive/negative. Sts compare answers with a partner. Check the answers as a class. Write all the answers on the board. (*Quick follow-on:* ask sts to change all the statements into questions and vice versa.)

> **Answers:** 1 They can't dance.   2 Can you swim?   3 He can speak Italian.   4 Can she drive?   5 Can you play golf?   6 I can't play the piano.   7 We can cook.   8 Can they use a computer?

b ▶ Refer sts to Reference page 57 for support before they do this exercise. Emphasise the need to use short answers, otherwise they will sound rude and impolite.

▶ **Real beginners** Ask sts to write out the questions first. Circulate and check they are correct. Then ask sts to read their questions to their partner and write down the response. Remind sts that they should use short answers.

▶ **False beginners** Ask sts to interview their partner and take notes. They then tell the class about their partner.

Pronunciation

6a ▶ **Real beginners** Ask sts to listen and tick *can* or *can't*. Play recording 5.10. Go over the answers by playing the recording again, item by item, and eliciting answers. Ask sts to repeat the sentences. Point out the pronunciation of unstressed *can* (/kən/).

> **Answers:** 1 can   2 can't   3 can   4 can   5 can't   6 can

b ▶ **Real beginners** Ask sts to listen and write the sentences. Play recording 5.10 again. Ask them to check their answers against the tapescript on page 147.

▶ **False beginners** Books closed. Go straight into b and use the recording as a dictation. Ask sts to listen and write the sentences. Play recording 5.10. Ask sts to check their answers against the tapescript on page 147. Play the recording again, item by item. Ask sts to underline the stressed syllables as they listen, and then repeat the sentence.

> **Answers:** 1 I can speak English.   2 I can't speak Italian.   3 Can you speak German?   4 He can speak Russian.   5 She can't speak Spanish.   6 Can they speak Portuguese?

c ▶ Ask sts what languages they can speak. Elicit answers from various sts and correct them if necessary. Then ask sts to write sentences about their family and friends on a piece of paper. Collect and redistribute them. Ask sts to read out the text they have been given. Sts guess who wrote it.

Vocabulary

7 ▶ Ask sts why they chose the class they are in. At least some sts are likely to say that it was because of the time. Ask them to look at the times given.

▶ **False beginners** Ask sts to try and say these times with a partner before listening.

▶ **All students** Ask sts to listen and repeat. Play recording 5.11.

8a ▶ Ask two sts to read the example to the class. Do a further example with the class, then ask them to practise with a partner.

b ▶ Ask: *When is our English course?* Write the times on the board and ask sts to say them. If times are not on the hour, introduce the *oh five/ten/fifteen/twenty*, way of telling the time (*six thirty, seven oh five*, etc.).

Language note Sts are likely to ask about the 24-hour-clock. Explain that it's not often used in everyday English conversation. With false beginners, go through the times in Ex. 7 and elicit a 24-hour-clock version.

Speaking

9 ▶ Ask sts to look at the adverts and decide what questions they'll need to ask. Ask them to interview five candidates and make notes. Sts mingle and ask each other questions. After a few minutes, put sts into groups of three and ask them to exchange ideas, e.g. *Susanne can swim, but she can't play golf. Stefan can sing and dance.* Ask each group to suggest a candidate for each job and present them to the group.

> **OPTIONAL WRAP-UP**
>
> Ask sts, in groups of three, to write a skills profile for a job advert in as much detail as they wish. Sts display them in the classroom, then they look at the exhibition of job adverts/skill profiles and decide which one they'd like to apply for. Ask them to write their personal profile to submit for consideration.

5 Communication: A Bed and Breakfast

In this lesson sts learn about a typical Bed and Breakfast and divide a room in one.

1a ▶ Write *Bed and Breakfast* on the board and ask sts what it is. If they don't know, play hangman for them to find out. Elicit/explain that a *Bed and Breakfast* (*B&B*) is a bit like a hotel, but smaller and normally with fewer facilities (no restaurant, swimming pool, etc.). With false beginners, extend the activity to brainstorm words by asking: *What do you find/need in a B&B bedroom?* Write ideas on the board.

b ▶ In pairs, ask sts to match the words in the box to the items in the picture. Ask sts to explain where the things are (*on the bed, under the table*, etc.).

> **Answers:** a shower   b towels   c blanket
> d television   e kettle   f fridge

c ▶ Ask sts to listen and check their answers to b.

d ▶ Give sts 30 seconds to have a good look at the picture, then ask them to close their books. With their partner, ask them to note down as many things as they can that are in the picture. Then ask them to make sentences, e.g. *There are some towels on the bed. There is a kettle on the table*.

▶ Put sts into new pairs and ask them to compare their results, then check against the picture.

2 ▶ Ask: *What time is breakfast and checkout?* Ask sts to answer the questions from memory, then play recording 5.12 again for them to check their answers.

▶ False beginners Ask sts to note down the times in the recording in words.

▶ Draw a clock face on the board and write/visualise *quarter to, quarter past, half past*.

> **Answers:** a 7.30–10.30   b 11.45

3a ▶ Ask sts to copy the clock face. Ask them to listen and repeat the times. Then add *five past*, etc. to the clock on the board. Play recording 5.13.

b ▶ Do the first few items as a class and write the times out in words on the board. Then ask sts to practise them in pairs. Circulate.

> **Answers:** a half past three   b quarter past five
> c quarter to nine   d half past eleven   e ten past
> seven   f quarter to eight   g twenty past six   h five
> past one   i twenty-five to ten   j quarter past eight
> k twenty-five past two   l five to five   m ten past ten
> n twenty to ten   o quarter past twelve

4a ▶ Ask sts to look at the words in the table and check that they know all of them. Explain *en-suite bathroom*. Ask them to add any information they like and to note down details about their B&B room. Circulate and support as necessary.

b ▶ Real beginners In groups of three, ask sts to read the dialogue in tapescript 5.12 on page 147. Then one of them is the B&B owner and shows the others their room. Sts change roles twice so that everybody gets a chance to be the B&B owner. Circulate and encourage sts to deviate from the tapescript once they feel confident enough to do so.

▶ False beginners Put sts in pairs and ask them to role play a situation like the one they've listened to.

Lifelong learning

Individual, unconnected vocabulary items are very difficult to remember. You can demonstrate this to your sts by giving the class a list of 10 unconnected items to remember. Write them on the board or on an OHT. Allow sts to see them for 30 seconds, then wipe the board/turn off the OHP and ask sts to note them down. Then do the same with a list of 10 vocabulary items that come in pairs or groups. Use vocabulary from the unit. Elicit ideas on how to create connections between words that help sts remember them (e.g. compound nouns, collocations, synonyms, antonyms, typical verb-noun connections, word fields). Encourage sts to write topic pages for their vocabulary folder to help them create word associations.

Tip Unless learners feel that they have achieved something, they are likely to give up or reduce their commitment. Encourage learners to set themselves goals and check whether they have reached them. Discuss possible goals and make sure that they are realistic. Use 'Can do' statements and every once in a while ask learners to look back on the way they've come.

Review and practice

1 ▶

Answers: 1 is   2 are   3 a   4 a lot of   5 is   6 some

2 ▶

Answers: 1 Are there any theatres in your town?
2 There isn't a nice restaurant near here.   3 There is a nice hotel near my house.   4 Is there a beach in Barcelona?   5 There are a lot of people in the cinema. 6 There aren't any galleries near here.   7 Are there any museums near this hotel?   8 There is a chemist/café next to this café/chemist.

3 ▶

Answers: 1 A: Is there an Italian restaurant near here?
B: Yes, there is.   2 A: Are there a lot of people in your hotel? B: No, there aren't.   3 A: Is there a car park in front of the hotel? B: No, there isn't.   4 A: Are there any good galleries near your hotel? B: Yes, there are.
5 A: Is there an Indian restaurant on this street? B: No, there isn't.   6 A: Are there any beautiful people in your office? B: Yes, there are.

4 ▶

Answers: 1 I can't use a computer.   2 They can play the piano.   3 Can she cook Italian food?   4 A: Can you drive? B: No, I can't.   5 We can sing but we can't dance.   6 Can you drive?   7 He's only 6 years old but he can play golf.   8 A: Can your dog swim?
B: Yes, he can.

5 ▶

Answers: 1 past   2 French   3 under   4 any   5 use
6 o'clock   7 some   8 play   9 quarter   10 blanket

Notes for using the Common European Framework (CEF)

CEF References

5.1 Can do: give a simple description of a place

CEF A1 descriptor: can produce simple, mainly isolated phrases about people and places (CEF page 58)

5.2 Can do: ask about a new town and where important places are

CEF A1 descriptor: can ask and answer simple questions, initiate and respond to simple statements in areas of immediate need or on very familiar topics (CEF page 74)

5.3 Can do: talk about general abilities

CEF A1 descriptor: can reply in an interview to simple direct questions spoken very slowly and clearly in direct, non-idiomatic speech about personal details (CEF page 82)

CEF quick brief

Usually people think about their learning progress as going from the lowest (A1) level to a higher one (A2, etc.). The CEF refers to this as *vertical progression*. However, the CEF provides a meta-language for a different sort of progression, namely from domain to domain. This is referred to as *horizontal progression*. Having looked at greetings and basic correspondence in a private context, one can extend vertically to a business context, thus widening the range of situations the student can deal with in that language without actually going to the next higher level.

The CEF identifies four basic 'domains' that help to understand this horizontal language, development: the public domain, the personal domain, the educational domain and the occupational domain.

CEF Portfolio task

Download the Total English Portfolio free from www.longman.com/totalenglish.

Objective: to introduce learners to the 'Your aims and objectives' section of the Language Biography.

The second section of the Portfolio is the 'Language Biography', which is for sts to think about and keep a record of their language learning history, objectives and progress through their coursebook.

This task could be done in the sts' first language.

1 ▶   If you think it will be useful, you could explain the names of the six CEF levels, as these are referred to in the table on page 10.

2 ▶   Give some examples of reasons for and objectives of your own language learning.

3 ▶   Encourage sts to list as many aims of their own, trying to make them as personal as possible. Do not insist on all five boxes being filled if sts run out of ideas.

People

Overview

Lead-in	**Vocabulary:** adjectives to describe people, intensifiers
6.1	**Grammar:** Present Simple *I/you ...*; object pronouns: *me, you, him, her, it, us, them*
	Can do: say what you like/don't like
6.2	**Grammar:** Present Simple *we/they*; *Wh-* questions
	Vocabulary: jobs and activities
	Can do: start and continue a conversation with someone you don't know
6.3	**Grammar:** Present Simple *he/she/it*
	Vocabulary: verbs of routine
	Can do: talk about the routines of people you know
Com. Focus	Finding presents for someone on www.findanicepresent.com

Summary

Lesson 1: Sts listen to an interview with a woman who talks about her likes and dislikes. Then they talk about their own likes and dislikes and interview each other about them.

Lesson 2: Sts talk to each other about their jobs, hobbies and personalities.

Lesson 3: Sts talk about people's habits and daily routines.

Communication: Sts look at a website which helps people to find suitable presents and ask and answer about a friend in order to find a present.

Film bank: The interview

A short film of an interview with Andy Platz, the lead singer in a band called *Mama's Gun*.

Possible places to use this short film are:
▶ after 6.3
▶ at the end of the unit

For ways to use this short film in class, see Students' Book page 121 and Teacher's Resource Book pages 137 and 144.

Lead-in

OPTIONAL WARMER

The purpose of this activity is to review job titles, *there is/are* and *some/any,* and to introduce the topic. Books closed. Write *Jobs* on the board and brainstorm job titles. Ask sts to pick one job title each and find out how many (e.g. *doctors*) there are in the class/group (split large classes into groups of four to five), by asking the other sts: *Excuse me, are you a/an ...?* Write this question on the board.

Pool information by asking sts/groups to report back to the class, using: *There are x doctors in our class/group,* or *There aren' t any doctors in our class/group.*

False beginners You could extend this by asking sts, working in pairs or small groups, to brainstorm adjectives they associate with the job title they chose for the first activity (e.g. *doctor – rich, actor – good-looking*). After three minutes, pool ideas, write the adjectives on the board and if opposites are mentioned, group them as opposite pairs.

Tip Explain that learning words as opposite pairs makes them easier to remember. Encourage sts to always find opposites when they learn an adjective. Point out that there may be more than one, depending on the context.

1a ▶ **Real beginners** Ask sts, in pairs, to try to find opposites and guess meanings before they look up the words. Elicit pairs of opposites and ask sts to demonstrate or visualise their meanings. Avoid translation.

b ▶ Ask sts to listen and check their answers. Play recording 6.1.

1a/b ▶ **False beginners** Books closed. Use recording 6.1 as a dictation. Play the recording and ask sts to check their spelling against the box in a.

▶ Play the recording again, or model pronunciation of the words in the box, and ask sts to repeat.

c ▶ **All students** Ask sts to work in pairs and play adjective 'ping pong' with opposites, by taking turns 'throwing' a word at their partner. Alternatively, in a group of up to eight, ask sts to stand in a circle. Nominate a student to say a word and throw a ball to someone who then gives the opposite, etc.

2a ▶ Read the sentences in the box to the sts and give them 30 seconds to put them in order, then ask them to compare ideas with their partner. Go over the answers.

Language note *not very* and *quite* are likely to provoke discussion/questions. Meanings vary, depending on stress and intonation. *He's not very rich* means he isn't rich, whereas *He's not very rich* means that he is, but not as rich as other people.

In British English, *quite* with gradable adjectives means something like *rather*, whereas in American usage, its meaning is closer to *very*. With non-gradable adjectives, *quite* in British English means *completely*, e.g. *That's quite true!* Sts may have experienced these different uses. Be prepared for questions, but don't give complicated explanations.

Answers: +++ He's very rich.   ++ He's rich.
+ He's quite rich.   – He's not very rich.

---

b ▶ Discuss the photos as a class. Sts may try to make comparisons – ask them to give you two contrasting sentences instead, e.g. *The girl is young. The woman is old.* Add relevant vocabulary if necessary, and find opposites.

3 ▶ Remind sts how to give opinions (*I think ...*). Ask pairs to choose eight very different people they both know from TV or films. Explain that sts should take turns to make sentences about one of the people, without saying his/her name. Their partner guesses who it is. They should describe two people each.

6.1 The 60-second interview

In this lesson sts listen to an interview with someone who talks about her likes and dislikes. They talk about their likes and dislikes and interview each other about them. Grammar: Present Simple *I/you*.

> **OPTIONAL WARMER**
>
> Write question openings (e.g. *What's ...? Where ...? What's your favourite ...? How old ...? How ...?*) on the board and ask sts, in pairs, to make as many questions as they can. After two minutes, rearrange the pairs and ask sts to interview their new partner. Circulate and monitor.

Listening

1a ▶ Pool questions from the optional warmer activity on the board if you did it. Or elicit the question openings from the optional warmer and write them on the board. Gather sts' questions on the board.

b ▶ Ask sts to look at the photo and elicit where Cynthia is. Explain that sts are going to listen to a radio programme called *The 60-second interview*. Ask: *How many questions can you ask and answer in 60 seconds?* Choose this number together from the questions on the board.

▶ Ask sts to try and find Cynthia's answer to their questions as they listen. Play recording 6.2. Go through the questions on the board and elicit sts' ideas: *Do we know the answer? What is it?* If the answer is not on the recording, encourage sts to speculate using *I think ...* .

c ▶ Draw a happy and an unhappy face on the board. Point to the appropriate face and say a few sentences about what you like/don't like. Read items 1–10 to the sts and ask them to draw happy/unhappy faces next to each one to show Cynthia's likes and dislikes. Play recording 6.2 again. Check the answers by having sts read out the item and point at the appropriate face on the board.

> **Answers:** 1 ☺ 2 ☹ 3 ☺ 4 ☺ 5 ☺ 6 ☺ 7 ☹
> 8 ☺ 9 ☺ 10 ☺

Grammar 1

2a ▶ Ask sts to find questions with *like* in the tapescript on page 147 and ask them to come up with a structure for the question (*Do you like X?*). Write *Do* in a different colour, if possible. Write *Yes, _ ____* and *No, _ ____* next to the question and ask sts to find the answers in the tapescript. Complete the short answers on the board. Show sts how *Do ...* and *do/don't* start and finish the question and answer. Explain that just answering *Yes* or *No* sounds quite rude.

▶ Ask a few sts questions starting with *Do you like ...?* and elicit answers. Then ask sts to write a list of five things they like and to find three people who like something on their list and three people who don't like something on their list. Remind them that the question is always *Do you like ...?* Circulate and correct as necessary.

Language note There is nothing similar to the English *do*-construction in many languages because questions are formed by inverting the verb and subject. Sts may find it difficult to understand the function of *do*. Written drills can be used to reinforce the structure, but speaking exercises are more likely to get sts used to it.

▶ Ask sts to complete the Active grammar box with a partner. Go over the answers as a class.

> **Answers:** Do   do   don't

b ▶ Ask sts to do this individually. If they finish early, ask them to make the sentences true for themselves by changing them as necessary. Go over the answers and write them on the board.

> **Answers:** 1 I like Rio.   2 I don't like chicken.
> 3 I like London.   4 I like yellow and green.
> 5 I don't like Mondays.   6 I like Spanish films.
> 7 I don't like Manchester United.   8 I don't like six o'clock in the morning.

c ▶ Ask sts to cover the Active grammar box as they write the questions, then compare them with a partner. Sts may ask how to form negative questions, or make *Don't you like ...?* questions. Explain that *Do you like ...?* can elicit a positive or a negative answer. *Don't you like ...?* is a rhetorical question. You may need to explain this.

Pronunciation

3a/b ▶ Books closed. Explain that this is going to be a dictation. Play recording 6.3 item by item. Ask sts to check their spelling against the tapescript on page 147. Ask them to listen again and repeat. Play the recording again. Demonstrate question intonation if necessary.

> **Answers:** 1 Do you like Italian food?   2 Do you like coffee?   3 Are you from Brazil?   4 Are you a student?   5 Do you like London?   6 Do you like Paris?   7 Are you happy?   8 Do you like this film?

Speaking

4a ▶ Ask sts to write their lists. (*Quick follow-on*: Ask sts to write sentences about each item. Circulate and help as necessary.)

b/c ▶ Play a pair finding game: make coloured cards, two of each colour, shuffle them up and give each student a card. Sts find their partner by asking: *Do you like (colour)?* Sts with the same colour work together.

▶ **Real beginners** Ask sts to first exchange sentences and then ask each other questions.

▶ **False beginners** Combine b and c so that sts have conversations about the categories, e.g. A: *I like Indian* food. *Do you like Indian food?* B: *No, I don't. But I like Italian food. Do you like Italian food?* A: *Yes, I do.*

Grammar 2

5a/b ▶ Ask sts to work out with a partner which picture matches which sentence. Explain that they are going to listen to the answers. Play recording 6.4.

> **Answers:** 1 b   2 e   3 d   4 a   5 f   6 c

c ▶ Ask sts to complete the chart. Explain that subject pronouns come before the verb and object pronouns come after the verb. Give a few examples by saying one or two sentences yourself, then prompt sts by giving them names of people.

> **Answers:** me   you   him   her   it   us   them

6a ▶ Explain that sts have lists of things and people that their partners will comment about. Put sts into pairs. Circulate and help as necessary.

b ▶ Ask a student to read the How to … box to the class. Elicit/explain that the reactions *Sorry?* and *Pardon?* mean that you haven't heard what the other person said, and that *Who's Salma Hayek?* means they don't know the person.

c ▶ Ask sts to stand in a circle. One student shouts out a name and throws a ball to someone else, who then has to react somehow.

Speaking

7a ▶ Ask sts to look back at the lesson and write eight questions. Circulate and support.

b ▶ Ask sts to stand in two concentric circles, the outer circle facing inwards, the inner outwards, so that everybody is facing a partner. The outer circle interviews first. Give them exactly one minute to interview their partner, then ask sts in the inner circle to move on one student to the right. The inner circle then interviews their new partner. This should be fast and fun!

> **OPTIONAL WRAP-UP**
>
> Write the words *I*, *like*, *English*, and *food* in large letters on separate pieces of A4 cardboard. Hand out the cards to four sts and ask them to stand up at the front to form a sentence. Give a student a piece of cardboard with a *?* on it and ask him/her to make a question. Provide cards with *do*, *don't*, *No*, *Yes* and *I* and ask sts to manipulate the sentence, question and answers. Discuss possible versions and write them on the board. Ask sts to copy these down. Emphasise that the main verb never moves. Make this very clear by providing a chair for the person holding *like*.

6.2 Making friends

In this lesson sts have conversations about people's jobs, hobbies and personalities. Grammar: Present Simple *we/they*; *Wh-*questions.

> **OPTIONAL WARMER**
>
> The purpose of this activity is to activate relevant vocabulary and prepare sts for new words. Write *buildings*, *newspapers*, *books*, *clothes*, *computers* and *Chinese food* on the board. Ask sts to interview each other about these things, using *Do you like …?* questions. Then ask sts in pairs to try and find related words for each item. Pool ideas and write them on the board. Group them according to their word class.

Vocabulary

1a ▶ Ask sts to match the pictures and jobs. Elicit the answers. Model pronunciation of job titles and ask the class to repeat.

> **Answers:** a designer   b reporter   c chef
> d builder   e architect   f sales rep.

b ▶ Write *Teachers teach subjects, for example English and German and Mathematics* on the board. Explain that this sentence makes it clear what a teacher does. Ask: *What do designers do?* Sts are likely to say *Designers design things.* Then ask sts to read the sentences and match the verbs.

> **Answers:** 1 design   2 sell   3 design   4 write
> 5 cook   6 build

c ▶ Ask sts to check their answers while they listen. Play recording 6.5. Play it again and ask sts to listen carefully. Then ask pairs of sts to read the questions and answers as mini-dialogues.

Language note The *do*-construction was introduced in 6.1, but sts may still find it difficult. *What do … do?* will be particularly confusing because *do* appears in two different functions here, as an auxiliary and a main verb.

▶ Write *What do … do?* on the board using a different colour for the auxiliary, if possible. Underline the second *do* and explain that this is a main verb.

▶ False beginners Ask sts to brainstorm words that could fill the gap (*students, teachers, children, singers*, etc.). Elicit verbs and write them on the board. Ask sts to write sentences using these verbs.

2a ▶ Ask a student to read the example. Elicit/explain the meaning of *too*. Explain that *too* comes at the end of a sentence after a comma. Ask for another example for one or two of the sentences in Ex. 1b and write them on the board. Then put sts in groups of three to think of more examples.

b ▶ Put sts from different groups into pairs to exchange definitions by asking the questions in Ex. 1b. Circulate and correct as necessary.

Listening

3a ▶ Ask sts to look at the photo. Ask them where this is and who they think the people are (hotel lobby, two couples). Explain that they are having a conversation about their jobs. Ask sts to find out who is who and to match the jobs to the people. Play recording 6.6. Elicit/discuss the answers.

> **Answers:** architect: Sharon, Pat
> sales rep.: Catherine   chef: Anthony

b ▶ Give sts two minutes to read the statements first and say from memory which are true and which false. Then play recording 6.6 again. Go over the answers, then elicit any other details sts can remember.

▶ Ask sts to go to the tapescript on pages 147–148 and read it as they listen again, then put sts into groups of four to read the conversation. Circulate and monitor.

> **Answers:** 1 T   2 T   3 F   4 T   5 F   6 F

Grammar 1

4a ▶ Ask sts to look at the Active grammar box with a partner and fill the gaps. Explain that they can look at lesson 6.1 for help if they wish. Check the answers. Write the examples on the board and use a different colour for the auxiliary. Ask sts to give you examples with *I* and *you* and add them to the board.

> **Answers:** don't   do   don't

▶ Ask sts to look back at the statements in Ex. 3b and to correct the false ones by using the negative. Elicit answers from the class and write them on the board.

b/c ▶ Ask sts to look at the sentences and mark them true or false individually, then to interview each other and note down the results. Ask pairs to report back to the class on what they have in common. Correct the grammar. Note: sts shouldn't present what they don't have in common because they need the third person form, which will be introduced next lesson.

Grammar 2

5 ▶ Ask sts to complete the Active grammar box. Tell them they can look at the questions in the tapescript on page 148. Go over the answers.

> **Answers:** Where   What   Who

6 ▶ Ask sts to do this individually. Write all the pairs of questions and answers on the board or prepare an OHT. Ask sts to underline the question words and the part of the answer that corresponds to the question word. Look at and discuss each question-answer pair in turn. As a result, the structure of *Who do you work for?* should become clear: *Who* is an object here, not a subject. You can also clarify that *What do you do?* means *What's your job?* Sts may think that it has a broader meaning, i.e. *What are you doing?*

> **Answers:** 1 What do you do?   2 What do you write?
> 3 Where do you work?   4 Who do you work for?
> 5 What do you design?   6 What do you do?
> 7 Where do you live?   8 What do you sell?

7 ▶ Ask sts in pairs to look at the How … to box and make their own dialogue by choosing from the options. Invite a pair to read their version. Model intonation of *Oh really?* and *Great!* and ask the class to repeat. Then have more pairs read their versions to the class.

> **OPTIONAL EXTENSION**
>
> Prepare sets of cards with *Excuse me., Sorry?, Oh really?, Great!, Pardon?, Who is …?* and *What is …?.* Give a set to each group of three to four sts. Ask them to put the cards in the middle and pick one each, then to ask and answer questions about who they are, where they live and work, etc. using the phrases on the cards.

Reading

8a ▶ Ask sts to look at the photo and elicit ideas about the two people. Explain that they are Clarissa and Martin. Ask sts to find their names, jobs and ages in the article. Give them two minutes to find the information. Check the answers.

> **Answers:** Name: Martin Dolan   Job: accountant
> Age: 23;   Name: Clarissa Hanson   Job: actor
> Age: over 60

b ▶ Ask a student to read out the adjectives. Clarify meanings if necessary. Explain that they apply to Clarissa, Martin, both of them or neither of them. Give sts four minutes to find the answers. Ask them to compare answers with their partner, then go over them as a class. Call on individual sts and ask them to give an answer and read the relevant sentence in the text.

> **Answers:** 1 rich N   2 young M   3 intelligent C/M
> 4 poor N   5 young-at-heart C

Speaking

9 ▶ Refer sts to the photo at the top of the page and review the situation: *Who are they? What do they discuss?* With real beginners, play recording 6.6 again to remind sts. Explain that sts will be given roles and role play a similar situation. Form groups of four and allocate roles. Remind sts to use the phrases from Ex. 7 – you could re-use the cards suggested in the optional extension activity. Circulate and support as necessary. Note down problems to follow up in a correction spot.

> **OPTIONAL WRAP-UP**
>
> Ask sts in groups of three to write a questionnaire. Circulate, checking question formation. Re-group sts and ask them to interview each other. At the end, pool all questions, write them on the board and answer them about yourself. Add a few sentences

on your daily routine, possibly on members of your family, to use language which sts will study in the next lesson.

Tip We tend to underestimate our sts. Provide language input at a level that is slightly higher than the sts'. Stephen Krashen, a linguist, has dubbed this n+1 level. By providing short texts about familiar topics (e.g. newspaper headlines) or by telling stories about yourself, you teach sts to listen for gist, and they will pick up language that in time they can use actively.

6.3 Daily routines

In this lesson, sts talk about people and their habits/daily routines. Grammar: Present Simple *he/she/it*.

OPTIONAL WARMER

Real beginners Draw a few clock faces on the board, between 6 a.m. and 10 p.m. Ask sts to say the times and try to make sentences with them, e.g. *the supermarket is open from 8 to 6. I work from 9 to 5.* Then tell them about your daily routine, using verbs that will come up in the lesson.

False beginners Give sts a multiple choice question, for example, say four daily routine verbs and ask sts to order them chronologically, e.g. *A go to bed, B have breakfast, C get up, D have a shower.*

Vocabulary

1a ▶ Read the sentences to the sts, then ask them to match the sentences and pictures and write in the phrases. Check the answers by asking one student to read the sentence and another to point at the picture and mime the action.

Answers: a 4 get up   b 7 finish work   c 5 watch TV
d 6 eat fast food   e 3 eat salad   f 1 start work
g 8 go to bed   h 2 have a shower

---

b ▶ Elicit a few examples, then ask sts to write true sentences about themselves. Circulate and help.

▶ Ask sts to give you some example sentences and model and correct intonation and pronunciation before they work in pairs. Encourage them to show the difference in meaning between their sentences by using contrastive stress. Then ask sts to find a new partner. Ask them to stand while they read their sentences to each other. Circulate and correct if sts make serious errors.

Reading

2a ▶ Ask sts to work in pairs to look at the photos. Ask them to brainstorm what sort of person they think each one is. Pool ideas and put vocabulary on the board. Then ask them to match the sentences from Ex. 1a to the people in the photos. Remind them of *I think ... .*

b ▶ Read the text to the sts and ask them to check

their answers. Go over the answers together, asking one student to read out the sentence from Ex. 1a and another to read out the sentence from the text. Leave out the negative sentences to begin with. Write all the positive sentences on the board. Underline the pronouns and verbs and circle the *s* in the third person. Watch pronunciation of *watches, finishes.*

▶ Add sentences 2, 5 and 8 (negatives), using the same procedure as above. Use a different colour for the auxiliary *do.* Ask sts: *Where has the 's' gone?* Elicit/teach that the *s* is attached to *do* unless the word *do* isn't there.

▶ Give sts a few minutes to read the text, then ask a few sts to read one paragraph each out aloud.

Answers: 1 Roberta   2 Frank   3 Elaine   4 Adam
5 Elaine   6 Frank   7 Roberta   8 Adam

OPTIONAL EXTENSION

Ask sts to go back to the sentences they wrote in Ex. 1b and exchange their notes with a partner. Ask them to re-write the sentences as if they were true for their partner, e.g. *Paul gets up at 7 o'clock.* Do an example or two with the class first. Circulate. Ask sts to present their partner to the group by reading out their sentences.

---

c ▶ Write *get up at eight?* on the board and ask sts to form a question. They'll probably say *Do you ...?* first. Write the *Do you* question on the board and ask sts to ask about Adam. See if they can construct the question. Write it on the board, using a different colour for *does,* and circle the *s.*

▶ Ask two sts to read the question and answer in the example. Call on individual sts to read the questions and elicit answers from the class. Ask sts to make more questions of this type about the text. Elicit ideas and get someone to answer each question.

Answers: 1 No, he doesn't.   2 No, he doesn't.
3 No, she doesn't.   4 Yes, she does.   5 Yes, he does.   6 No, she doesn't.

Grammar

3 ▶ Ask sts to complete the Active grammar box individually and then compare their answers with a partner. Go through the answers as a class. Point out the pronunciation of *finishes* and elicit similar examples (*watches, kisses*). To show why these endings are pronounced /ɪz/, ask a few sts to try and add the *s* directly to the verb – you can't! Elicit/teach the spelling rule.

Answers: starts   finishes   doesn't   doesn't   Does

4a ▶ Read the verbs in the box to the sts. Then ask them to give you the third person form. Ask sts to shout them out. Then ask sts to fill in the gaps individually. Go over the answers by having sts read whole sentences aloud.

► You can use this text for an exercise on intonation. Call on two or three sts to read the whole text to the class. Ask them to sound convincing, as if they are really talking about their friend. Then put sts in pairs and get them to practise reading the text convincingly.

Answers: 1 works   2 gets   3 has   4 watches
5 starts   6 eats   7 finishes   8 likes

b ► Ask sts to write the sentences individually. Circulate and support as necessary. Go over the answers. Ask sts to explain their answers to the class.

Answers: 1 doesn't like   2 Do, work   3 does, do
4 doesn't write   5 does, finish   6 Do, start
7 don't go   8 does, write

Speaking

5a/b ► The notes are to spark ideas and to help sts structure them. Read through a and b with the sts to clarify the task, then ask them to make notes individually. Circulate and help with vocabulary. Real beginners could write full sentences. False beginners should produce notes.

c ► Put sts into pairs and ask them to tell each other the four names of the people they wrote about. They then ask each other about these people. Real beginners read their texts to each other; false beginners answer the questions with full sentences using their notes.

Listening

6a ► Write *soulmate* on the board and ask sts what they think it means. Elicit ideas, then explain that *soulmates* are people who love each other and who are very alike or very close. Explain that sts are going to listen to a song. Ask them to note down what the two people in the song do (i.e. the verbs). Play recording 6.7.

Answers: get up   eat   love   need   finish   watch
do   drink

b ► Ask sts to listen again and check/complete their notes. Pool ideas and write them in a table on the board. Put what she does in one column and what he does in another. Clarify the contrasts, but note that *work – watch TV* is less obvious than *get up early – get up late*.

c ► Ask: *Does Emma like the song? What does she like/ doesn't she like about it?* Pool ideas. Then put sts into pairs and ask them to discuss what they think about the song. Introduce *because*.

► Depending on how sts like the song, they can either re-write it or add lines. Ask them to find a rhythm for their lines. After a few minutes, ask a few pairs to perform or read out their songs.

Writing

7a ► Ask sts to turn to page 128. Read the letter to the sts and ask questions about it to ensure sts understand. Ask them to make notes about what information Fran includes. Then point out the structure of the letter and the language used to start and finish it.

b ► Ask sts to make notes about their life, using the notes they made about Fran's letter. You could set the letter for homework/self study.

OPTIONAL WRAP-UP

Sts could add verbs of routine to their vocabulary folders and word boxes. In their groups, they could put the verb cards in the middle (or write the verbs on separate pieces of paper) and take turns to pick up a card and ask another student a question using that verb.

6 Communication: www.findanicepresent.com

In this lesson sts look at a present-finding website and discuss choosing suitable presents.

OPTIONAL WARMER

Ask sts to write down the names of three friends or family members on a piece of paper. Revise third person *s* by asking sts to work in groups with the verb cards they made at the end of last lesson (see optional wrap-up). They put the cards in the middle and take turns drawing a card and making a sentence using that verb about one of the three people on their list.

1a/b ► Ask sts in pairs to look at the words in the box and explain to each other the ones they know. Pairs then try to match words to photos. Check the answers and clarify the meanings of all the words.

Answers: 1 travel iron   2 saucepans   3 DVD
4 suitcase   5 candles   6 book   7 CD   8 tie
9 pen

2 ► Ask sts to look at the website. Ask: *Do you use this sort of website? Do you search the net to find presents?* Pool ideas. Ask: *How can this website help you find the right present?* Sts will guess that the half questions make up some sort of questionnaire.

► Ask sts to listen for what the problem is. Play recording 6.8 and elicit the answer.

Answers: Josef doesn't know what to buy Nisha for her birthday.

3a ► Ask various sts to read out the words/questions on the website. Clarify meanings as necessary.

b/c ► Explain that Josef uses the website to find a present for Nisha. Ask sts to note down the answers to the questions. Play recording 6.9. Check the answers by one student asking the complete question and another one answering. Ask sts to consider Nisha's profile and make suggestions, e.g. *I think the right present for Nisha is ... .* Pool ideas. Then ask sts to go to page 148 to see what the computer found.

> **Answers b:** Work long hours? Y   Married? N
> Have children? N   Travel a lot? Y   Can cook? N
> Watch a lot of films? N   Listen to a lot of music? Y

> **Answers c:** a pen   a suitcase   a CD

4a ▶ Ask: *Do you think these questions are enough?*
Put sts into groups of three and ask them to find more
questions to ask about someone, and to add more
possible presents.

b ▶ Rearrange sts into pairs from different groups. One
student thinks of someone and answers questions, the
other asks questions and selects three possible items.

Lifelong learning

Write *kettle, towel, blanket, skirt, shirt* and *map* on the
board. Ask sts to give meanings. Ask a student to read
the Lifelong learning box to the class. Tell sts that the
words were taken from Units 3 and 5, but that they need
them in Unit 6.

> **OPTIONAL WRAP-UP**
>
> Ask sts to select three or four items and write a
> short advertisement for them. Describe the item
> (using adjectives), and describe people who use
> it, e.g. *A career woman has a stylish bag, and she
> writes with a designer pen. She reads books. She
> doesn't cook – she eats in restaurants.*

Review and practice

1 ▶

> **Answers:** 1 Do you like   2 I like   3 Do you like   4 I like
> 5 I don't like   6 I like   7 I like   8 Do you like

2 ▶

> **Answers:** 1 her   2 it   3 them   4 me   5 you   6 him
> 7 us

3 ▶

> **Answers:** 1 Where   2 Who   3 What   4 What   5 Where
> 6 What

4 ▶

> **Answers:** 1 designs   2 gets up   3 doesn't have a
> shower   4 doesn't eat   5 watches   6 starts   7 doesn't
> work   8 works   9 finishes   10 goes

5 ▶

> **Answers:** 1 I don't like French food.   2 She gets up
> at 8 o'clock.   3 Do they start work early?   4 Thomas
> doesn't eat salad.   5 Does Clara watch TV every day?
> 6 Paul and I write articles for Newsmag.   7 Where does
> Lorraine live?   8 Jo and Ian don't go to bed late.

6 ▶

> **Answers:** 1 f   2 c   3 d   4 a   5 h   6 e   7 b   8 g

Notes for using the Common European Framework (CEF)

CEF References

6.1 Can do: say what you like/don't like

CEF A1 descriptor: can reply in an interview to simple direct
questions spoken very slowly and clearly in direct non-
idiomatic speech about personal details (CEF page 82)

6.2 Can do: start and continue a conversation with
someone you don't know

CEF A1 descriptor: can establish basic social contact by
using the simplest everyday polite forms of: greetings
and farewells; introductions; saying *please, thank you,
sorry*, etc. (CEF page 122)

6.3 Can do: talk about the routines of people you know

CEF A1 descriptor: can produce simple, mainly isolated
phrases about people and places (CEF page 58)

CEF quick brief

The CEF was produced by specialists in the theory and
practice of language testing and language teaching.
It was commissioned by the Council of Europe in
order to promote multilingualism and to come to an
understanding of functional, communicative language
competence in a Europe where linguistic and cultural
diversity and international/intercultural communication
are not mutually exclusive. The CEF is not a syllabus, but
a guideline for teachers, authors or test designers who
would like to put together a course or test at a particular
level. It does not prescribe a way to teach or an order to
teach in. The CEF specifications (e.g. can give and ask for
personal information) provide a framework for selecting
the language that needs to be taught (vocabulary,
grammar, phrases, e.g. *What's your name? Where are
you from?* and corresponding answers).

CEF Portfolio task

Objective: to encourage a reflective and independent
approach to the learner's own learning.

The task could be completed in class.

1 ▶ Refer sts to the *Can do* section of the Language
Biography (downloadable from www.longman.com/
totalenglish), and to the *Can do* statements which apply
to Unit 6.

2 ▶ After sts have filled in the grid by ticking the
appropriate box, you may like to ask them which two of
the *Can do* skills are most important for them and why.
At this level, this could be done in the sts' first language.

3 ▶ If you feel it is appropriate and likely to generate
useful discussion, you could ask sts if they have ever
been in a situation where they have needed or wanted to
be able to do any things in the unit's *Can do* statements.
You could ask for the name of a song in English they
would like to be able to (or already can) understand.

Overview

Lead-in	**Vocabulary:** places where people work, jobs
7.1	**Grammar:** imperatives
	Vocabulary: months
	Can do: understand simple written and spoken instructions
7.2	**Grammar:** adverbs of frequency
	Vocabulary: work phrases
	Can do: say how often you do something
7.3	**Grammar:** *would like*
	Vocabulary: ordinal numbers
	Can do: welcome a visitor to your place of work
Com. Focus	Take the lift to the third floor

Summary

Lesson 1: Sts learn how to give simple instructions and talk about classroom etiquette. They also practise how to greet people in a business/formal context and have short telephone conversations.

Lesson 2: Sts talk about how often they do certain things, especially typical work activities.

Lesson 3: Sts talk about appointment times and dates and birthdays. They also learn how to offer visitors food and drinks, and how to respond to offers of refreshments.

Communication: Sts practise asking for and giving information and simple directions within a building.

Film bank: The company

A short film which gives brief details of the working days of four employees of a company: the receptionist, the chef, a designer and a post room worker.

Possible places to use this short film are:
- ▶ after 7.2
- ▶ after 7.3
- ▶ at the end of the unit

For ways to use this short film in class, see Students' Book page 122 and Teacher's Resource Book pages 138 and 145.

Lead-in

OPTIONAL WARMER

The purpose of this activity is to review job titles and activities and to introduce the topic. Books closed. Ask sts in groups to brainstorm jobs and related activities. Ask them to write each job on a separate piece of paper and add an activity for each one. Groups give one of their ideas to a student from a

different group. This student has to mime the activity and his/her group tries to guess the job and activity. Collect all the papers and put them up on the board or classroom wall. Ask: *Where do these people work?*

1a ▶ Ask sts to look at the photos. Ask: *Who are these people? Where is this?* Elicit ideas.

b ▶ **Real beginners** Ask sts to work with a partner to match the words in the box to the pictures. Check the answers with the whole class. Read the words to the class to model pronunciation and ask sts to repeat.

▶ **False beginners** See below.

Answers: A call centre   B office   C hospital
D university   E shop   F restaurant   G factory
H school

2a ▶ **Real beginners** Read the words to the class and ask sts to repeat. Then ask sts to match people to places individually. Go over the answers.

Answers: 1 restaurant   2 office   3 factory
4 hospital   5 shop   6 university   7 call centre
8 school

1b/2a ▶ **False beginners** Put the words on cards and do the matching exercise as a partner finding game. Pairs then match the other words. Don't go over the answers, but explain that sts are going to listen to the answers.

2b ▶ **All students** Play recording 7.1 for sts to correct their answers. Ask: *Who works in a school?* Elicit *A teacher works in a school.* Ask a student to ask the next question. Repeat around the class.

c ▶ **Real beginners** Ask sts to look at the words in Ex. 1b again and then to cover them. Ask them to listen to the recording and write the jobs in the gaps. Play recording 7.2.

▶ Ask sts to check their spelling and look at the words in a. Again, ask them to cover the words as they listen and complete the sentences. Play recording 7.2 again.

▶ **False beginners** Write the sample sentences on the board. Ask sts to close their books and write similar sentences about the people they can hear on the recording. Play recording 7.2. Go over the answers. Ask sts to check their writing against the words in Exs. 1b and 2a.

Answers: 1 She's a shop assistant. She works in a shop.   2 She's a call centre worker. She works in a call centre.   3 He's a teacher. He works in a school.   4 He's a waiter. He works in a restaurant.   5 She's a PA. She works in an office.   6 He's a lecturer. He works in a university.   7 He's a factory worker. He works in a factory.   8 She's a nurse. She works in a hospital.

7.1 A new teacher

In this lesson sts learn how to give simple instructions and talk about classroom etiquette. They also practise how to greet people in a business/formal context and have short telephone conversations. Grammar: imperatives.

OPTIONAL WARMER

This job-guessing game reactivates job vocabulary and practises question formation with *do*. Ask a student to think of a job and to write it on a piece of paper which he/she hands to you. The group then asks questions that must be answered with either *Yes* or *No* in order to find out what job it is. Model a question, e.g. *Does this person write books?*

Listening and vocabulary

1a ▶ Ask sts to look at the pictures and explain that they are a sort of picture story. Establish who the people are and where these situations take place. Elicit ideas as to the sort of conversation that may take place in these scenes. This will be guesswork, of course, but it will prepare sts for the listening text. Stronger sts may even be able to put together short dialogues.

b ▶ Explain that sts are going to listen to three dialogues. Each relates to one picture. Ask sts to listen and note down names, then play recording 7.3.

Answers: 1 Jake Parker   2 Alice Fischer   3 Steven

c ▶ Ask sts to look at the phrases first and note down answers as they listen. Play recording 7.3 again. Go over the answers.

Answers: a 2   b 1   c 3   d 3   e 3   f 3   g 2

d ▶ Give sts a few minutes to match the phrases from c to the pictures, then go over the answers. You can make this into a partner finding game by putting the words and pictures on cards – the advantages are that it gets sts moving, and that they will work with a different partner for the Active grammar box exercise.

Answers: a 6   b 4   c 5   d 7   e 1   f 2   g 3

Grammar

2 ▶ Ask pairs of sts to find a verb for each gap. Ask sts to find formulae for the imperative for positive and negative sentences (verb + X; *Don't* + verb + X). Insist that sts use *please* to soften the imperative. Demonstrate, using tone of voice, that *Sit down!* is very different from *Please sit down.*

Answers: Look   come   sit

3 ▶ Ask sts to work individually on the first set of sentences, then go over the answers as a class. Ask sts whether they think these rules should apply in their English class. In groups or as a class, brainstorm further

classroom rules. You could write these on a poster to put up in the classroom entitled *Our classroom do's and dont's.* Then ask sts to read the short text silently and elicit what sort of text it is. Give sts two minutes to fill in the gaps. Ask a student to read the note to the class to check the answers.

Answers: 1 Don't be   2 Speak   3 Turn off   4 Use
5 don't get up   6 don't watch   7 eat   8 Don't eat

OPTIONAL EXTENSION

Ask sts to think of a similar situation in which they would write a note to a friend, family member, colleague, etc. to give them instructions, or give sts situations to use. Ask sts to write a note. Circulate and support. Ask a few sts to read their notes to the class. Correct the grammar.

(If you have a class email list, you could exchange notes like these through email!)

4 ▶ Give sts a moment to look at places a–e. Explain that they are going to listen to five recordings and need to decide where each one takes place. Play recording 7.4. Ask sts to exchange ideas with a partner. As you go over the answers, ask sts to reconstruct as much of the recording as they can manage.

Answers: 1 d   2 e   3 a   4 b   5 c

5 ▶ You could link imperatives for how to learn English to the work you do on lifelong learning and the language portfolio. *How to succeed at work* will probably be more interesting for sts who learn English primarily for business reasons. By this time, you'll know your group quite well – pick one of the topics as a focus and one for individual writing practice.

▶ For your focus topic (see above), elicit from the class or provide sub-topics, e.g. for learning English: how to learn vocabulary, how to practise pronunciation, how/where to find real-life situations in which you can practise English (see Lifelong learning below); for succeeding at work: how to get things done efficiently, how to find a job, how to manage your time, how to deal with difficult colleagues, etc.

▶ Split the class into pairs or groups of three and give a subtopic to each group. Ask them to think of as many ideas as possible. Circulate and help with vocabulary. Provide groups with a basic grid for giving presentations (welcome, introducing oneself, content, invite questions and discuss ideas). Give sts 10 minutes (with a five-minute warning), then ask them to present their ideas. Write them on the board or, if possible, on a poster that you can put up in the classroom.

▶ For the individual writing practice, ask sts to write sentences individually and pool/discuss a few ideas. (*Alternative:* ask sts to write sentences via the class email list and invite an email-based discussion. A simple mailing list will do for this if everybody uses 'Reply to all'.)

Speaking

6a ▶ If you like acting, you could get out your mobile phone at this stage, apologise to the class and explain that this is urgent, and pretend you are ringing the head/director of your school. Use the language A uses in the How to … box and add some details. Obviously, this should only take a minute or two.

▶ Alternatively, or after your improvisation, ask three sts to read the How to … box to the class as a role play. Ask sts who they think the people are, e.g. *B = secretary, A = a pupil's mother, C = head teacher*. B is quite clear. For A and C quite a bit of variation is possible. Elicit a few ideas and make notes on the board.

b ▶ Group sts in threes and ask them to role play one of the ideas on the board, then the three situations given. Sts should take on a different role in each role play.

> **OPTIONAL EXTENSION**
>
> Develop one of the situations into a longer role play, including the reason for calling and possibly more detail. Give sts time to work out ideas. Circulate and support. Ask a few groups to perform their role plays.

Lifelong learning

▶ Possible activities depend partly on what you did in Ex. 5. Pick one or two ideas from the lists groups created about learning English and convert them into specific tasks for sts to do (see below). Alternatively, try the following activity. Ask sts: *Can you book a flight on the internet?* They're likely to say *Yes*. Ask: *Can you book a flight on the internet in English?* Explain that everything will look almost exactly the same, and ask them to find (not book!) a flight to London for the following week as homework. Ask them to look for the cheapest one they can find, and to bring a printout the following week. You could bring in a prize for the person who finds the cheapest direct flight.

▶ Remind sts of a few things they now can do in English, e.g. order food in a restaurant, help English-speaking tourists by giving directions, and elicit ideas where they can do these things in English in their home town.

Reading

7 ▶ Books closed. Explain that sts will read a text about a teacher's (Tim's) daily schedule. Read the questions to the class and ask them to note down spontaneous ideas. Pool ideas.

▶ Ask sts to scan the text for answers to the questions. The first student to finish should shout *Bingo!* Go over the answers. Call on individual sts to read a question and give their answer.

▶ Give sts two minutes to re-read the text, then ask them to close their books. Explain that you are going to read the text to them but that you will pause in places. In the pauses, sts should shout out the word that follows as a class. Suggested pauses: before prepositions, times, months and important content words.

> **Answers:** 1 eight o'clock 2 He looks at students' books and prepares lessons. 3 in his classroom 4 He teaches football or works in his classroom. 5 half past nine in the evening 6 in July and August

Cultural note Because of the differences between teachers' routines in different countries and the description in the text, sts may be surprised, confused or even have problems understanding it. Some explanation of this may be necessary, and this may even provoke a discussion about full-time schooling, working hours, etc. Some of the key differences are: teaching hours, length of holidays, whether they stay in one classroom or move about, where they do lesson preparation, and marking.

Vocabulary

8a ▶ **Real beginners** Ask sts to underline the stressed syllables as they listen. Play recording 7.5.

▶ **False beginners** Books closed. Ask sts to write the words as they listen and to underline the stressed syllable. Play recording 7.5 item by item. Ask sts to check spelling against the book.

> **Answers:** January February March April May June July August September October November December

b ▶ Play the recording again, item by item, and ask the class to repeat.

c ▶ Sts may find it difficult to guess the exact month, but they will probably be able to guess the season. Supply vocabulary if necessary. With false beginners, discuss ideas and ask sts to give reasons. They'll need to describe the pictures for this.

> **Answers:** a April b January c October d July

d ▶ If you have very creative/artistic sts, you may ask them to draw a calendar picture for their month. Then they work in pairs and ask their partners to guess which one it is before telling them. You may also bring a selection of pictures for them to choose from, and again partners guess which is the other's favourite month. If sts find it difficult to decide, make the question more specific, e.g. sts' favourite month for a holiday.

▶ Ask sts to complete the sentences individually first,

> **OPTIONAL WRAP-UP**
>
> Ask sts to write a text about themselves, similar to the text in Ex. 7. Sts exchange texts with their partner. Then ask sts to give their partners some advice on what they should change/do, e.g. if someone writes about their stressful job, the other student could say/write *Take yoga classes*. Circulate and support as necessary.

7.2 Do you give presentations?

In this lesson sts discuss how often they do certain things, particularly job-related activities. They also learn to understand and write request notes or emails. This is a job-oriented lesson. You could cover the same ground with free-time related vocabulary if this suits your class better, but ensure you work with verb + X constructions (e.g. verb + time/place/object).

> **OPTIONAL WARMER**
>
> This activity reactivates vocabulary related to daily routine and introduces the word order for adverbs of frequency. Write on the board *It never rains in California!* Say: *I never get up at 4 o'clock in the morning.* Ask sts to think of something they never do at a certain time and tell the class. Encourage absurd or funny ideas, correct grammar and write ideas on the board.

Vocabulary

1a▶ Have a class brainstorming of jobs.

b▶ Read the work phrases in the box to the class and ask sts in pairs to match them to the pictures. Discuss ideas picture by picture and clarify meanings of all phrases (e.g. to work from home – a housewife/househusband works *in* the home, but not *from* home).

> **Answers:** 1 travel abroad   2 work from home   3 answer the phone   4 take work home   5 work outdoors   6 have meetings   7 call customers   8 write reports   9 give presentations   10 help people

2a▶ Explain that the *What's your job?* board is the basis for a game show, like a questionnaire. Elicit one or two questions. Then ask sts to listen and write down *Yes* or *No* for each activity for John. Play recording 7.6. Go over the answers by asking *Does John ...?* for each activity. At this point, don't go into any more detail – this would involve adverbs of frequency. Write the questions on the board or prepare an OHT and write *Y* or *N* against them as you go over the answers.

> **Answers:** work from home N   have meetings Y   give presentations Y   call customers N   write reports Y   take work home N   travel abroad N   answer the phone Y   work outdoors Y

b▶ Ask sts to open their books and look at the tapescript. Read the adverbs of frequency in the box to them and ask them to complete the tapescript as they listen. Play recording 7.6 again. Clarify the meaning of the adverbs of frequency by drawing a diagram like the one in the Active grammar box on the board and adding the adverbs on a scale of 0%–100%. Ask sts to read the dialogue aloud with a partner. Circulate and correct pronunciation.

> **Answers:** never   often   sometimes   never   usually   usually   never   often   often   always

Grammar

3 Ask sts to look at the Active grammar box first and then to find the sentences in Ex.2b to complete it. Elicit the answers.

> **Answers:** 'm always   usually write

4a▶ Sts should correct the sentences individually. Ask them to decide for each sentence which type it is, and then to correct it. Go over the answers and write them on the board.

▶ Ask sts: *Do we need another formula for negative sentences?* Sts may see straight away that the basic formulae are still valid, but you could write negative formulae as well (verb *be* + *not* + adverb of frequency; *don't/doesn't* + adverb of frequency + verb).

> **Answers:** 1 I never work from home.   2 She doesn't often travel abroad.   3 I usually take work home.   4 We always call customers.   5 We sometimes write reports in the evening.   6 He never works outdoors.   7 I don't often give presentations.   8 They always call their customers in the evening.

b▶ Ask sts to write the sentences individually. In a business-oriented class change this task to a job-related topic. You may need to give more vocabulary for this. Circulate, support and correct.

Pronunciation

5a▶ Explain that this is a dictation. Play recording 7.7 item by item. Ask sts to check their spelling against the tapescript on page 148.

> **Answers:** 1 I usually have a meeting on Monday morning.   2 I often take work home.   3 I don't usually answer the phone.   4 I don't often give presentations.

b▶ Ask sts to listen again, this time concentrating on pronunciation and intonation. Play the recording again. Ask individual sts and the class to repeat the sentences. 'Conduct' stress and intonation.

Speaking

6▶ Play a guessing game about jobs, similar to the one in recording 7.6. One student thinks of a job, the other asks questions using *How often ...?* Answers will be sentences like the ones in Ex. 4a. Demonstrate this by thinking of a job yourself and answering the sts' questions. Sts then play the game in pairs or groups. Each student should prepare by writing sentences about a job first. Then the question and answer phase begins. Circulate and monitor.

Writing

7a ▶ Ask sts in pairs to discuss which picture goes with which note. Elicit the answers. You may need to explain that the people in the pictures are doing what the notes ask them to do.

> **Answers:** 1 b   2 c   3 a

b ▶ Ask sts to re-read the notes and find differences between them and to mention anything they find surprising. Point out that the name of the addressee is not followed by a comma, and that the first word of the note is capitalised. Point out the comma after *thanks*.

Language note Discuss the different ways of addressing people and explain that the second note is not unfriendly, though it could be rude in some cultures. In informal email replies you sometimes leave out the addressee altogether.

▶ As you discuss these points, refer sts to the How to … box. Then ask sts to write the note to Benita individually and ask a few sts to read theirs to the class. Write a sample answer on the board. (*Alternative:* Ask sts to send their note to the email list or to write you/their learning partner an email.)

> **Possible answer:**
> (Benita)
> Can you come to my office at 7 o'clock tomorrow morning?
> Many thanks.

> **OPTIONAL WRAP-UP**
>
> Ask sts to write a sentence about each job that they have learnt so far, e.g. *Teachers never work outdoors, but they often take work home,* to add to their vocabulary folders.

7.3 Would you like a coffee?

In this lesson sts talk about appointments and birthdays (dates, ordinal numbers) and learn how to offer and ask for food and drink. Grammar: *would like*.

> **OPTIONAL WARMER**
>
> This activity reviews months and introduces ordinal numbers. Ask sts to stand in a circle and count to twelve, then to say the months together. Then give a ball to a student and explain that sts should say a number from 1 to 12 and throw the ball to another student. This student says the appropriate month, says another number and throws the ball to someone else. Sts tend not to mix the order unless you encourage them to. Play the game for a few minutes. If you want to extend this to introduce ordinal numbers, ask sts to go back to their seats. Write *1st class, 2nd hand* on the board. Elicit *first, second* and ask: *Which one is the first month of the year?* Elicit the answer and write *January is the*

first month of the year. Ask sts in pairs to write sentences for the other months, then go over the sentences and elicit/teach ordinal numbers.

Listening

1a ▶ You could use the optional warmer activity here or alternatively, ask pairs to say the months of the year together.

b ▶ Ask sts to look at the picture and guess who the two people are and what they are discussing. Explain that they are the boss, who doesn't know what happens when, and her PA, who does. Explain that sts are going to listen to their conversation. Read the rubric to the sts and ask them to find the dates as they listen. Play recording 7.8. Check the answers and elicit any other information sts can remember.

> **Answers:** 1 6th June   2 8th June   3 14th June
> 4 24th June   5 6th June

2 ▶ Ask sts who Mr Rogers is and explain that the PA (Personal Assistant) is going to welcome him. Encourage sts to think about the sort of situation, and what these people are like. Put sts into groups of three and ask them to write a conversation, referring to the How to … boxes from the book for help. In a small class, ask groups to perform for the class, otherwise circulate as sts act out the conversation.

Vocabulary

3a ▶ Ask sts to look at the dates that have been mentioned so far and try and remember how to say them. Elicit a few ideas and correct as necessary. Ask sts to listen and repeat the ordinal numbers. Play recording 7.9 item by item. Elicit a rule for forming ordinal numbers. Sts should be able to pick out -th from listening. Practise pronunciation by asking individual sts to repeat numbers you model for them. Sts tend to find -th in *fifth, twelfth, sixth* and *eighth* and -ieth in *twentieth* difficult.

b ▶ Ask sts to look at the chart on page 77 and explain/ elicit why some numbers are colour-coded. Explain what the irregularities are. Then ask sts to practise pronunciation in pairs. Circulate and correct.

4 ▶ Ask sts to read the How to … box. Read the dates to sts and ask them to repeat.

Language note Sts may have come across other versions, e.g. AE versions (April 3rd) and may ask questions about them. If they do, explain.

5a ▶ Ask: *What's the date today?* Elicit the answer and write it on the board in numbers and in words. Circle *the* and *of*. Put sts in pairs and suggest that they each write five dates that mean something to them, e.g. national holidays, festivals or similar. They show these dates to their partner, who says the dates and guesses what the dates are. Circulate and correct as necessary.

b ▶ Explain that in one corner of the classroom it's January, and in the other it's December, and ask sts to line up according to their birthday by asking each other when their birthday is. Start this off by asking a student when her/his birthday is and asking them to stand in a certain spot. Sts then get up and ask each other when their birthday is until they form a line. Check that this has worked by asking each individual student to give their birthdays. You could follow this up by writing up a birthday list and writing birthday cards for sts.

Grammar

6a ▶ Ask sts: *What do you do when you welcome a visitor?* Elicit ideas. Sts are likely to come up with *offer a drink*. If some sts included the idea in their dialogue in Ex. 2, ask the group who did so to perform their conversation again. Explain that Michelle had the same idea. Ask sts to complete the dialogues as they listen. Play recording 7.10. Don't check the answers yet – see b.

> **Answers:** 1 to   2 like   3 Would   4 thank

b ▶ Ask sts to listen again and check. Play recording 7.10 again. Check the answers and write them on the board. Clarify meaning as necessary. Model pronunciation of new words and intonation.

c ▶ Ask three sts to read the conversation to the class. Then put sts into groups of three and ask them to read the conversation. Circulate and correct pronunciation/ intonation. Note that sts may ask what the difference is between *Do you want …?* and *Would you like …?* This is explained in the Active grammar box.

7 ▶ Ask sts to complete the Active grammar box by looking back at Ex. 6. Check the answers. Model and practise intonation. Ask a student to read the comment on *Would you like …?* vs. *Do you want …?* to the class. Ask sts in what situations they would use each form.

> **Answers:** Would   'd

8 ▶ Sts write the sentences individually. Go over the answers by asking pairs of sts to read the mini-dialogues to the class. Read the first one yourself to model pronunciation/intonation.

> **Answers:** 1 B: I'd like   2 A: Would you like
> B Yes, please.   3 A: What would you like?   B: I'd like   4 A: Would you like a   B: No, thank you.
> 5 A: Would you like   B: No, thank you.   6 A: What would you like   B: I'd like

Listening and vocabulary

9a ▶ Ask sts to match pictures and words with a partner. Go over the answers with the class. You could use pictures to elicit/teach further vocabulary.

> **Answers:** a salad   b snacks   c fruit   d soup
> e main courses   f desserts   g vegetables
> h starters   i drinks

b ▶ If you feel it is necessary, you could briefly review prepositions by talking about where sts sit in the classroom, e.g. *Peter is next to Karin. Anna is opposite*

Karin. Establish that the diagram is a sort of map of a canteen. Ask sts where they would put the other items mentioned in a, then ask them to listen and check their ideas. Play recording 7.11. Go over the answers as a class. You could extend this by discussing sts, alternative plans, e.g. *I would like to put the drinks next to the fruit.*

> **Answers:** a snacks   b starters   c salad   d desserts

Speaking

10 ▶ Ask sts to work in pairs and role play a situation similar to the one in Ex. 6.

OPTIONAL WRAP-UP

Say a few sentences like the following and write one or two on the board: *I would like a theatre ticket for Hamlet for the 22nd of September. I would like an appointment for a massage on the 5th of June. I would like a holiday from the 1st of July to the 30th of October.* Ask sts to write similar sentences about things they would like. Some of these should be for the following week, some for the following month. Circulate and support. Go back to these the following week/month and check what happened to the plans/wishes.

---

7 Communication: Take the lift to the third floor

In this lesson sts practise asking for and giving information and simple instructions.

1 ▶ Ask sts to look at the picture with the receptionist and visitor and elicit what sort of situation this is. Elicit ideas as to what the visitor may need to know. Then ask sts what they can find on the different floors of the building. Ask two sts to read the example to the class, then repeat it around the class with further questions and answers. Clarify meaning as necessary.

2a ▶ Explain that some of these phrases are things a receptionist would say, and others are what a visitor would say. Give sts three minutes to decide which is which. Elicit ideas. Don't give the correct answers because sts are going to listen to the dialogue to find out.

> **Answers:** 1 v   2 r   3 r   4 r   5 v   6 r   7 r

b ▶ Ask sts to check their answers as they listen. Play recording 7.12. Elicit what the visitor asks, and what the receptionist explains. Elicit/clarify *left* and *right*.

3 ▶ Ask sts to answer from memory before listening, then play recording 7.12 again for them to check their answers. Ask sts to check against the tapescript on page 149 and read the dialogue with a partner.

> **Answers:** 1 b   2 d   3 a   4 c

4a/b ▶ Ask sts to note down a name and to decide which office that person is in. Then ask sts to work with a different partner for this exercise. After they have acted out the situation, sts move on to another partner. Make sure all sts practise both roles by allocating roles A and B and telling sts B to move on to the next partner.

Review and practice

1 ▶

> **Answers:** 1 Please sit down. 2 Turn off your mobile phone. 3 Please don't be late. 4 Hold the line, please. 5 Please look at page 50. 6 Don't get up late.

2 ▶

> **Answers:** 1 never 2 often 3 never 4 often 5 doesn't often 6 always

3 ▶

> **Answers:** 1 Francis always works from home.
> 2 I often have meetings on Monday mornings. 3 She doesn't usually watch TV in the evening. 4 He is never late for work. 5 She sometimes sings in the shower. 6 You aren't usually at home in the evenings.
> 7 Sales reps. don't often work from home.
> 8 Her boyfriends are always rich.

4 ▶

> **Answers:** 1 c 2 a 3 e 4 b 5 d

5 ▶

> **Answers:** 1 Please sit *down*. 2 This *is* Mr Smith.
> 3 Nice *to* meet you. 4 Nice to meet *you*, too. 5 Would you like *a* coffee? 6 Black, *no* sugar, please. 7 No, thank *you*. 8 What would you *like* to eat? 9 I'd like a piece *of* chocolate cake … 10 I'd *like* some fruit, please.

6 ▶

> **Answers:** 1 May 2 dessert 3 home 4 rep. 5 August 6 phone 7 worker 8 November 9 home 10 worker 11 seventh 12 twenty-first

Notes for using the Common European Framework (CEF)

CEF References

7.1 Can do: understand simple written and spoken instructions

CEF A1 descriptor: can understand instructions addressed carefully and slowly to him/her and follow short, simple directions (CEF page 67)

7.2 Can do: say how often you do something

CEF A1 descriptor: can write simple phrases and sentences about themselves and imaginary people, where they live and what they do (CEF page 62)

7.3 Can do: welcome a visitor to your place of work

CEF A1 descriptor: can establish basic social contact by using the simplest everyday polite forms of: greetings and farewells; introductions; saying *please*, *thank you*, *sorry*, etc. (CEF page 122)

CEF quick brief

The CEF is concerned with both the study of major international languages such as English and the preservation of regional languages spoken by smaller numbers of people. It sees linguistic and cultural diversity throughout Europe as an important part of the continent's heritage.

It aims to encourage greater co-operation between and respect for different cultures, '*better access to information, more intensive personal interaction, improved working relations and a deeper mutual understanding*'. (CEF page 5)

Its three main aims are:

- assisting co-operation between educational institutions in different countries
- facilitating the mutual recognition of language qualifications gained under different educational systems
- helping learners, teachers, course designers and assessors to co-ordinate their efforts.

CEF Portfolio task

Download the Total English Portfolio free from www.longman.com/totalenglish.

Objective: to introduce learners to the 'Your language learning history' section of the Language Biography.

1 ▶ Ask sts to reflect on and record their experience of learning another language, if this is applicable. At this level, it is likely that some of the sts may not have had any prior tuition in English, in which case ask them to reflect on their experiences to date on this course.

2 ▶ This may be a good opportunity to gauge from sts what kind of learning experiences they have found useful, either on previous courses or on the one you are teaching on.

8 Leisure

Overview

Lead-in	**Vocabulary:** leisure activities
8.1	**Grammar:** *like + ing, want* + infinitive
	Vocabulary: adjectives for describing activities
	Can do: explain why you want to do something
8.2	**Grammar:** *have got/has got*
	Vocabulary: rooms and furniture
	Can do: say what things you possess
8.3	**Grammar:** question words
	Vocabulary: food
	Can do: suggest and book a restaurant; order food in a restaurant
Com. Focus	Addresses

Summary

Lesson 1: Sts discuss choosing a hotel/holiday location which offers the leisure activities they enjoy.

Lesson 2: Sts talk about the things they have in their homes and about their attitude to technology.

Lesson 3: Sts discuss restaurants and eating out. They book a table and order food.

Communication: Sts play a game in which they find out people's identity through asking questions.

Film bank: Change your life

A short film showing 10 exciting adventure activities. A short description is given of each activity.

Possible places to use this short film are:
► after 8.1
► after 8.3
► at the end of the unit

For ways to use this short film in class, see Students' Book page 123 and Teacher's Resource Book pages 139 and 145.

Lead-in

OPTIONAL WARMER

This reviews leisure activities, ordinal numbers and imperatives. Books closed. Explain that sts will give short presentations entitled *10 steps towards a happy and healthy life*. Elicit/provide the basic structure of a presentation (welcome, introduction, presentation, conclusion, questions). Explain that sts should use *Your first/second step* to structure the presentation. Give sts a few prompts, e.g. sports, food and drink, sleep. Put sts into groups and ask them to brainstorm ideas and then to put together a presentation. Groups then present their ideas. Everyone should present at least one step.

1a ► Ask sts to match the words and pictures with a partner. Pairs then match the other items. Don't go over the answers yet – see b.

Answers: 1 go to the theatre   2 eat out   3 play chess   4 go swimming   5 play football   6 go for a walk   7 watch TV   8 go sightseeing   9 read a book   10 play tennis   11 go cycling   12 do exercise

b ► Ask sts to listen and check. Play recording 8.1. Re-play the recording item by item and ask sts to repeat.

c ► Elicit answers by asking: *Which activity can you see in photo A (etc.)?*

Answers: A go to the theatre   B play chess   C go cycling   D read a book

2 ► Ask sts, in pairs, to practise collocations or do this as a ball game. Sts stand in a circle. Ask one student to give an activity and the next student to react by giving the verb plus the activity.

3a ► Write on the board: *How often do you go swimming?* Ask a few sts and elicit answers. Ask sts to work in pairs and use the pictures in Ex. 1a as a basis for their questions. Sts should make notes.

b ► In a small class, sts report back to the class. In a large class, ask sts to work with a different partner and tell him/her about their first partner. Circulate and correct grammar.

OPTIONAL WRAP-UP

Sts write a short text either about themselves or their partner, using the pictures in Ex. 1a as a guide, e.g. *I often go to the theatre. I never play football. I go swimming every morning.*

8.1 I don't like walking

In this lesson sts discuss choosing a hotel/holiday location which offers the leisure activities they enjoy. Grammar: *like + ing; want* + infinitive.

OPTIONAL WARMER

This activity introduces the topic. Ask sts: *How do you chose a place and hotel to go to for your holiday?* Brainstorm ideas. Say: *I like Wales (because) I like walking*. Ask sts to feed back their ideas using similar sentences.

Speaking

1a ► Ask sts to look at the brochures of hotels. Ask three different sts to read the names, phone numbers and email addresses to the class.

b/c ▶ Elicit what sts can see in the photos and make notes on the board. Ask: *What can you do at the X hotel?* Refer sts to the How to ... box for model sentences.

▶ Ask sts which of these hotels they like and why. Give an example: *I like the Blue Sea Hotel. You can go swimming.*

> **Answers:** Langston Hotel – You can go for a walk, play golf, play tennis and play chess.   New Metro Hotel – You can eat out, go sightseeing, go to the theatre and go swimming.   Blue Sea Hotel – You can go for a walk, go swimming, go cycling and eat out.

2 ▶ Say: *Think of hotels you know. Which of them do you like? What can you do there?* Elicit a few ideas/ sentences from various sts, then group sts in threes to exchange ideas. Circulate, support and correct grammar.

Listening

3a ▶ Explain that sts are going to listen to a conversation between Gary and Annie, who have a problem. Play recording 8.2. Ask: *Are Gary and Annie happy? What does Gary like doing? What does Annie think about this? What do you think?*

> **Answers:** Annie isn't happy. She and Gary never go out.

Language note Point out that possessive *s* is added to the phrase *Gary and Annie*, not to each individual noun. Explain that this means the problem is theirs together, not just Annie's.

b ▶ Explain that in the following conversation, Gary and Annie look at the three hotels. Ask sts to note down where they want to go, and any other information they understand. Play recording 8.3. Elicit the answers.

> **Answers:** 1 Langston   2 New Metro   3 Blue Sea

c ▶ Ask sts what leisure activities Gary and Annie talk about. Elicit what sts remember and make notes on the board, then ask them to listen again. Play recording 8.3 again. Pool information and write the activities (including the verbs) on the board as infinitives (see example). Write them in a column and leave space for adding the *ing* version.

> **Answers:** play golf   go sightseeing   go swimming do exercise   go for a walk

▶ Ask: *What does Gary like doing?* Write: *He likes playing golf* next to *play golf* on the board. Ask sts to form similar sentences about Gary and Annie with the verbs + activities you've written on the board. Write all ideas on the board and correct the grammar (not content). Ask sts to go to the tapescript on page 149 to check whether the sentences on the board are true or false. Go through the sentences and ask individual sts to comment on/correct content. Underline *like* and *ing*.

Grammar

4 ▶ Ask sts to complete the Active grammar box individually. Elicit the answers. Elicit/explain that *like* is a general statement, and *want to* is what you want to do at the moment. Clarify by giving an example such as *I like doing X, but I don't want to do X at the moment.*

Language note Some learners tend to find the *like + ing* structure strange (and may misunderstand it as *I would like to ...*). Many other languages use a completely different structure, so clarify the difference between *want to* and *like + ing* from the beginning.

Sts may have come across *I like to do X*, which is a common American English way of talking about habits; and may also have heard *I'd like to ...* and be unaware of the *'d* in it and its meaning. These structures may also cause confusion.

In lesson 7.3, sts learned that in the context of accepting offers, e.g. of food and drink, *I want* is informal (and can be impolite), as opposed to *I'd like*.

▶ Ask sts to go to the tapescript for recordings 8.2 and 8.3 on page 149 and find all instances of *like + ing* and *want to* + infinitive. Ask two sts to read the dialogues to the class. Then ask sts to read the dialogue with a partner.

> **Answers:** want   want   like   like

5a ▶ Ask sts to do the exercise individually, then go over the answers as a class.

> **Answers:** 1 going out with friends   2 watching TV 3 to play tennis   4 going sightseeing   5 to eat out 6 playing chess   7 swimming   8 to read

b ▶ Ask sts to complete the conversations individually. To go over the answers, ask two sts to read the dialogue to the class. Write all the answers on the board. Then ask sts to practise the conversations in pairs.

> **Answers:** 1 swimming   2 watching   3 to play 4 playing   5 going   6 to go   7 to go   8 to go 9 going   10 to go

6 ▶ Before sts work with a partner, ask a few sts the questions and elicit answers. Then ask sts to note down ideas or to write sentences individually. Ask them to talk to a partner for two minutes, then to move on to the next person. (You could organise this like a speed-dating event where you have two rows of chairs facing each other, and sts move to the next chair clockwise when you give the signal.)

> **OPTIONAL EXTENSION**
>
> Write on the board: *tennis: Tuesday 22nd September, 7 o'clock*. Ask a student: *Do you like playing tennis?* Hopefully, he/she will say yes. Say: *Do you want to play tennis with me on Tuesday the twenty-second of September at seven o'clock?* Ask sts to note down four activities they like doing, and a date and time for each. Then ask them to try to find someone who shares their interest, and suggest a time.

Vocabulary

7a ► Read the words in the box to the sts. Ask them to repeat as a class. 'Conduct' the stress. Ask individual sts to repeat and correct their pronunciation.

Language note The adjectives introduced here express attitudes and emotions. Pronunciation and intonation are particularly important here. Typical mistakes are: *interesting* with four syllables rather than the correct three – the first *e* is silent; *difficult* has an unstressed *u* /ə/; *exciting* – sts may try to pronounce the *xc* separately.

► Ask sts to match the pictures and words with a partner. Don't go over the answers yet – see b.

> **Answers:** 1 exciting 2 boring 3 fun 4 easy
> 5 interesting 6 difficult

Tip To practise intonation, you could ask sts not to use words but sounds, e.g. *dadedadedada* and emphasise intonation to convey meaning.

b ► Say: *I think learning English is fun* and write the sentence on the board. Ask sts to look at page 79 and elicit further examples from individual sts. Correct their intonation and pronunciation. Then ask sts to exchange ideas with a partner or in a group of three. Circulate, support and correct pronunciation/intonation.

Speaking

8 ► Ask sts to decide which hotel they'd like to go to and to write a statement similar to the example. Then ask sts to get up and tell other sts where they want to go. False beginners could ask the other sts whether they want to go to the same place: *Do you want to go to X hotel?* Explain that sts should find two others to go with them. In their groups, they discuss what they like doing. They present their plans to the class: *We like doing X, X and X. We want to go to the X hotel.*

Writing

9a ► Remind sts of the work you've done on writing notes, memos and emails and elicit how to begin/end an email. Then ask them to look at the Writing bank to check and expand these ideas. Discuss and elicit that an email to a hotel is a relatively formal email.

b ► Ask sts to write an email to the hotel they have chosen to book rooms for the weekend they planned in Ex. 8. Refer sts back to Unit 5, Communication, for further questions they may want to ask about their room. For homework, you could ask sts to write a real email to a hotel – they would have to find one on the internet first.

> **OPTIONAL WRAP-UP**
>
> Ask sts to find a hotel or resort on the internet that offers a number of activities. Ask them to write an email or letter to a friend (or to you) to tell them about their next holiday: where they want to go, what they can do there, and whether they like/don't like these activities and why (using adjectives from Ex. 7). Correct sts' work. The corrected

version could go into the portfolio section of their vocabulary folders.

8.2 We've got a small garden.

In this lesson sts talk about things they have in their homes, and about their attitude to technology. Grammar: *have got/has got*.

> **OPTIONAL WARMER**
>
> The purpose of this activity is to practise telling the time, to revise verbs of daily routine and to introduce rooms. Draw a clock face on the board and write *sleep* against *12*. Ask sts to get together in groups of three, make a poster of a clock face and write verbs against each hour. Circulate and help with vocabulary. Ask sts to put up their posters on the wall and to briefly present them. Ask questions to clarify the information they're giving. Alternatively, collate all ideas on the board. Ask: *Where do you do these things?* Go through all the relevant verbs, elicit ideas and provide vocabulary as necessary. Write places next to the verbs.

Vocabulary

1a ► Give sts two minutes to look at the activities and come up with sentences. Ask a student to read out an activity and someone else to say the appropriate sentence. Elicit alternatives, as different sentences may be true for different sts (*watch TV – living room, bedroom, kitchen*). If you used the optional warmer activity, add any activities and places that haven't been mentioned in the warmer activity to the items on the board. Elicit more sentences using the words on the board. Again, elicit/discuss alternatives.

Language note *You* is impersonal here. This is worth pointing out and explaining if sts' own languages use a different construction.

> **Answers:** a in the kitchen b in the living room
> c in the bathroom d in the bedroom e in the garage f in the garden

b/c ► Give sts three minutes to match the words and pictures. Ask them to listen and check. Play recording 8.4. If the rooms/places haven't been mentioned in the optional warmer activity or earlier in this exercise, add them to the items on the board.

► Model pronunciation of the words in the box and ask the class to repeat. Watch compound stress. Model a sentence: *Picture a is a mirror. It's in the bedroom.* Only accept answers that use the same sentence structure.

► Describe one of the rooms saying: *There's an X in this room*, and ask sts to tell you what the room is called. Ask sts to practise this in pairs, using *there is/there are* (refer sts to the Active grammar box in Lesson 5.1 if necessary).

Answers: a mirror b bed   c wardrobe d bath
e toilet f basin g cooker h sink i washing
machine j fridge k sofa l lamp m coffee table
n armchair o car p bicycle

2a ▶ Ask a student to read the two questions to the class. Brainstorm things you can find in a hotel room as a class and circle the items on the board. Then ask sts to restrict themselves to seven items for their new house and make a list individually.

b ▶ Ask sts to discuss their lists with a partner. Explain that they should try and agree on the seven most important things and rank them according to importance. Pairs then present their list to the class: *First on our list is X, second ...*, etc., possibly adding reasons (e.g. *a cooker – cooking is important*).

c ▶ Ask sts: *Do you like your house/flat?* Tell them about your own house/flat and mention a few things you like and a few you dislike, using similar sentences to the example. You may add a sentence or two using *I want to ...* to mention things you'd like to change. Then ask sts to tell each other about their houses/flats. Encourage them to expand this and talk about things they want to change.

Listening

3a ▶ Explain that sts are going to listen to a conversation between Paul and Jo, and that Paul wants to buy a present for someone. Elicit a few ideas how to find the right present (remind sts about Unit 6 Communication). Ask sts to note down possible presents they talk about. Play recording 8.5. Elicit the answers.

Answers: an armchair   a lamp   a wardrobe
a bed   a bicycle

b ▶ Ask sts to look at the questions and note down their answers from memory, then to listen and check. Re-play recording 8.5. Elicit the answers. Ask sts to guess what the present is going to be.

Answers: 1 next week   2 doing things at home, watching TV, cooking   3 an armchair, a lamp
4 a wardrobe, a bicycle

c ▶ Discuss with the class whether this is a good idea. Ask sts to give opinions. Write *I (don't) think it is a good idea because ...* on the board. Encourage sts to suggest alternatives.

d ▶ Discuss the question as a class or in groups. If you form groups, make sure that, in a multinational class, you form mixed groups to discuss the question.

Grammar

4a ▶ Ask: *Has Paul's sister got a bicycle?* Elicit the answer. Write *has got* and *have got* on the board. Ask sts to turn to page 149 and to find all instances of *have/has got* in the tapescript. Ask them to listen again and pay particular attention to the relevant sentences. Play recording 8.5 again. Pause after each of the relevant sentences and ask sts to repeat. Point out the voiced *'ve*.

b ▶ Ask sts to complete the Active grammar box without looking at the tapescript again. Go over the answers. Write out the Active grammar box on the board, and complete the gaps as you elicit the answers.

▶ Write *I like my flat. My flat is perfect. I can sit on my balcony* on the board. Ask sts to write questions and negative sentences from these. Elicit answers and write them on the board. Elicit similarities and differences between these structures and *have got*: *have* functions like an auxiliary or a modal in negatives because *not* is added directly to the verb and in questions because the subject and verb are inverted. This helps to explain that *have got* and *do* are never combined. Unlike a modal, however, it changes in the third person.

Answers: have has Have Has have has
have(n't) has(n't)

5a ▶ Before sts work in pairs, ask a few sts questions, e.g. *Have you got an armchair?* and elicit answers. Write *Have you got ...? Yes, I have. No, I haven't* on the board to support sts. Ask them to work in pairs. Circulate and correct grammar.

b ▶ Ask sts to complete the texts individually. Don't go over the answers yet – see Ex. 6.

Answers: 1 've   2 've   3 haven't   4 's   5 haven't
6 've   7 's   8 's   9 hasn't   10 's   11 's   12 hasn't

Pronunciation

6a ▶ Ask sts to check their answers to Ex. 5b as they listen. Play recording 8.6. Go over the answers and write them on the board.

b ▶ Focus sts' attention on the question and ask them to listen again. Re-play recording 8.6 (or read the texts to the sts) and ask sts to mouth the text as they listen.

Answers: I've /aɪv/   we've /wiːv/   she's /ʃiːz/
(Note: /s/ in *it's* /ɪts/)

c ▶ Ask two sts to read the texts to the class. Some sts find voiced sounds difficult to produce. Practise these, then ask sts to work in pairs. Sts decide which syllables they should stress. One student reads the text, the other listens and gives feedback on pronunciation and intonation. Sts then change roles. Make sure all sts understand the procedure before they begin.

Speaking

7 ▶ Ask sts to make notes about their own home individually and prepare a little presentation, then organise them into pairs. Ask pairs to present their ideas to each other. Partners can then ask additional questions. To round this off, ask pairs to find things they have in common and to report back to the class.

Reading

8 ▶ Ask sts to answer the questions for themselves first. Then form pairs or small groups and have sts interview each other and make notes about their partner's answers.

9a/b ▶ Ask sts to calculate their own and their partner's scores and to read the corresponding profiles. Ask them to go through the text and check which of the sentences are true for them, and which aren't.

c ▶ Ask sts to get together with their interviewees and to check the profile they found for their partner by asking a question about each sentence in the text: *Do you like new technology? Do you sometimes buy new things?*, etc.

d ▶ You could set this for homework or self-study. Ask sts to write a true profile about themselves. Explain that they can either keep the structure and change the sentences to make them true, or they can add other things and write a completely new text.

▶ Ask sts to exchange texts with a partner. Sts then present their partner to the class using the information in the text.

OPTIONAL WRAP-UP

Ask sts to draw a diagram of their ideal home, including furniture, and to label it. Ask them to write a text to go with it, entitled *Ideal and real home*. Give some sentence openings, e.g. *In my ideal home, there is/are ... . In my real home I have got ...* . Collect the texts and correct them. The corrected texts and labelled diagrams could go into the portfolio section of sts' vocabulary folders.

8.3 Eating out

In this lesson sts discuss restaurants and eating out. They book a table and order food. Grammar: question words.

OPTIONAL WARMER

This activity introduces the topic, reactivates relevant vocabulary and reviews the unit's language. Write on the board: *eat out, order a pizza, get food from a take-away, go to a fastfood restaurant, cook food in a microwave oven, heat tinned soup*. Ask:

Do you like doing these things? Why/Why not? How often do you do them? Ask sts to interview a partner about these questions and then to present their partner to the group.

Reading

1 ▶ The optional warmer activity covers the first question. Describe your favourite restaurant to the class, e.g. *It's an Italian place. They've got fresh salads and my favourite dish is their tomato soup. Of course, they've got pasta, too, but they haven't got pizza. They've got nice wooden furniture and interesting modern lamps with coloured shades. I often go there at lunchtime. It's near my office.*

▶ Ask sts, in groups of three, to describe their favourite restaurants to each other. Give sts these prompts: *location, people who go there, people who run/own it, service, furniture, prices* and *food*. Circulate and support.

2a ▶ In the same groups as Ex. 1, ask sts to look at the photos of the top restaurants in the world. Ask sts to decide who's A, B and C and to read their information. Remind them of the work you have done on presentations and ask them to prepare a mini-presentation of their restaurant. In a business-oriented class, you could tell sts they are the PR person of their respective restaurant and want to win customers.

b/c ▶ Sts give their mini-presentations in turn. They then discuss which restaurant to choose. Ask them to present their decision to the class and to give reasons for it. Again, a business-oriented class can slightly change perspective here; the focus could move away from personal likes and dislikes and focus on other aspects.

Listening

3a ▶ Explain that Mark and Alda want to go to a restaurant to celebrate. Ask sts to note down where they want to go. Encourage them to note down any other detail, e.g. why they want to go there. Play recording 8.7 and elicit the answer.

Answer: c

---

b ▶ Ask sts to try to order the questions from memory. Ask them to check their answers and note down who says which question as they listen. Check the answers. Go through the questions in the correct order and ask sts who said what, and what the answer was in the dialogue.

Answers: 1 How about dinner next Friday?
2 Which restaurant do you want to go to?
3 Where's that?   4 What food do they serve at *Wasabi*?   5 How big is it?   6 What about *Carlitto's*?

4a ▶ Ask a student to read the questions in the How to ... box to the class. Watch intonation. Give answers yourself and ask the class to repeat.

b ▶ Ask sts to suggest restaurants to each other in pairs.

Grammar

5 ▶ You could put the questions and answers on cards and do the matching exercise as a pair finding game. Ask a pair to read the questions and answers to the class to check the answers. Ask another pair to read them and focus on intonation this time. Correct/model, then ask pairs to practise asking and answering.

> **Answers:** 1 b 2 f 3 c 4 a 5 e 6 d

6 ▶ In the pairs they formed in Ex. 5, ask sts to complete the questions.

▶ Ask sts to look at the questions using *which* and *what* and elicit the difference between the two question words. Sts may not spot the difference. Explain, using the examples given on Reference page 87.

> **Answers:** 1 How 2 What/Which 3 What
> 4 Where 5 Who 6 What 7 How 8 Which

7 ▶ You could ask sts to prepare this exercise by working in groups to draw up a questionnaire. Then pair sts from different groups to interview each other. Sts could write all the questions up as a questionnaire before they interview each other for practice in writing questions. For the actual interviews, they could use only key words. To round this off, ask sts to write a profile of their interviewee for homework.

Listening

8a ▶ Ask sts: *Before you go to a restaurant, what do you do?* Elicit ideas and tell them that Alda books a table. Ask sts to listen for the time. Play recording 8.8. Check the answer.

> **Answer:** nine o'clock

b ▶ Ask sts to look at the How to ... box and note down ideas for the gaps on a separate piece of paper, then to listen again. Play recording 8.8 again. Check the answers.

> **Answers:** like How What What

c ▶ Ask sts to read the How to ... box again carefully, then to role play the situation. Circulate and correct.

Vocabulary

9a/b ▶ Give sts two minutes to match the words and pictures. Ask them to listen and check their answers. Play recording 8.9.

> **Answers:** 1 chicken 2 chocolate 3 seafood
> 4 pasta 5 fish 6 beef 7 potatoes 8 lamb
> 9 cheese 10 rice

c ▶ Remind sts of the difference between *I like* and *I want*. Write *I like potatoes* on the board for this exercise. Then ask them to tell their partner what they like from the menu.

d ▶ Ask various sts what their favourite starter, main course and dessert is. Elicit how they can order food (using *I'd like*, see Lesson 7.3).

10a ▶ Ask sts to note down what Mark and Alda order – the exact phrases, if possible. Play recording 8.10. Elicit the answers. Then ask sts to give you the phrases. Don't correct or write them at this stage.

> **Answers:** Mark: starter – fish soup, main course – lamb chops Alda: starter – seafood cocktail, main course – vegetable pasta bake

b ▶ Play recording 8.10 again and ask sts to follow it in the tapescript. Then ask them to practise the conversation with different items from the menu.

Speaking

11 ▶ Ask sts to enact a similar situation to the one in Ex. 10. Encourage them to stand at the beginning of the conversation – then only the customers sit down. Bring in a few paper napkins and arrange tables to create a slightly restaurant-like atmosphere. Ask sts to do three role plays. Everybody should play the waiter once.

8 Communication: Addresses

In this lesson sts play a game in which they find out people's identity through questions.

1a/b ▶ Ask sts in pairs to describe what people have got in their flat, and what they like doing. The purpose of this activity is to make sure sts remember both *have got* and *like + ing*. Write an example sentence and a *Yes/No* question and answer for each structure on the board. Circulate and provide any vocabulary sts need.

2 ▶ Explain that the postman has a letter for each of the people who live in the building and that he needs help. Put sts into pairs, A and B. Then explain that each of them will find five addresses. Ask them to look at their information and complete the addresses.

> **Answers:** See SB pages 111 and 114.

3 ▶ Go through the 'Important' notes together. Sts mustn't ask questions such as *Is Mr X in apartment 12a?* When sts think they've worked out all the correct names, they shout *Bingo!* Then all sts finalise their notes with the information they have. Reveal the answers and allow sts a point for each correct one.

> Answers: See SB pages 111 and 114.

OPTIONAL UNIT WRAP-UP

Ask sts to draw up a questionnaire that a dating agency might use to find out about people, including questions about family background, work, hobbies, likes/dislikes, possessions, plans and ideas for the future, ideas about their prospective partner. Check them for accuracy and hand them back to the sts to keep in their portfolio.

Review and practice

1 ▶

> Answers: 1 to go   2 to watch   3 watching
> 4 swimming   5 to go   6 to do   7 to go   8 to take

2 ▶

> Answers: 1 I've got   2 It's got   3 It hasn't got   4 it's
> got   5 I haven't got   6 my friends have got   7 Have
> you got   8 My husband has got

3 ▶

> Answers: 1 A: Has your sister got a washing machine?
> B: Yes she has.   2 A: Have you got a car? B: No, I
> haven't.   3 A: Have your parents got a TV? B: No, they
> haven't.   4 A: Has James got a bath? B: Yes, he has.
> 5 A: Have they got a new email address? B: No, they
> haven't.   6 A: Has she got a good dictionary? B: Yes,
> she has.

4 ▶

> Answers: 1 Which restaurant do you like?   2 *What* do
> you do? Are you an accountant?   3 Where do you live?
> 4 How intelligent *is she*?   5 *What* time is it?   6 Who
> do *you work for*?   7 There are two armchairs. *Which*
> armchair do you like?   8 Where *is your brother*?

5 ▶

> Answers: 1 What do you do?   2 How tall is she?
> 3 What food do you like?   4 *Which* coffee table do you
> like?   5 Where do you live?   6 Who is she?

6 ▶

> Answers: 1 eat out   2 playing chess   3 reads
> 4 boring   5 fun   6 fridge   7 garden   8 How
> 9 potatoes   10 chocolate

Notes for using the Common European Framework (CEF)

CEF References

8.1 Can do: explain why you want to do something

CEF A1 descriptor: can interact in a simple way but communication is totally dependent on repetition at a slower rate of speech, rephrasing and repair (CEF page 74)

8.2 Can do: say what things you possess

CEF A1 descriptor: can reply in an interview to simple direct questions spoken very slowly and clearly in direct, non-idiomatic speech about personal details (CEF page 82)

8.3 Can do: suggest a restaurant; book a restaurant; order food in a restaurant

CEF A1 descriptor: can ask people for things and give people things (CEF page 80)

CEF quick brief

The CEF sees language learning as a process of developing one's communicative competence. This is a composite of other competences:

* linguistic competence (lexis, phonology, syntax and the four skills)

Total English Starter contains a wide range of vocabulary, pronunciation and grammar, as well as plenty of opportunities for sts to develop their skills. The *Total English Starter* Portfolio lists several discrete competences, grouped under five skills-based headings: listening, reading, spoken interaction, spoken production and writing.

* sociolinguistic competence

This entails an awareness of politeness and sensitivity appropriate to the level. For example, in the How to … box on page 84 of the Students' Book, sts are shown how to make, accept and reject suggestions politely, and then given an opportunity to practise.

* pragmatic competence

This refers to the ability to get things done with the linguistic resources at your disposal, in other words, the successful performance of speech acts. For example, the restaurant role play on page 85 of the Students' Book provides an opportunity for sts to practise the speech acts of making requests.

CEF Portfolio task

Download the Total English Portfolio free from www. longman.com/totalenglish.

Objective: to encourage sts to pay attention to English they encounter outside the classroom, and to use it as a learning opportunity.

1 ▶ Ask sts how they rate their ability to understand menus (one of the reading *Can do's* from Unit 8), and to tick the appropriate column.

2 ▶ In addition to the menu in *Total English Starter*, bring in a real menu if you can get hold of one, and use this as a way of extending sts' vocabulary.

The past

Overview

Lead-in	**Vocabulary:** saying years (1975, 2006), historical events and headlines
9.1	**Grammar:** past of *to be*: affirmative
	Vocabulary: occupations
	Can do: make simple statements about people from history
9.2	**Grammar:** past of *to be*: negatives and questions
	Vocabulary: *yesterday, last, ago*
	Can do: give a short description of a past experience
9.3	**Grammar:** *Can/Could you ...?; Can/Could I ...?*
	Vocabulary: housework
	Can do: make a simple request and ask permission
Com. Focus	School days

Summary

Lesson 1: Sts talk about celebrities' and historical personalities' past, and about their own childhood activities and skills.

Lesson 2: Sts talk about the things they have in their homes and about their attitude to technology.

Lesson 3: Sts discuss who does the housework in their home and talk about past experiences.

Communication: Sts talk about subjects they were good or bad at at school.

Film bank: 100 years ago

A short film giving some details of what life was like in the north of England in 1901. The film looks at work routines, the streets, technology and free time activities.

Possible places to use this short film are:
▶ after 9.1
▶ after 9.2
▶ at the end of the unit

For ways to use this short film in class, see Students' Book page 124 and Teacher's Resource Book pages 140 and 146.

Lead-in

OPTIONAL WARMER

This activity reviews dates/numbers and introduces the topic and the past tense of *to be* (for understanding only). Books closed. Write some recent headlines in English on the board. Explain that they are headlines and ask sts if they can say the date on which they were in the news. Elicit/ clarify meaning as necessary and ask sts to explain

what the story behind each headline is. Elicit a few guesses as to the date for each, then say: *This was in the paper on the X of X in 200X.*

1 ▶ Say one of the years and ask sts: *Which picture and headline matches?* Elicit some background about each event. To sum up, say: *X was in (year).*

> **Answers:** A 2000 B 1929 C 1989 D 1994

2a ▶ Ask sts to look at the years as they listen and repeat. Play recording 9.1 item by item.

Language note If sts say *19 hundred 22*, etc., always correct this mistake. Sts need to be told that *1901* is *19 oh 1* (when this comes up) and *2002* is generally said *two thousand and two*. *20 oh 2* and *twenty ten* (for *2010*) are possible but not widely used (yet).

b ▶ Ask sts to read the headlines individually and to match them to the years. Point out the use of capital letters and incomplete sentences. Check that sts understand the quotation marks (in f), that the colon in f means *says* and in g *is*. Clarify other meanings as necessary.

> **Answers:** a 1957 b 1981 c 2002 d 1912
> e 1990 f 1963 g 1946 h 1977

c/d ▶ Ask sts to compare ideas in pairs or groups of three. Circulate and help with language, but don't give them the correct answer. Ask them to listen and check. Play recording 9.2. Elicit some detail about these events from the class. Teach *I remember* (e.g. *Princess Diana's dress*). In this way, you can avoid past verbs at this stage.

3 ▶ To demonstrate how to write a headline, think of some memorable event that took place in the English course and write a headline for it, e.g. *Youngest Course Member Turns 40!, Traffic Jam: Teacher Late for Class,* and ask sts when this was. Then ask them to write three to five headlines about themselves. Sts then talk to their partner and guess the years. Sts report back to the class – one headline and year per student.

9.1 20th-century icons

In this lesson sts talk about celebrities' and historical personalities' past, and about their own childhood activities and skills. Grammar: past of *to be*: affirmative.

OPTIONAL WARMER

This activity introduces the topic. Write *Once upon a time ...* on the board. Elicit/explain that this is how fairy tales begin. You could give an example from a well-known fairy tale. Ask sts: *What are the ingredients for a fairy tale?* (e.g. *prince, princess, adventure, live happily ever after, the evil witch, someone who is poor but good/honest,* etc.). Elicit ideas from the class. Sts may even want to try and tell a tale. Then ask sts what modern-day fairy tales are, and where they can read them (tabloid newspapers, gossip and celebrity magazines).

Reading

1a ▶ Books closed. Read the four famous quotes to the sts (not the whole texts) and ask them what sort of person may have said these things. Elicit ideas (man/woman, job, where from, sort of background or upbringing, sort of situation, etc.). Then ask sts to open their books and look at the photos and guess who said the quotes.

▶ Ask sts to read the texts individually and look up words. If sts don't have dictionaries with them, invite questions about the texts and clarify the meaning of the underlined words.

b ▶ Elicit which text matches which picture, then ask a student to read a text and elicit further information about the person from the class. Follow this procedure for each text in turn.

> **Answers:** 1 Elvis Presley   2 Princess Grace
> 3 Bruce Lee   4 Princess Diana

c ▶ Sts should write the sentences individually. Go over the answers by asking individual sts to read sentences. Ask sts to read the relevant sentences from the texts to support their statements.

> **Answers:** 1 Diana and Grace   2 Elvis, Grace and Bruce   3 Elvis, Grace and Bruce   4 Elvis and Bruce
> 5 Grace and Diana

d ▶ Give sts one minute to look at the texts again, then ask them to close their books and brainstorm in pairs what they can remember about the four people. Explain that they should make notes first. After three minutes, ask sts to write sentences on the basis of their notes. Ask each student to read or say one sentence.

Grammar

2a/b ▶ Ask sts to complete the Active Grammar box individually. Don't go over the answers yet, but ask sts to listen and check. Play recording 9.3. Prepare an OHT with the Active grammar box and write in the answers, or write the sentences out on the board.

> **Answers:** was   were   was   was   was   were

3a ▶ Ask sts to complete the sentences individually. Go over the answers by asking individual sts to read the sentences. Write the answers on the board.

> **Answers:** 1 was   2 were   3 was   4 were   5 were
> 6 were   7 was

> **OPTIONAL EXTENSION**
>
> Give sts one minute to prepare three sentences about themselves. Give prompts, e.g. *born, job, family*. Ask each student to read their sentences to the class.

b ▶ Give sts a few minutes to think of a 20th-century icon and make notes. Then group sts in pairs or threes and ask them to tell each other about who they have chosen. You can do this as a guessing game. Sts tell the others without mentioning their icon's name, and the others guess.

4a/b ▶ You could introduce this by playing Eric Burdon's *When I was young*. Give sts the text of the first verse (*The rooms were so much colder then/my father was a soldier then/and times were very hard/when I was young.*) Ask sts to read the How to ... box and then write sentences about themselves, two true and one false.

c ▶ Prepare sentences about yourself and read them out to the class. Ask sts to guess which one is false. Write *I think X is false. I don't think you were a good singer* on the board. Ask various sts to comment on your sentences, using this structure. Then ask them to present and discuss their sentences in pairs or groups of three.

Listening and vocabulary

5a/b ▶ Explain that sts are going to listen to a quiz show called *Who am I?* There are statements about a famous person, and contestants guess who the person is. Play recording 9.4 up to the sentence *Let's play 'Who am I?'* (i.e. the host's instructions). Explain that sts can interrupt and shout a name if they think they know who the person is (i.e. join in as if they were contestants).

▶ Write *I think it is ...* on the board. Play the rest of recording 9.4, pausing briefly after each sentence. If sts don't find the right answer before the end of the recording, ask them to give ideas after the recording ends and discuss them before sts check their answer.

> **Answer:** John Lennon

c ▶ Ask sts to read the statements and write *T* or *F* from memory, then to check as they listen. Re-play recording 9.4. Go over the answers, asking sts to correct the false statements. Elicit any further information about John Lennon and his art, and sts' likes/dislikes/attitudes.

▶ You could bring and play a recording, e.g. of *Imagine* (sts may have been reminded of the line *You may say I'm a dreamer ...* in Ex. 1 – Elvis Presley's famous quote).

> **Answers:** 1 F   2 T   3 T   4 F   5 F

> **OPTIONAL EXTENSION**
>
> The *Who am I?* game show works well as a classroom game. Split the class into four to five teams who each write statements about one group member. Each group presents their statements and a representative of each of the other groups guesses.

6a ▶ Read the words in the box to the sts. Elicit/teach that these are prepositions. Ask sts to complete the texts individually, then to compare answers with a partner.

▶ Ask a student to read the texts aloud. Write the answers on the board, always in context (*married to, in 1929, friends with,* etc.). Explain that sts need to learn these collocations. Brainstorm other collocations with prepositions (e.g. *on* + day of the week, *at* + the weekend, *at* + o'clock) and write these on the board.

> **Answers:** 1 in   2 at   3 to   4 of   5 on   6 for
> 7 with   8 to

b ▶ Ask sts to play preposition 'ping pong' in pairs using the collocations.

7a ▶ Ask sts to look at the statements on John Lennon again (tapescript 9.4 on page 150) and to think of someone they can find similar information about. Insist that sts talk about a well-known person. Give them a few minutes to write their statements. Circulate and support while they are writing. Sts may find it difficult to think of someone – you could provide some short texts on important people to help them. Explain that it is important in what order the statements are given.

b ▶ Put sts in pairs or small groups and ask them to present their statements while the other sts guess.

> **OPTIONAL WRAP-UP**
>
> Ask sts to look back at Ex. 2b in the Lead-in and pick one or two of the events to write sentences about. Where relevant, they should include what they can remember about this event, and where they were at the time. Alternatively, ask sts to make notes and then interview someone about one or two of the events.

9.2 My first, my last …

In this lesson sts talk about past experiences (first teacher/last holiday). Grammar: past of *to be*: negatives and questions.

> **OPTIONAL WARMER**
>
> The purpose of this activity is to practise saying dates and years and to introduce and activate relevant vocabulary. Elicit/teach what a *CV* is and brainstorm what sort of things you include in a *CV*. Make notes on the board and write a few sample questions, e.g. *When were you born? What was your first job? When were you at university?* etc. Ask sts to interview a partner. Circulate and support.

Speaking

1 ▶ Books closed. Ask sts whether they would put their hobbies on their CV. Explain that on a CV in the UK it is considered important. Discuss the reasons for this. This point will be more important in a business-oriented class than in a general class. Ask sts in groups to note down as many hobbies that belong to different categories as they can think of in two minutes. Elicit ideas from the class and write any games sts mention on the board. Ask sts to look at the pictures. Elicit what games these are (snakes and ladders, Scrabble, Trivial Pursuit, chess, Monopoly).

▶ Ask: *Do you know how to play these games?* (Indicate the ones on the board as well as in the book.) *Do you like playing them?* Discuss the questions as a class. Snakes and ladders will require some explanation – it is very specific. The other games on the page are

known internationally. For one of the games, elicit how to play it (how many players, what you do first, second, how you win/score a point, etc.).

Listening

2a ▶ Explain that sts are going to listen to three people playing a game.

> **Answer:** She talks about her last meal at a restaurant.

b ▶ Ask sts to look at the sentences for *Christof's first teacher* and *Jasmine's last holiday* and to note down what they can remember, then ask sts to listen again to check or make further notes. Re-play recording 9.5. Elicit answers.

> **Answers:** Cristof's questions: 1 Mrs Lloyd   2 fifty
> 3 good   4 Francoise
> Jasmine's questions: 1 two   2 Greek   3 a friend
> 4 beautiful beaches

> **OPTIONAL EXTENSION**
>
> Ask sts, in groups of three, to write cards like the ones given for other firsts and lasts. See Ex. 9 for ideas. Circulate and support.

Grammar

3 ▶ Ask sts to complete the Active grammar box individually. Write the sentences from the Active grammar box on the board. Elicit the answers and write them in.

> **Answers:** wasn't   weren't   wasn't   weren't
> weren't   Was   Were   Was   Were   Were

4a ▶ Explain the meaning of the ticks and crosses before you ask sts to complete the sentences. Go over the answers by asking individual sts to read out the sentences/questions. To make this a little more lively, ask sts to answer the questions about themselves and to say whether the statements are true or false for them.

> **Answers:** 1 was   2 wasn't   3 were   4 was
> 5 weren't   6 weren't   7 Were   8 was

b ▶ Ask sts to work in pairs to ask and answer the questions on the *My first teacher* card. Encourage them to give further detail to keep the conversation going.

> **OPTIONAL EXTENSION**
>
> If you used the optional extension activity above, ask sts to pick one or two of the cards they wrote and to interview two different sts, using these. Circulate and monitor.

Pronunciation

5a ▶ Ask sts to look at the sentences and guess which syllables are stressed, then to listen and underline the stressed syllables. Play recording 9.6. Ask individual sts to tell you which syllables were stressed. Write and underline the sentences on the board.

> **Answers: 1** I was a <u>good</u> <u>student</u>. **2** I <u>wasn't</u> very <u>intelligent</u>. **3** Was she a <u>good</u> <u>teacher</u>? **4** <u>Who</u> was your <u>best</u> <u>friend</u>?

b ▶ Model the pronunciation of stressed vs unstressed *was/wasn't*. Point out the different vowel sounds, /ɒ/ and /ə/, and ask sts to decide which variant they heard in which sentence. Re-play the recording for them to check and repeat.

6a ▶ Explain that this is going to be a dictation. Ask sts to write the sentences, then play recording 9.7. Ask sts to mark the stress and listen again to check. Re-play recording 9.7. Elicit that in negative sentences, *wasn't* is stressed – /wɒznt/ – but in affirmative sentences, *was* is generally /wəz/.

> **Answers: 1** You were my <u>best</u> <u>friend</u>. **2** You <u>weren't</u> a <u>good</u> <u>student</u>. **3** Were you <u>happy</u> at <u>school</u>? **4** <u>Who</u> were your <u>favourite</u> <u>teachers</u>?

b ▶ Ask sts when *was* and *were* were stressed and unstressed. Re-play recording 9.7 for them to check and repeat.

7 ▶ Reorganise sts into new pairs/groups of three and ask them to ask and answer about their last holiday. Before they begin, ask them to think about additional questions and detail they'd like to add. Ask them to sound as natural as possible (i.e. question intonation). Circulate and monitor.

Vocabulary

8a ▶ Ask sts: *What's the date today?* Write this on the board. Say a sentence about the day before, using the date, and elicit how to say this more simply (*yesterday*). Ask sts to read the tapescript of recording 9.5 and find time expressions with *ago* and *last*. Elicit the answers and ask sts to give you the full sentences.

b ▶ Ask sts to complete the chart individually. Go through the expressions and explain their meanings by giving the corresponding exact dates.

> **Answers: 3** last **5** ago **6** last **7** last **8** ago **9** last **10** ago

Speaking

9a ▶ Ask sts to write sentences first, then to interview their partner and make notes. Ask sts to report back to the class about their partner.

b ▶ You can ask sts to practise sentences in pairs as suggested. Alternatively, invent things that happened yesterday, two weeks ago, etc. and write them on cards, e.g. *Yesterday at 3.30 p.m./car accident in front of the main station*. Give one or two to each student and explain that they are checking alibis/looking for witnesses. Ask sts to get up and ask two other sts their question (e.g. *Where were you at 3.30 yesterday afternoon?*), then to swap their card for a new one and ask two more sts, etc. This makes them think on their feet. Circulate and correct as necessary. This should be fast – to add pace, you can tell sts when to move on.

10a ▶ Establish the rules for the game *My first, my last* (see below) and write them on the board as imperatives.

▶ Rules for playing *My first, my last*: You roll the dice and move your counter. You land on a topic. You talk about a topic for 30 seconds. The other players ask you questions. You can't say *Yes* or *No*. If you say *Yes* or *No*, you lose. If you speak for 45 seconds without saying *Yes* or *No*, you win and you roll the dice again.

b ▶ Ask sts to play the game on page 115. Provide dice!

Writing

11 ▶ Write *How was your last holiday? – Nothing to write home about!* on the board and elicit/explain the meaning. Ask sts: *Would you say this about your last holiday?* Ask them to write a letter or email about their last holiday. If sts wish, they can write about some other first or last experience.

9.3 How was your day?

In this lesson sts talk about who does the housework in their home, and talk about past experiences. Grammar: *Can/Could you ...?; Can/Could I ...?*

> **OPTIONAL WARMER**
>
> Write *A woman's job – A man's job* on the board and ask groups of sts to brainstorm jobs and activities. Pool ideas. This should provoke a discussion as to whether there is such a thing as a woman's/man's job or sphere. Ask: *Who does the housework in your family? Do you like doing housework?* You may need to clarify the difference between *housework* and *homework*! Elicit ideas. Move into Ex. 1 when sts want to be more specific, e.g. *I like cooking, but I don't like cleaning.*

Vocabulary

1a/b ▶ Give sts one minute to match the phrases and pictures, then ask them to listen and check. Play recording 9.8. Ask sts to listen again, mark the stress and repeat. Play recording 9.8 item by item.

> **Answers:** 1 vacuum the house   2 clean the bathroom   3 wash the dishes   4 do the laundry   5 iron a shirt   6 cook dinner

2a ▶ Put sts in groups of three to four and ask them to discuss who does what in their home. Appoint one person who takes notes and someone else who reports the results back to the class. Ask sts to report back statistics for their group.

b ▶ Ask groups to discuss who likes doing what and to imagine they were to share a flat/house. Ask them to make a plan about who does what according to their likes and dislikes (and to find some solution for the things no one likes doing). Don't allow them to say they would hire a cleaner. Again, ask someone to take the 'minutes' and someone to report back to the class. Also appoint someone who checks that the grammar is used correctly (*like + -ing, can + infinitive*). Circulate, listen in and support as appropriate.

Reading

3a ▶ Ask sts to look at the photos and guess what the text is about. Elicit ideas, then ask sts to read the text silently and find the phrases from Ex. 1a. Ask individual sts to read out the relevant sentences.

b ▶ Ask sts to read the questions first, then the text. Go over the answers by calling on various sts for answers. Ask them to read relevant passages from the text to support their answer.

> **Answers:** 1 over 21,000   2 Yes, he does.   3 She's an architect.   4 vacuuming the house and cooking dinner   5 He was a sales rep.   6 No, not now. He wants to get one in the future.

c ▶ Organise sts into groups of three to four. In a multinational class, mix up the different nationalities. Try to have groups with different ages and genders. Ask groups to discuss the questions and to come up with some group results. Allocate roles as in Ex. 2. Circulate and support. After a while, ask sts to report back to the group. This can be a controversial topic, so be aware that sts may hold strong opinions. Remind sts of the language for giving opinions and add *I agree, you're right* and *I don't agree.* Write these on the board to help sts.

Listening

4a ▶ Ask sts to look at the pictures and guess what sort of situations they show. Then play recording 9.9 for sts to listen and match the pictures to the conversations. Go over the answers and, for each conversation, ask sts whether their predictions were correct. Ask: *What does Jeff mean by 'Oh dear!'?*

> **Answers:** 1 b   2 c   3 d   4 d

b ▶ Ask sts to listen again to identify who's who in the pictures and to write down all the questions beginning with *How*. Ask them to check against the tapescript and ask pairs of sts to read the dialogues to the class.

> **Answers:** a The man is Jeff's friend.   How was your week?   b The woman is Jeff's aunt.   How was your flight?   c The boys are Jeff's sons.   How was school?   d The woman is Jeff's wife.   How was your day?

5a ▶ Read the How to ... box to the class. Model pronunciation and intonation.

b ▶ Put sts into groups of three to four and ask them to find out about each other's weekend, etc. Refer them back to *My first, my last* for further ideas for events. Ask sts to add some details when they answer.

Grammar

6a ▶ Ask sts to go back to the tapescript for 9.9 on page 150 and find the questions with *Can/Could*. Alternatively, ask sts to listen for them and replay recording 9.9. Ask sts to complete the questions individually, then go through them as a class.

> **Answers:** carry   have   turn   pass

b ▶ Ask sts to complete the Active grammar box, then check the answers together. Elicit/explain that *can* and *could* mean almost exactly the same, and ask sts what they think the difference is (formality/politeness). Explain that it is a good idea for sts to use *could*. You may need to explain that using *can* here is not expressing ability. Establish which sentences are polite requests, and which ask for permission.

> **Answers:** I   you   you   you   I

7 ▶ Ask a few sts questions with *Can/Could*, e.g. *Could you come here, please?* which involve sts doing something to respond rather than just replying. Put sts into pairs and ask them to practise using the ideas from the book. Then play 'Remote control'. One student 'controls' the other by asking him/her to do certain things. After a few minutes, sts change roles.

Speaking

8a/b ▶ Ask sts to tick the items in the box that they have got (a discussion on what's a good English dictionary may result from this exercise – have some ideas/criteria ready!). Ask: *What can you do with these things?* and refer sts to the phrases in b. Give sts a minute to match the words and phrases, then go over the answers. As you elicit answers, ask sts to make sentences like *With my MP3 player, I can listen to music.*

c ▶ With a weaker class, ask sts to write out the requests first. A stronger class can go straight into the activity.

> **OPTIONAL WRAP-UP**
>
> Ask sts to draw up a *Household* page for their vocabulary folders, with relevant phrases, and to add *Can/Could you …?* below them.

9 Communication: School days

In this activity sts talk about subjects they were good or bad at at school.

> **OPTIONAL WARMER**
>
> This activity practises times and numbers and introduces the topic. Prepare an OHT with a school timetable for a language school. Ask sts: *When is the English class?* Elicit *It's on Monday from 10.00 to 12.30,* etc. After sts have given you all the times, elicit/explain that this is a timetable, just like at school. Explain that the different languages and other things you study at school are called *subjects.*

1a ▶ Ask sts to match the subjects and pictures. Alternatively, put these on cards as a pair finding game. Pairs then match the other pictures.

> **Answers:** 1 science   2 music   3 art   4 sport
> 5 maths   6 languages

b ▶ Ask sts to listen and check their answers, then to repeat. Play recording 9.10.

Language note Sts tend to find the pronunciation of *maths* difficult.

c ▶ Ask: *Which subjects did you like when you were at school?* Elicit a few answers. Respond to *I liked X* by asking: *Were you good at X?* Then ask sts to complete the sentences about themselves.

2a/b ▶ Explain that sts are going to hear Louise talking about her school days. Give sts a moment to look at the chart, then ask them to listen and take notes. Play recording 9.11. Ask sts to compare notes with a partner, then to listen again. Re-play the recording.

> **Answers:** Where: Oxford   Years: 1981 to 1986
> Good/bad school: good   Good/bad student: not
> good   Good at: sport and art   Bad at: maths,
> science and languages   Favourite lessons: art
> Best friend: Sarah Jenkins

Lifelong learning

▶ Ask sts to read the Lifelong learning box. Remind them that people who speak to them in English won't know how much English they (the sts) know. Elicit how to interrupt someone politely and how to ask for repetition or explanation. Then tell the group about your school days. Speak at almost natural speed and don't simplify your language too much. Use visuals and/or gesture, some repetition and pauses. This should be a three-minute talk. Only explain if sts ask.

▶ In your role as a teacher, elicit what sts understood – allow them to use their own language if necessary (they may have understood things they can't say in English). Clarify questions and write relevant words on the board.

3a/b ▶ Explain that sts are going to prepare a short presentation about their school days. Ask them to use the chart as a basis. The Lifelong learning activity will have provided additional vocabulary. Ask sts to prepare a short presentation from their notes and to present it to their partner. After both presentations, pairs find things they have in common to present to the class.

4 ▶ Organise sts in groups of four and ask them to talk about their school days – teachers, subjects, friends, etc. Encourage them to practise small talk strategies: showing interest, asking about detail, talking about similarities and differences. Alternatively, play *cocktail party*. Ask sts to walk around as you play music and, when the music stops, talk to the person nearest to them about their school days. Explain that at a cocktail party you want to keep the conversation going, i.e. you must show interest, comment, ask about details, etc.

> **OPTIONAL UNIT WRAP-UP**
>
> Ask sts to write about an imaginary society that existed once upon a time, and about its idols and celebrities.

Review and practice

1 ▶

> **Answers:** 1 was   2 were   3 was   4 was   5 were
> 6 were

2 ▶

> **Answers:** 1 Sally wasn't late. She was early.   2 My
> parents weren't at home. They were in a restaurant.
> 3 I wasn't at the theatre. I was at the cinema.   4 Ian
> wasn't born in 1981. He was born in 1979.   5 It wasn't
> a good film. It was very boring.   6 We weren't rich.
> We were quite poor.   7 You weren't my best friend.
> You were a good friend.   8 Kerry and Mark weren't in
> Bogota. They were in Cali.

3 ▶

> **Answers:** 1 Were   2 wasn't   3 Were   4 was   5 was
> 6 were   7 Was   8 was   9 were   10 weren't

4 ▶

> **Answers:** 1 When were you born? c   2 Who was your
> manager? d   3 Where was your school? e   4 What was
> your first job? a   5 How was your weekend? b

5 ▶

> **Answers:** 1 you   2 you   3 I   4 I   5 you   6 you   7 you
> 8 I

6 ▶

> **Answers:** 1 last   2 to   3 does   4 to   5 ago   6 for
> 7 yesterday   8 vacuum   9 with   10 at

Notes for using the Common European Framework (CEF)

CEF References

9.1 Can do: make simple statements about people from history

CEF A1 descriptor: can indicate time by such phrases as *next week, last Friday, three o' clock* (CEF page 81)

9.2 Can do: give a short description of a past experience

CEF A1 descriptor: can produce simple, mainly isolated phrases about people and places (CEF page 58)

9.3 Can do: make a simple request and ask permission

CEF A1 descriptor: can ask people for things and give people things (CEF page 80)

CEF quick brief

As mentioned earlier, the *Can do* statements for each unit are by no means an exhaustive list, just as the Portfolio competences are no more than a representative sample of the content of *Total English Starter*. Likewise, not all of the CEF A1 descriptors feature in the CEF References section of *Total English Starter Teacher's Book*.

For any class you teach, materials you produce or assessments you devise, it may be worth referring back to the A1 descriptors in the CEF (downloadable from www.coe.int) and using these to set or check learning goals. You may also like to make reference to these in any lesson plan or course documentation if it is appropriate to your teaching situation.

CEF Portfolio task

Download the Total English Portfolio free from www.longman.com/totalenglish.

Objective: to reflect on sts' individual preferred learning styles.

1 ▶   This activity could be made into a kinaesthetic activity by photocopying the 21 ways of studying and learning on page 12 of the Portfolio and cutting them into separate pieces of paper. Put sts into small groups, give each group three to four of the pieces of paper and ask them to discuss the merits of each particular strategy for them. When they have talked about these strategies, ask them to swap papers with another group, but do not try to make them discuss all 21 or to continue this activity for too long.

2 ▶   Refer sts to page 12 of the Portfolio and ask them to tick, asterisk or cross the methods as instructed.

10 Stories

Overview

Lead-in	**Vocabulary:** verbs relating to events in people's lives
10.1	**Grammar:** Past Simple (regular verbs)
	Can do: understand a simple narrative of past events
10.2	**Grammar:** Past Simple (irregular verbs)
	Vocabulary: high numbers
	Can do: give a simple summary of a news event
10.3	**Grammar:** *going to*
	Vocabulary: future plans
	Can do: talk about immediate and long-term plans
Com. Focus	Holiday of a lifetime

Summary

Lesson 1: Sts learn about the story of Leonardo da Vinci's famous painting, the Mona Lisa.

Lesson 2: Sts talk about good and bad things which happened to people. They also exchange information about their past week.

Lesson 3: Sts discuss past events and future plans. They listen to a story about future plans and happiness.

Communication: Sts discuss past holidays and plan a holiday.

Film bank: Cucumber sandwiches

A short film about the British game of bowls, which is mainly played by older people and enjoys many traditional elements such as a break for afternoon tea half-way through the game.

Possible places to use this short film are:
- ▶ after 10.2
- ▶ after 10.3
- ▶ at the end of the unit

For ways to use this short film in class, see Students' Book page 125 and Teacher's Resource Book pages 141 and 146.

Lead-in

OPTIONAL WARMER

The purpose of this activity is to review the past tense of *to be* and to introduce the topic. Books closed. Write *lost and found* on the board and elicit/explain the meaning. Write two short lost and found notices, e.g. one about a wallet and one about a mobile phone, on the board. Read them to the sts, then ask them to write a notice for something lost. Then ask them to work in pairs or small groups and interview each other about the lost item (description

of the item, where it was and when, etc.). Circulate and support.

1a ▶ Read the verbs in the box to the sts. Ask them to match the verbs and phrases in pairs. You could use this as a pair finding game by putting the verbs and phrases on cards. Explain that sts will listen to check their answers.

> **Answers:** 1 lose   2 steals   3 stay   4 win   5 get
> 6 find   7 arrests   8 move   9 break   10 meet

b ▶ Play recording 10.1. once for sts to check their answers.

c ▶ Elicit from the class which phrase matches which picture. Then ask sts to describe what they can see in each picture. Elicit ideas from the class and write any new or relevant vocabulary on the board.

> **Answers:** A 5   B 7   C 10   D 9

2a ▶ Put sts into pairs and ask them to put the phrases in Ex. 1a into either of the two categories. Elicit answers from the class. Check whether everybody agrees. Opinions may vary. If they do, invite discussion.

> **Possible answers:** Good experiences: you win the lottery, you get married, you find €10 on the street, you meet your favourite actor   Bad experiences: you lose your wallet, a thief steals your mobile phone, a police officer arrests you, you break your arm   Good or bad experiences: you stay in bed all day, you move to a new house

b ▶ Ask pairs of sts to read the examples to the class. Model and correct intonation. Then ask sts to work in pairs to find new words for each 'experience'.

10.1 The story of the Mona Lisa

In this lesson sts learn about Leonardo da Vinci's famous painting. Grammar: Past Simple (regular verbs).

OPTIONAL WARMER

This activity introduces the topic. Bring in postcards or pictures of a range of works of (modern) art (include graffiti, Cubism, etc.) that are likely to provoke reactions such as *That's easy – I could do that!* Ask sts to decide which of these are art and why. This will stimulate a class discussion and a general introduction to the topic.
(*Alternative*: bring in leaflets/flyers of (past) exhibitions. Give one or two to each group of three sts and ask them to present them to the class, e.g. *There was an exhibition of ... at the Tate Gallery from ... to ... . Opening times were ...,* etc. Provide relevant vocabulary and write it on the board. After sts have presented their exhibitions, ask the class when they were last in a museum, what exhibition was on and if they liked it.)

Speaking

1 ▶ Discuss question 1 as a class. Elicit what sts know about Leonardo da Vinci. Then ask sts to work in pairs to answer questions 2 and 3. Ask individuals to report back on their partner's answers.

Reading

2a ▶ Ask sts to read the text silently as you read it to them. Ask them to underline the stressed syllables and to mark any pauses. Then ask sts in pairs to read the text aloud to their partner, who then gives feedback. Sts change roles. Circulate and listen in.

b ▶ Ask sts to complete the information, then elicit answers from the class. Remind sts how to say years and correct them if necessary.

> **Answers:** Place (now): the Louvre, Paris
> Artist: Leonardo da Vinci   Started: 1503
> Finished: 1507   Moved to France: 1516

Grammar 1

3a/b ▶ Ask sts to underline all the verbs. Elicit them and write them on the board in the order they appear in the text. Elicit which refer to the past and draw a dividing line between the past and present verbs.

c ▶ Elicit the rule and underline -ed in the verbs on the board. Ask sts to spell the infinitives for you and point out that in *like* and *move*, only -d is added.

4 ▶ Ask sts to complete the sentences in the Active grammar box individually. Go over the answers by asking individual sts to read sentences. At this point, don't correct voiced vs voiceless pronunciation, but do correct /ɪd/ and any intrusive sounds sts may pronounce that shouldn't be there.

> **Answers:** stayed   worked

> **OPTIONAL EXTENSION**
>
> Say: *I started my first job in 1987*, or something similar. Give sts a minute to prepare two sentences about themselves, using *started*. Remind them of *My first, my last* in Lesson 9.2 and give prompts, e.g. *school, first job*. Ask each student to tell the class. Correct any mispronunciation of *started*.

5 ▶ Give sts a few minutes to complete the texts individually, then go over the answers by asking individual sts to read out sentences. Correct any mispronunciation of *started*.

> **Answers:** 1 wanted   2 asked   3 started
> 4 finished   5 lived   6 played   7 moved
> 8 worked   9 moved

Pronunciation

6a ▶ Ask sts to read the verbs in the box and predict and write down the past forms. Then ask them to listen carefully to how the past forms are pronounced and repeat them. Play recording 10.2 item by item.

b ▶ Write *asked, moved* and *wanted* on the board and model pronunciation. Ask individual sts to repeat, then give sts the phonetic symbols and explain the difference between /d/ and /t/. Then ask sts to categorise the verbs. Elicit the answers and pay close attention to pronunciation.

> **Answers:** /t/ asked   finished   worked   cooked
> talked   walked   /d/ moved   lived   played
> closed   listened   /ɪd/ wanted   started   arrested

7a/b ▶ Ask sts to look back at the texts in Ex. 5 and decide how to pronounce the past forms, then call on individual sts to read the texts to the class. Correct pronunciation. Then ask sts to work in pairs, with one student reading a text, the other giving feedback. Sts then change roles. Play recording 10.3 for sts to check their pronunciation. You may want to stop the recording before each verb and ask sts to say the verbs, then continue with the recording. You could use recording 10.3 as a model for sts before they read the texts aloud themselves.

Listening

8 ▶ Ask various sts to read the statements aloud to the class. Correct any mispronunciation. Ask sts to guess whether these statements are true or false, then to check their ideas by listening to Part 2 of the Mona Lisa story. Play recording 10.4. Elicit answers from the class.

▶ Ask sts to correct the false statements by finding the relevant sentences in the tapescript on page 151. Elicit the answers. Write the negative forms on the board. Clarify that this is the past negative form. Elicit/explain that *did* is the past tense of *do*. Elicit the Present Simple of the same sentences to clarify that the structures are the same.

> **Answers:** a F   b F   c F   d T   e F

Grammar 2

> **OPTIONAL GRAMMAR LEAD-IN**
>
> To lead in, ask a few topic-related *Do you ...?* questions, e.g. *Do you like the Mona Lisa? Do you know the Louvre? Do you think the Mona Lisa is happy?* Then write a question and answers on the board to remind sts of how *do* is used.

9a ▶ Ask a pair of sts to read the first question and answer aloud. Then ask the next pair of sts to do the next question and answer. Write both questions and answers on the board and underline *did/didn't*. Ask sts to write the remaining answers individually and elicit answers.

> **Answers:** 1 Yes, he did.   2 No, it didn't.   3 Yes, they did.   4 No, they didn't.

b ▶ Ask sts to complete the Active grammar box individually. Go over the answers. Ask sts to write the same sentences in the Present Simple to make sure they use *he/she/it*. Point out that there is no *s* in the third person in the past. Explain that it is *do* which shows the past in the negative and in questions, i.e. there is no *-ed* added to the main verb.

> **Answers:** didn't   didn't   Did   did   didn't

10a/b ▶ Ask sts to write the sentences, questions and answers individually. Check the answers by asking individual sts to read their sentences.

> **Answers a:** 1 Picasso didn't like the Mona Lisa.
> 2 Leonardo da Vinci didn't live in Spain.   3 The Mona Lisa didn't stay in Italy.   4 Picasso didn't move to New York.

> **Answers b:** 1 A: Did Marcel Duchamp play chess?
> B: Yes, he did.   2 A: Did the police arrest Picasso?
> B: No, they didn't.   3 A: Did Andy Warhol work for *Vogue*? B: Yes, he did.   4 A: Did Van Gogh move to London? B: Yes, he did.

c ▶ Explain that sts can write questions with answers in the text, or other questions. If sts wrote questions they don't know the answer to, ask them to put the questions to the class at the end. If nobody knows, appoint sts to find out the answer for the next lesson. Note that they may be answered in Ex. 11.

Speaking

11a ▶ Read the questions to the class and ask pairs of sts to write down their ideas on a separate piece of paper. Ask them to put their names on it. Collect them in.

b ▶ Ask sts to read the story quickly and elicit answers to the questions. Check who got the answers right. You could bring in a small prize for the ones who did.

> **Answers:** 1 Vencenzo Peruggia was the thief.
> 2 It was in his apartment.   3 He walked out of the Louvre with the Mona Lisa under his coat.

> **OPTIONAL WRAP-UP**
> Ask sts to interview each other about things they did in the past. Ask groups of sts to draw up questionnaires (minimum 10 questions) and then reorganise the class into pairs from different groups for the interviews. To extend this, sts could write a text about their partner.

10.2 Good week, bad week

In this lesson sts talk about news items of good and bad things that happened to people. They also talk about their past week and give a brief account of what others tell them. Grammar: Past Simple (irregular verbs).

> **OPTIONAL WARMER**
> This activity practises past forms and introduces the topic. Bring in a current news item – either a headline or a short text or, preferably, a recording from the radio/internet. This should be short, clear and current so that sts will be able to understand it. Present the news item and ask sts: *What was this about?* Elicit what sts understood and then ask them to share any further information they know about it.

Reading

1a/b ▶ Books closed. Ask sts in small groups to brainstorm other current news stories . Ask them to present their ideas to the class, giving details but not giving opinions about what happened. Circulate and help as sts prepare their presentations. After each presentation, ask the class to decide whether it was a good or a bad week for that person.

2a/b ▶ Give sts four minutes to scan the texts and decide which of these events are good and which bad. Ask sts to listen and check. Play recording 10.5.

> **Answers:** 1 It was a good week for Romero Cline.
> 2 It was a good week for Mr and Mrs Blatt from the UK.   3 It was a bad week for Emiliana Rotman.
> 4 It was a bad week for pop group Gilt.

c ▶ Ask sts to read the statements and check them against the text. Go over the answers by asking different sts to read a statement, say whether it is true or false and give evidence from the text. Clarify vocabulary as you go over the answers. (*Alternative*: ask sts to close their books. Dictate the statements to them, then play the recording for them to decide whether they are true or false. Go over the answers as above.)

> **Answers:** 1 T   2 T   3 T   4 F   5 F   6 F   7 F   8 F

3 ▶ Books closed. Ask sts to brainstorm as much detail as possible with a partner, then to form sentences. Elicit stories from different pairs and ask the other sts to comment, correct and add ideas. Correct as necessary.

Grammar

4a ▶ Ask sts to underline all the Past Simple verbs and to write a list of the infinitives and past forms. Go over the answers together.

b ▶ Ask sts to complete the Active grammar box. Check the answers. Clarify that *did* is used in the same way as for regular verbs: *did* + infinitive.

> **Answers:** took   take   take

5a ▶ Ask sts to cover the list of verbs they wrote in Ex. 4a. Check they understand *across* and *down* and give them a few minutes to complete the crossword. Ask them to compare with a partner before you check the answers. Make sure that you model and practise pronunciation of all verbs.

Answers: Across: 3 came   5 played   8 saw
9 bought   12 finished   14 had   15 moved
16 went   Down: 1 met   2 asked   4 listened   6 got
7 won   10 found   11 said   13 lost

b ▶ Ask sts to complete the text individually, then call on individual sts to read out the answers and spell the verbs for you. Write all the answers on the board.

▶ Ask sts in groups of three to write 10 *Did … ?* questions about the texts in Exs. 2 and 5b. Ask them to play 'question ping pong': members from different groups form pairs. One student asks another a question, and they answer in a full sentence, and vice versa.

Answers: 1 found   2 won   3 didn't find   4 said
5 came   6 saw   7 didn't have   8 took

6 ▶ Ask sts to write sentences about themselves. Ask them to add detail, e.g. *What did you lose? Why did they come late? What day did X happen?* etc. Circulate and help as necessary.

▶ Ask sts to work in pairs. Explain that the idea is that they don't just ask and answer, but have a conversation. Remind them of the phrases you use to show interest (see the How to … box in Lesson 6.2). Circulate, listen in and support as necessary.

Vocabulary

7a ▶ Ask sts to look at the How to … box. Ask a student to read the examples aloud. Point out the use of the comma in English. Remind sts how to say years, and that there is a difference between saying numbers in general and years.

Answers: *And* is used in high numbers before numbers less than 100.

b ▶ Ask sts to look at the picture and elicit that this is an advert. Ask what a sale is, and whether the sale price is lower or higher than the normal price. Then ask them to listen and write the prices. Play recording 10.6. Check the answers and write them on the board. Ask sts whether they think these prices are realistic, cheap or expensive.

Answers: 1 €119   2 €1050   3 €465   4 €1750
5 €427   6 €325

8 ▶ Ask sts to write new sale prices and to tell their partner. (*Alternative*: after they have written in new sales prices, allocate a virtual sum of money to each student and explain that they can now go shopping, and that they should try to get the best possible value for money. Sts then get up and move around the class, asking other sts for prices and buying items. Each student can only sell each item once, i.e. sts need to be quick and economical. Set a time limit. Afterwards, ask sts what they bought, and how much they spent on each item and in total.)

Speaking

9a ▶ Ask sts: *How was last week for you? What did you do? What did you miss? What did you enjoy?* Give them two minutes to make notes. Then ask sts to speed-interview five people. Give them a time limit and explain that they need to find out something general and two details about five people. Circulate and monitor.

b ▶ Ask sts to give their partner a brief account about what they found out. Ask them to be concise. If something happened to more than one person, they should put this into one sentence. Circulate and listen in. To wrap this up, draw together a general picture of the class – was the past week more on the positive or more on the negative side for the class as a whole?

Writing

10 ▶ Ask sts to look back at their ideas from Ex. 1a – or to think of other news items and write a short news story like the ones in Ex. 2. Ask them to use the same structure. Circulate and support as necessary. Ask sts to read their news stories to the class without mentioning the name of the person involved. The class then guesses who it is about.

OPTIONAL WRAP-UP
Ask sts to write a list of all the irregular verbs they know so far, with a sample sentence for each. Then ask sts, in pairs or small groups, to write an irregular verb rap which they could perform at the beginning of the next lesson. Check them for accuracy.

10.3 What are you going to do?

In this lesson sts discuss past events and future plans. They listen to a story about future plans and happiness. Grammar: *going to*.

OPTIONAL WARMER
If you used the optional wrap-up idea at the end of lesson 10.2, ask groups to perform their irregular verb raps as a warmer. Write irregular verbs that come up on the board.

Alternatively, elicit irregular verbs in pairs (present – past) and write them on the board. Start a story by saying *Once upon a time there was …* and use the first verb on the board to describe something which happened. Ask individual sts to continue the story with a new sentence/event using the next verb, etc.

Listening

1 ▶ Books closed. Ask sts: *How was your week?* Put them in pairs or small groups and ask them to tell each other what they did, where they went, and about something special or dramatic that happened – something about every day of the past week. Circulate and help with vocabulary.

2a ▶ Books still closed. Explain that sts are going to listen to a conversation between four friends about last week – one had an exciting week, one an interesting week and two of them had a busy week. Ask them to note down what each person's week was like. Play recording 10.7, then elicit the answers.

> **Answers:** 1 Orla   2 Nick   3 Charlie and Abby

b ▶ Ask sts to look at the chart. Ask: *What did Nick do? What's his plan?* and ask a student to read the example. Ask them to make notes as they listen again. Play recording 10.7 again. Go over the answers by asking questions as above, avoiding *going to* at this stage.

> **Answers:** Nick: talked to manager; find a new job Abby: someone stole her mobile phone; go to the police tomorrow   Orla: Daniel asked her to marry him; get married next year   Charlie: moved to a new flat; buy a house next year

▶ Books closed. Ask sts to listen for a third time and try to note down the exact sentences the people on the recording say about their plans. Elicit answers using *going to* and write them on the board. Ask sts to explain the structure to you. Elicit *be + going to +* infinitive as a formula. Write it on the board, using different colours if possible.

> **OPTIONAL EXTENSION**
> Call on individual sts to make sample sentences about themselves, using the structure on the board and the notes they made in Ex. 1.

Grammar

3 ▶ Ask sts to complete the Active grammar box with a partner. Go over the answers. Using the example on the board from Ex. 2b, demonstrate and write down question formation – only the auxiliary verb changes position, everything else remains the same. The structure may look complicated at first because it creates long sentences but if you make the construction of it clear, students will find it easy to use.

> **Answers:** 'm She's not not Are Is are is

4a ▶ Ask sts to go back to Ex. 2b and write the sentences individually. Check the answers together and write them on the board. Ask a few sts to read the sentences aloud and correct/demonstrate intonation.

> **Answers:** 1 Nick is going to find a new job.   2 Abby is going to go to the police tomorrow.   3 Orla is going to get married next year.   4 Charlie is going to buy a house next year.

b ▶ Read the example to the sts, using contrastive stress. Ask the class to repeat it. Elicit one or two more sentences from the class, then ask sts to write the sentences and read them to their partner. Circulate, correcting grammar and intonation.

> **Answers:** 1 Nick's not going to play football tomorrow. He's going to play tennis.   2 Orla and Daniel aren't going to eat out tomorrow. They're going to stay at home.   3 Nick's not going to write a report next Sunday. He's going to stay in bed all day.   4 Orla and Daniel aren't going to go for a walk next Sunday. They're going to have lunch with friends.   5 Nick's not going to work from home next Monday. He's going to visit a customer.   6 Orla and Daniel aren't going to work next Monday. They're going to have a holiday.

c ▶ Ask sts one or two questions from the chart, then put them in pairs to practise. At this stage, discourage negative questions (*Isn't he going to play ...?*) because they often aren't real questions but expressions of surprise or speculation.

d ▶ Ask sts to make notes first about their plans and then to tell their partners about their plans for next week. (*Quick follow-on:* You could expand this into a game where everybody tries to find someone to join him/her. Give sts two questions: *I'm going to go to the cinema next Wednesday. Would you like to come?* or *What are you going to do next Wednesday? Would you like to go to the cinema with me?*)

Pronunciation

5a ▶ Explain that sts are going to do a dictation from the recording. Ask them to write the sentences as they listen. Play tapescript 10.8 item by item, twice if necessary. Ask sts to compare notes with a partner, then check their spelling against the tapescript on page 151.

> **Answers:** 1 A: Are you going to buy her a present? B: Yes, I am.   2 A: Is he going to stay with us? B: No, he isn't.   3 A: What are you going to do tonight? B: We're going to watch a film.   4 A: Where is she going to live? B: She's going to live in Ireland.

b ▶ Ask sts to listen again and mark the stressed syllables in the tapescript. Ask individual sts to read the sentences out loud. Remind them that unstressed vowel sounds are reduced to schwa /ə/. Then ask them to practise with a partner. Circulate and correct as necessary.

> **Answers:** *to* is pronounced with a schwa /ə/– no stress.

Speaking

6 ▶ Give sts a few prompts, e.g. holidays, job, presents, parties, things they are going to buy or sell, do or stop doing. Then give them a few minutes to make notes. Put sts into pairs or small groups (with new partners) and ask them to interview each other about their plans. Circulate and support as necessary.

Vocabulary

7a ▶ Give sts one minute to match the vocabulary items to the pictures, then elicit the answers. Clarify meanings as necessary.

> **Answers:** 1 have a child/children 2 go to university
> 3 get fit 4 retire 5 start a business 6 learn to drive

b ▶ Ask sts: *Which of these things did you or someone you know do in the past? When?* Make one or two sentences about yourself and a third person. Elicit a few sentences from the class before you ask sts to exchange ideas in small groups. Ask sts to make notes.

c ▶ Read through the examples with the group and elicit a few more example sentences. Then ask sts to work in the same groups as for b and find someone in their group who is going to do something some other group member did in the past, e.g. *Petra retired two years ago. Hugh is going to retire in 10 years' time.* Give groups five minutes to discuss ideas and produce six pairs of sentences for their group. Ask groups to present their sentences to the class.

Listening

8a ▶ Explain that sts are going to listen to a story. Ask them to read the items and elicit guesses as to what the story is going to be about. Then ask sts to number the phrases in the correct order as they listen. Play recording 10.9. Give sts one minute to compare with a partner, then check the answers as a class. (*Quick follow-on:* With confident sts, you can ask the class to try and reconstruct the dialogue at this stage.)

> **Answers:** 1 go to university 2 start a business
> 3 make a lot of money 4 be rich 5 enjoy my life
> 6 go fishing

b ▶ Play recording 10.9 again, then elicit the questions and write them on the board. Ask individual sts to repeat them. Correct pronunciation and intonation.

> **Answers:** 1 What are you going to do in life?
> 2 (And) Then what are you going to do? 3 (And)
> How are you going to do that?

9 ▶ With confident sts, ask them to reconstruct and practise the dialogue in pairs. Ask one or two pairs to perform their dialogues in front of the class. With less confident sts, reconstruct the dialogue as a class and then ask pairs of sts to practise it together.

> **OPTIONAL EXTENSION**
> Discuss with the class what the grandfather means by his final sentence. You can use this as a starting point for a discussion of lifestyles – competition, contemplation, new vs old jobs, how important is money, how precious is free time, etc.
>
> You could also use the fisherman's story as a starting point for a writing task, e.g. an exchange of emails between grandfather and grandson. Sts would need to flesh out the story a bit. It could be developed into a larger writing project by setting up an email exchange through which sts develop the story further (the son tells his grandfather about his first day at university, his graduation, etc.), to review what sts have learnt so far.

Speaking

10 ▶ Write *3,000,000* on the board and ask a student to try and read the number out loud. You may need to explain the use of commas. Ask: *Do you play the lottery?* Then ask half the class to imagine they win three million euros on the lottery. Ask: *What are you going to do/ change/stop doing?* Ask the other half of the class to imagine they are journalists who are going to interview the person who won three million. Give sts a few minutes to discuss ideas and possible questions, then put sts together in journalist–winner pairs and ask the journalists to interview winners.

10 Communication: Holiday of a lifetime

In this lesson sts discuss past holidays and plan a holiday.

> **OPTIONAL WARMER**
> This activity practises telling a story using the Past Simple tense. Write a news story headline on the board. Elicit what questions the news story will need to answer (*Who? What? Where? When? Why?*) and write the questions words and questions on the board. Either make up a story as a class or give different headlines to different groups and ask them to think up questions and a story. Don't ask them to write a news item – this follows certain rules that require more complex language. Ideas for headlines: *The Wedding of the Year, Family of 6 Die in Fire, The Prisoner on the Roof, Soccer: Triumph of Strong Women.* It makes sense to use something that was in the news a day or two before you teach the class as an example, then imaginary ones.

1a ▶ Books closed. If you are teaching this class at the end of a course just before the holidays, ask: *What starts (tomorrow/next week)?* and elicit *holidays.* Ask sts to look at the pictures and decide which of these they like best, and to rank them, then to compare ideas in groups and agree on a group ranking.

b ▶ With a strong class, ask sts to look at the questionnaire and think of two questions they would like to add. Then ask them to interview their partner about their last holiday and to take notes. Explain that before a journalist can publish an interview, the interviewee checks what they have written, and ask sts to give the notes they wrote to their partner. Alternatively, ask sts to write their own notes to answer the questions.

c ▶ Reorganise the class into new pairs or small groups. Explain that each student has two to three minutes to tell their story, and afterwards the others can ask questions. Circulate and support. Gently correct mistakes with the Past Simple.

2a ▶ Write *Holiday plans* on the board and elicit where and on what sort of holiday sts would like to go.

b ▶ Explain that sts have won a holiday of a lifetime. Ensure they understand that this is not a *life-long* holiday. Ask a student to read the rules and check that everyone understands them. Bring a map of the world or a globe to demonstrate rules 2 and 3.

c ▶ Ask pairs of sts to look back at the questions in Ex. 1b to help them organise their plans. To give sts ideas, it may be useful to bring in a few leaflets and/or postcards. You could encourage sts to visualise their plans by making a poster/collage, which would help them to speak freely as they present their ideas.

3 ▶ If pairs of sts have produced a poster, ask them to present their poster to the class. Sts should be given two to three minutes for their presentation, then the class can ask further questions (or even make suggestions, e.g. *In Krakow, you must visit the old university*). Without posters, reorganise pairs and ask sts to present their holiday plans to their partners.

Review and practice

1 ▶

> **Answers:** 1 worked 2 cooked 3 watched 4 played 5 visited 6 stayed 7 talked

2 ▶

> **Answers:** 1 My friend started a new job. 2 Did Louise move to America? 3 I didn't talk to my boss. 4 Did you play chess with Michelle? 5 Quentin and I cooked dinner. 6 Pietro didn't like his present. 7 The artist started a new painting in 1994. 8 Do they want to eat out tonight?

3 ▶

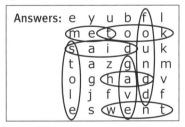

4 ▶

> **Answers:** 1 did, break 2 won 3 did, arrest 4 didn't buy 5 went 6 saw 7 did, have 8 got

5 ▶

> **Answers:** 1 Who's going to retire? 2 What are you going to buy? 3 Where are they going to go? 4 What are you going to see at the cinema? 5 Who's going to get fit? 6 Who are you going to call? 7 Which university is Lucy going to go to? 8 Where are Tom and Minnie going to move to?

6 ▶

> **Answers:** 1c 2g 3e 4h 5b 6a 7f 8d

Notes for using the Common European Framework (CEF)

CEF References

10.1 Can do: understand a simple narrative of past events

CEF A1 descriptor: can follow speech which is very slow and carefully articulated, with long pauses for him/her to assimilate meaning (CEF page 66)

10.2 Can do: give a simple summary of a news event

CEF A1 descriptor: can link words or groups of words with very basic linear connectors like *and* or *then* (CEF page 125)

10.3 Can do: talk about immediate and long-term plans

CEF A1 descriptor: can reply in an interview to simple direct questions spoken very slowly and clearly in direct, non-idiomatic speech about personal details (CEF page 82)

CEF quick brief

The Common European Framework (CEF) is used by examining bodies, academic institutions and employers across Europe as a yardstick to determine what level of language proficiency a particular qualification represents. It allows comparisons to be made between language objectives and qualifications in the same and in different languages, and is used as a policy-making tool by European Union member states.

Increasingly, exam boards such as Cambridge ESOL are mapping their qualifications to the CEF levels.

Common European Framework level Cambridge ESOL qualification

A1	–
A2	KET
B1	PET, BEC Preliminary
B2	FCE, BEC Vantage
C1	CAE, BEC Higher
C2	CPE

CEF Portfolio task

Download the Total English Portfolio free from www.longman.com/totalenglish.

Objective: to review the portfolio as it nears completion.

1 ▶ Remind sts that they could show their portfolio to a potential employer as evidence of their progress in English, and ask them what they would like to add to it or change.

2 ▶ Ask them to look back at the assessments they made some time ago of their competence across the various descriptors, and amend any they feel they can do better by ticking the 'I can do this' box.

3 ▶ Now would be a suitable time to talk about when and how the sts intend to continue their studies, and how this course has helped them.

photocopiable worksheets

contents

The hotel game

Student A **START**	Student B **START**	Student C **START**
Hotel Québec	**Hotel Bordeaux**	**Hotel Perth**
Hotel Ontario	**Hotel Montmartre**	**The Alice Springs Hotel**
Hotel Vancouver	Hotel Cannes	*Hotel Sydney*
The Pacific Hotel	Hotel Seine	**The Antarctic Hotel**
Hotel Toronto	Hotel Strasbourg	Hotel Brisbane
Hotel Montreal	**Hotel Paris**	Darling River Hotel
The Cameron Hotel	**Hotel Marseille**	The Gold Coast Hotel
Cold Lake Hotel	*Hotel Toulouse*	*The Darwin Hotel*
The Atlantic Hotel	**Hotel Loire**	**Hotel Melbourne**
Edmonton Hotel	**Hotel Lyon**	Hotel Canberra
FINISH	**FINISH**	**FINISH**

Room 265 · Room 473 · Room 198 · Room 467 · Room 920 · Room 723

Room 155 · Room 354 · Room 128 · Room 537 · Room 206 · Room 439 · Room 816

Room 574 · Room 639 · Room 608 · Room 417 · Room 159 · Room 306 · Room 784

Cities and countries

✂

Warsaw	**Rome**	**Berlin**
Poland	**Italy**	**Germany**
London	**Rio de Janeiro**	**New York**
the UK	**Brazil**	**the US**
Tokyo	**Buenos Aires**	**Sydney**
Japan	**Argentina**	**Australia**
Delhi	**Moscow**	**Venice**
India	**Russia**	**Italy**

Nice to meet you.

Core cards

Jaime: Hi, Natalia.	**Jaime:** Where are you from, Birgit?	**Jaime:** I'm from Spain.
Natalia: Hi, Jaime. This is Birgit.	**Birgit:** I'm from Sweden.	**Birgit:** Where are you from in Spain?
Jaime: Nice to meet you, Birgit.	**Natalia:** Where are you from in Sweden?	**Jaime:** I'm from Vigo.
Birgit: Nice to meet you, too.	**Birgit:** I'm from Gothenburg. Where are you from?	

Extension cards

Birgit: Is Vigo in the south of Spain?	**Birgit:** It's in the south west of Sweden. It's on the coast.	**Birgit:** Let's have a drink, Jaime.
Jaime: No, it's in Galicia. Where exactly is Gothenburg?	**Jaime:** Oh! Vigo's on the coast, too!	**Jaime:** Great idea!

Name cards

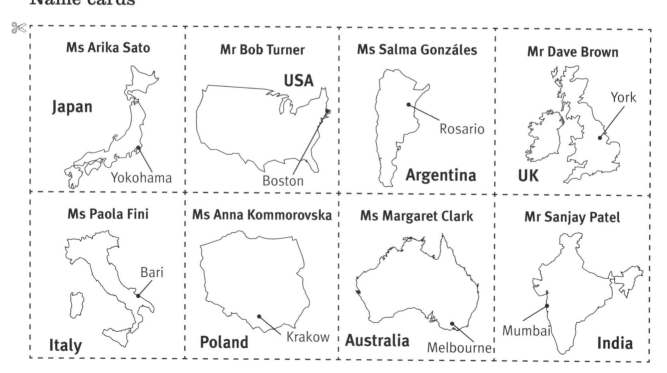

Ms Arika Sato — Japan — Yokohama

Mr Bob Turner — USA — Boston

Ms Salma Gonzáles — Argentina — Rosario

Mr Dave Brown — UK — York

Ms Paola Fini — Italy — Bari

Ms Anna Kommorovska — Poland — Krakow

Ms Margaret Clark — Australia — Melbourne

Mr Sanjay Patel — India — Mumbai

Family tree puzzle

Core version

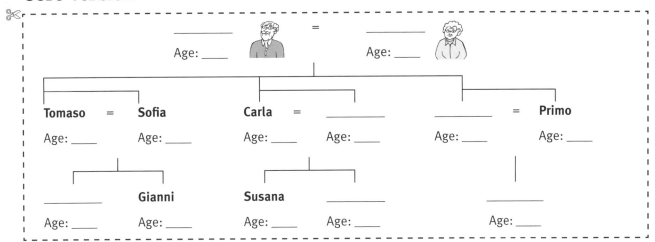

Core cards

I'm Tomaso (♂). Paolo is my father. He is 85.	I'm Sofia (♀). My husband is 41 and my daughter is 18.
I'm Elisabeta (♀). I'm 82. Carla is my daughter.	I'm Luigi (♂). I'm 34. Carla is my wife.
I'm Susana (♀). I'm 10. My mother is 35.	I'm Raffaella (♀). I'm 8. Susana is my sister.
I'm Primo (♂). I'm 29. Enzo is my son. He is three.	I'm Gianni (♂). My mother is 43.
I'm Michaela (♀). Gianni is my brother. He is 16.	I'm Carla (♀). Berta is my sister. She is 27.

Extension

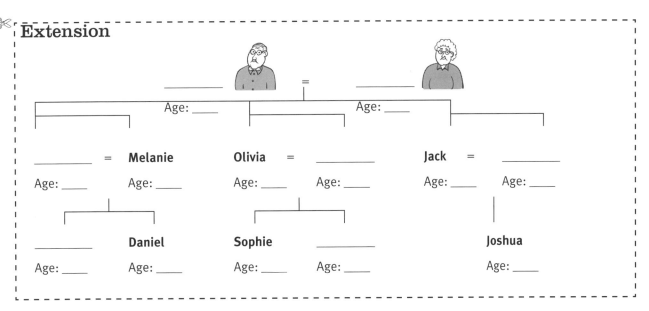

Extension cards

Joshua (♂) is four. Chloe is his grandmother. She is 82.	Sophie (♀) is 15. Sue is her cousin. She is 13.
Mike (♂) is 46. Jack is his brother. He is 35.	Daniel (♂) is 11. Tom is his uncle. He is 41.
Melanie (♀) is 47. James is her father-in-law. He is 84.	Ben (♂) is 12. Melanie is his aunt.
Olivia (♀) is 40. Emily is her sister-in-law. She is 30.	

What's your email address?

Student A

1 Answer your partner's questions.

2 Ask your partner questions. Fill in the form.

FORM

Name:	Padma Gandhi
Country:	India
Age:	44 years old
Job:	teacher
Address:	45 Apollo Street, Mumbai
Email address:	padma8@hotline.in
Home phone number:	0091 376 40 94
Mobile phone number:	404561337
Favourite city:	New Delhi
Favourite singer:	Manna Dey

FORM

Name:	
Country:	
Age:	
Job:	
Address:	
Email address:	
Home phone number:	
Mobile phone number:	
Favourite city:	
Favourite singer:	

Student B

1 You start. Ask your partner questions. Fill in the form.

2 Answer your partner's questions.

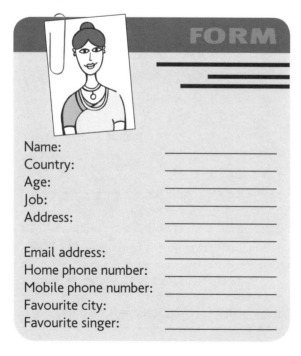

FORM

Name:	
Country:	
Age:	
Job:	
Address:	
Email address:	
Home phone number:	
Mobile phone number:	
Favourite city:	
Favourite singer:	

FORM

Name:	John Brown
Country:	England
Age:	36 years old
Job:	actor
Address:	45 Baker Street, London
Email address:	John.brown@yahoo.com
Home phone number:	0044 20 725846
Mobile phone number:	665432094
Favourite city:	London
Favourite singer:	Van Morrison

Who's Joe?

Student A

1 an important number (a house number, a phone number, etc.)	number:
2 the name of a friend	person:
3 the name of a relative	person:
4 another important number (a car number, a room number, etc.)	number:
5 the name of your home town or city	place:
6 the name of your favourite restaurant	place:
7 the day of your birthdate (for example, 31)	number:
8 the name of your favourite singer	person:

Student B

1 the name of a relative	person:
2 the name of your home town or city	place:
3 the day of your birthdate (for example, 31)	number:
4 the name of your favourite restaurant	place:
5 the name of your favourite singer	person:
6 an important number (a house number, a phone number, etc.)	number:
7 the name of a friend	person:
8 another important number (a car number, a room number, etc.)	number:

What's in your suitcase?

Student A

Tell your partner what is in your suitcase.

Draw your partner's suitcase.

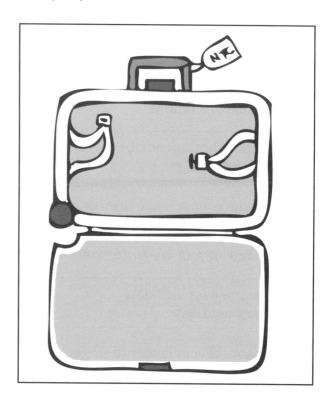

✂ -

Student B

Draw your partner's suitcase.

Tell your partner what is in your suitcase.

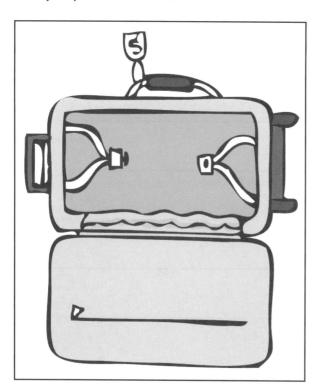

Information swap

Information sheets

Student A

The Beatles Story is a small museum about the Beatles. It is in Liverpool. It is open from Monday to Sunday. It isn't free.

Petticoat Lane is a market in London. It is famous for clothes. It is open on Sundays. It is free.

Student B

The Metropolitana is a beautiful cathedral. It is in Mexico City. It is open from Tuesday to Sunday. It isn't free.

Galerías is a new and very big department store. It is in Guadalajara, Mexico. It is open from Monday to Saturday. It is free.

Student C

The **Boquería** is a big food market. It is in Barcelona. It is open from Monday to Saturday. It is free.

The **Centro de Arte Reina Sofía** is a modern art museum. The paintings by Picasso and Dali are great. It is in Madrid. It is open from Monday to Sunday. It isn't free.

Student D

Dumbarton Oaks is a big park. The library inside the park is old. It is in Washington. It is open from Tuesday to Sunday. It isn't free.

Saint Louis is a beautiful cathedral. It is in New Orleans. It is open from Monday to Sunday. It is free.

Question sheets

Student A

Boquería
1 (art museum)
2 (Madrid)
3 (open/Thursdays)

Centro de arte Reina Sofía
1 (market)
2 (modern)
3 (free)

Student B

Dumbarton Oaks
1 (palace)
2 (open/Mondays)
3 (big)

Saint Louis
1 (museum)
2 (beautiful)
3 (open/Fridays)

Student C

The Beatles Story
1 (shop)
2 (big)
3 (open every day)

Petticoat Lane
1 (department store)
2 (famous for food)
3 (open/Saturdays)

Student D

Metropolitana
1 (shop)
2 (Mexico City)
3 (free)

Galerías
1 (museum)
2 (open on Sundays)
3 (old)

Where are you?

Student A

1 **Ask Student B:**

1 hotel good?

2 hotel small?

3 food nice?

4 room big?

5 city ugly?

6 How/you?

7 hotel beautiful?

8 cold?

9 traffic bad?

10 hotel old?

Then ask: Where are you?

2 **Answer Student B's questions and complete the puzzle.**

1 No, it's _____ .

2 No, it's _____ .

3 No, it's _____ .

4 No, it isn't _____ .

5 We're _____ .

6 No, it's _____ .

7 Yes, it's _____ .

8 No, it's _____ .

9 Yes, it's _____ cold.

10 Yes, it's _____ .

Student B

1 **Answer Student A's questions and complete the puzzle.**

1 No, it's _____ .

2 No, it's _____ .

3 Yes, it's _____ .

4 No, it's _____ .

5 No, it's _____ .

6 We're _____ .

7 No, it's _____ .

8 No, it's _____ .

9 Yes, it's _____ .

10 No, it's _____ .

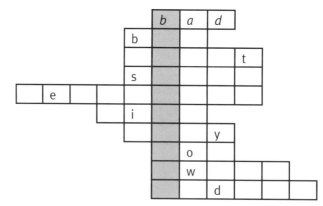

2 **Ask Student A:**

1 room small?

2 hotel old?

3 hotel restaurant good?

4 hot?

5 How/you?

6 hotel big?

7 city old?

8 city ugly?

9 cold?

10 traffic bad?

Then ask: Where are you?

Can I have a ... , please?

Student A

Dialogue 1

You are the waiter. You speak first.

You: Good _____ . Can _____ help _____ ?

Customer: (student A)

You: Certainly.  or  ?

Customer: (student A)

You: Sure. _____ else ?

Customer: (student A)

You: _____ . _____ else ?

Customer: (student A)

You: Eat _____ or _____ _____ ?

Customer: (student A)

You: That's € _____ . Thank _____ .

Dialogue 2

You are the customer. Your partner speaks first.

Waiter: (student B)

You: Yes. Can , please?

Waiter: (student B)

You: One and one , please.

Waiter: (student B)

You: Yes. Can , please ?

Waiter: (student B)

You: No, _____ you.

Waiter: (student B)

You: _____ in, please.

Waiter: (student B)

Student B

Dialogue 1

You are the customer. Your partner speaks first.

Waiter: (student A)

You: Yes. Can , please?

Waiter: (student A)

You: A , please.

Waiter: (student A)

You: Yes. Can , please ?

Waiter: (student A)

You: No, _____ _____ .

Waiter: (student A)

You: _____ away, please.

Waiter: (student A)

Dialogue 2

You are the waiter. You speak first.

You: _____ afternoon. _____ I help _____ ?

Customer: (student A)

You: or ?

Customer: (student A)

You: Sure. _____ else ?

Customer: (student A)

You: _____ . Anything _____ ?

Customer: (student A)

You: _____ in or _____ away ?

Customer: (student A)

You: That's € _____ . _____ you.

Menu

Sandwiches

€2.20

€2.00

Drinks

€1.99

€3.50

€1.75

€3.00

Cakes

€ 3.50

€ 3.70

How much is ... ?

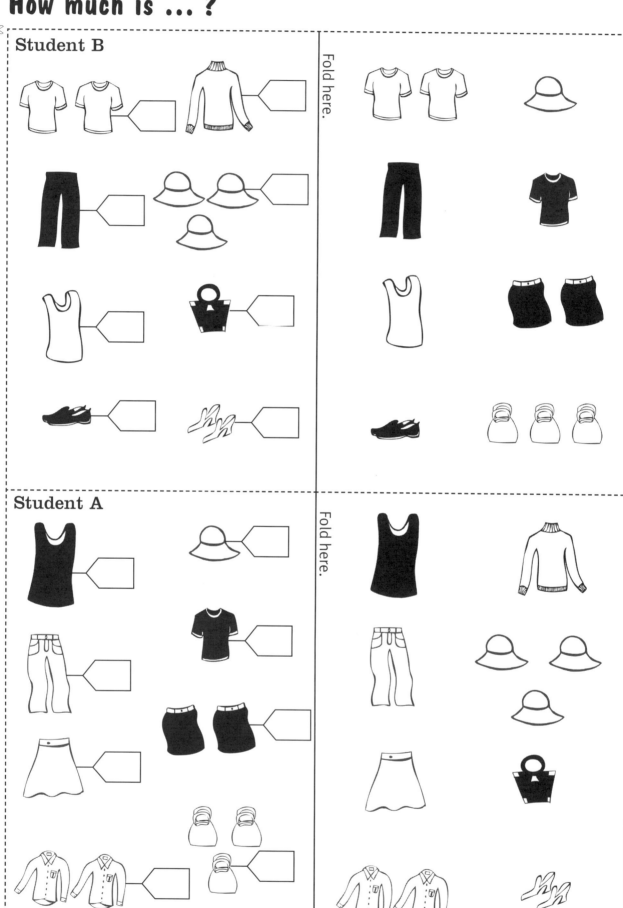

Student B

Fold here.

Student A

Fold here.

Answer the question.

START

FINISH

1 A
How much are *these/those* shoes?

1 B
Can I have *a/an* coffee?

2 A
How much *is/are* this red shirt?

2 B
Can I have *a small salad/a salad small*, please?

3 A
What's email address *Tom's/Tom's email address*?

3 B
Pete and Dave are Australian *man/men*.

4 A
Here you *are/have*. That's €20, please.

4 B
Is/Are these your books?

5 A
Ben and Jenny are *childs/children*.

5 B
How much is *that/this* blue jacket?

6 A
Can I have *a/an* orange juice and a coffee, please?

6 B
That's *Henry's/the Henry's* credit card.

7 A
These are my cinema *tickets/cinemas tickets*.

7 B
That's/That are $40, please, Sir.

8 A
It *not is/isn't* red, it's brown.

8 B
I'm sorry. I *don't know/know not your* name.

9 A
Can I have *a cappuccino large/a large cappuccino*, please?

9 B
Are these your train *tickets/trains ticket*?

10 A
How much is *this/that* hat?

10 B
How much are *these/those* shirts?

11 A
I *know not/don't know* your telephone number.

11 B
These shoes *not are/aren't* black, they're blue.

12 A
Can *I a return ticket have/Can I have a return ticket*, please?

12 B
Can I help you?/Can I you help?

Answers for A questions. Give to student B.	**Answers for B questions. Give to student A.**
1 these; 2 is; 3 Tom's email address; 4 are; 5 children; 6 an; 7 cinema tickets; 8 isn't; 9 a large cappuccino; 10 this; 11 I don't know; 12 Can I have a return ticket	1 a; 2 a small salad; 3 men; 4 are; 5 that; 6 Henry's; 7 That's; 8 I don't know; 9 train tickets; 10 those; 11 aren't; 12 Can I help you?

Where are you?

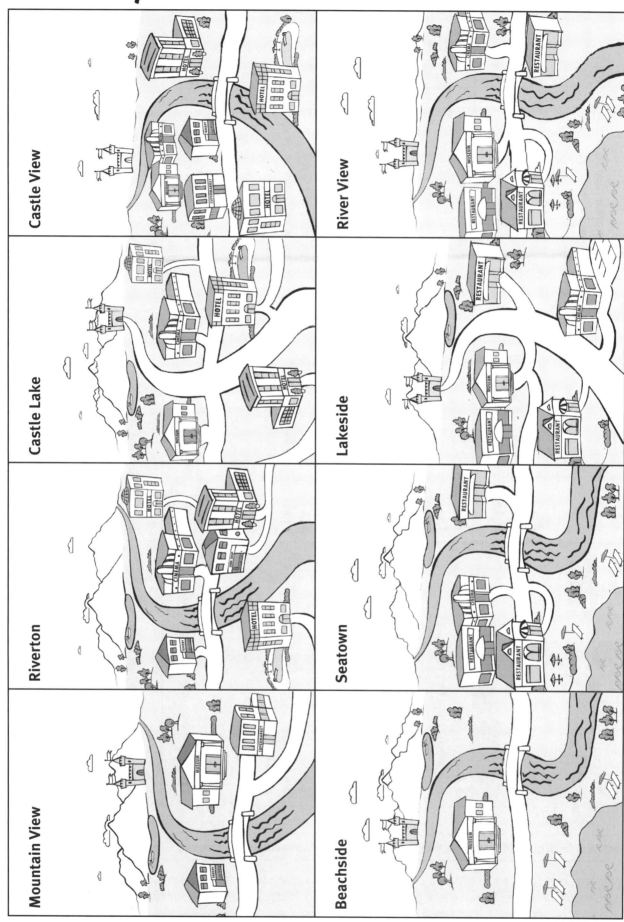

Castle View

River View

Castle Lake

Lakeside

Riverton

Seatown

Mountain View

Beachside

Find the differences.

Student A

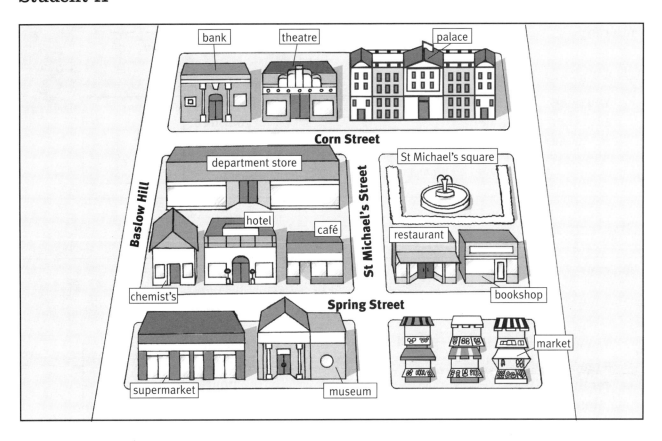

Student B

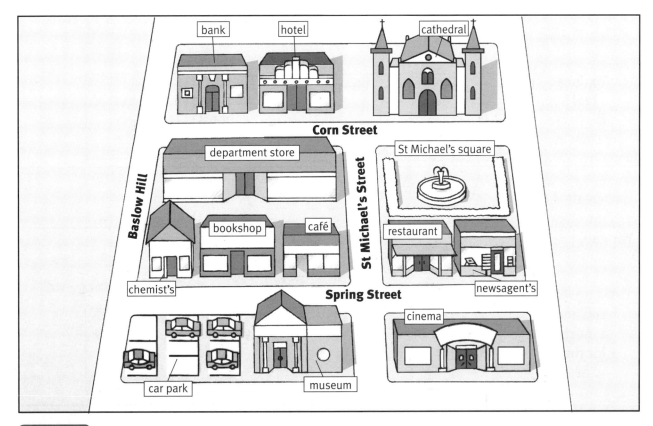

Find a teacher.

Student A

You can:

You need a teacher for these classes:	Time	Class	Teacher		These are your free hours:	Free hours
	8.00–8.45	Italian				8.50–9.35
	9.40–10.25	Dance				11.20–12.05
	13.50–14.35	Golf				12.10–12.55
	16.20–17.05	Swimming				13.00–13.45

Student B

You can:

You need a teacher for these classes:	Time	Class	Teacher		These are your free hours:	Free hours
	10.30–11.15	French				8.00–8.45
	11.20–12.05	Piano				9.40–10.25
	14.40–15.25	Cooking				13.50–14.35
	15.30–16.15	Dance				15.30–16.15

Student C

You can:

You need a teacher for these classes:	Time	Class	Teacher		These are your free hours:	Free hours
	8.50–9.35	German				9.40–10.25
	9.40–10.25	Singing				14.40–15.25
	13.00–13.45	Football				15.30–16.15
	17.10–17.55	Golf				18.00–18.45

Student D

You can:

You need a teacher for these classes:	Time	Class	Teacher		These are your free hours:	Free hours
	8.50–9.35	Cooking				8.50–9.35
	12.10–12.55	Football				10.30–11.15
	15.30–16.15	Singing				16.20–17.05
	18.00–18.45	Italian				17.10–17.55

Friendfinders

1 Sports

Do _____ ?

What _____ favourite _____ ?

_____ ?

2 TV programmes

_____ ?

What _____ favourite _____ ?

_____ ?

3 Restaurants

Do_____ ?

What _____ favourite _____ ?

_____ ?

4 Cities

_____ ?

What _____ favourite _____ ?

_____ ?

5 Famous songs/singers

_____ ?

What _____ favourite _____ ?

_____ ?

Prefer

Example: *Do you prefer the countryside or the city?*

1 _____ or _____ ?

2 _____ or _____ ?

3 _____ or _____ ?

What do builders do?

buildings.	things, for example computers and books.	shoes.	articles.	food.	buildings.
designs	sells	designs	writes	cooks	builds
architect	sales rep.	shoe designer	reporter	chef	builder
An	A	A	A	A	A

Question and answer bingo

do/Jenny and Rob/what/do	in an office/work/you/do	like/Peter/you/do
favourite food/wife's/is/your/what	Anne/work/does/at 7.30/start	car/what/your/is/favourite
what/mean/*brunch*/does	how/your/is/old/father	different/you and your brother/are/how

which/for/work/does/Pete/company	what/mean/*brunch*/does	is/favourite food/your/what
in an office/work/you/do	different/you and your sisters/are/how	you/work/start/at 7.30/do
do/you/films/Alfred Hitchcock's/like	how/your/old/is/daughter	favourite/country/what/your/is

company/for/work/you/which/do	in an office/Mary/does/work	your/tall/son/is/how
actor/is/favourite/your/who	time/do/work/what/you/finish	you/work/start/at 7.30/do
favourite food/wife's/is/your/what	live/England/Pamela/does/in	do/you/films/Alfred Hitchcock's/like

actor/is/favourite/your/who	what/mean/*brunch*/does	different/you and your brother/are/how
favourite food/wife's/is/your/what	how/your/old/is/daughter	time/do/work/what/you/finish
do/Jenny and Rob/what/do	which/for/work/does/Pete/company	Anne/work/does/at 7.30/start

actor/is/favourite/your/who	favourite food/wife's/is/your/what	how/your/is/old/father
which/for/do/company/work/you	do/you/films/Alfred Hitchcock's/like	bed/you/go/do/early/to
in an office/do/work/you	live/England/Pamela/does/in	do/Jenny and Rob/what/do

Question race

Student A START	Student B START
1 How old he is?	1 Does she like fast food?
2 Does he watch a lot of films?	2 What does she does?
3 Which company do he work for?	3 Works she work long hours?
4 Does he has breakfast early?	4 Who does she work for?
5 Can he cook?	5 Is married?
6 Does he have got any children?	6 Does she listen to a lot of music?
7 Does he have a shower every day?	7 She travels a lot?
8 What time does he gets up?	8 What time does she finishes work?
9 Do he eat fast food for breakfast?	9 Does she get up at 8 o'clock?
10 Does he start work at half past seven?	10 Do she watch TV?
FINISH	**FINISH**

Student A	Student B
1 Does she like fast food?	1 How old is he?
2 What does she do?	2 Does he watch a lot of films?
3 Does she work long hours?	3 Which company does he work for?
4 Who does she work for?	4 Does he have breakfast early?
5 Is she married?	5 Can he cook?
6 Does she listen to a lot of music?	6 Does he have any children?
7 Does she travel a lot?	7 Does he have a shower every day?
8 What time does she finish work?	8 What time does he get up?
9 Does she get up at 8 o'clock?	9 Does he eat fast food for breakfast?
10 Does she watch TV?	10 Does he start work at half past seven?

Imperatives mime

Students A and B

Please turn off your mobile phone.	Don't eat!	Sit down!
Please close the door.	Have a shower.	Don't watch TV!
Turn off your MP3 player.	Don't come in!	Please don't play the piano.
	Hold the line, please.	
	Go to bed!	
	Turn on your computer.	

Students C and D

Open your books.	Please listen to me.	Look left.
Please don't sing.	Please read this book.	Complete this form.
Don't answer the phone!	Don't get up!	Be quiet!
	Please look at this picture.	
	Please open the door.	
	Come in!	

Reading – writing relay

Student A – Part 1

Sally Jones

I'm a reporter. I get up at 6.00 in the morning. I have a shower, but I don't have breakfast. I leave the house at 7.30. I work at the office from 8.00 to 5.00. In the morning, I have meetings and make phone calls. I have lunch at a restaurant near the office. In the afternoon, I talk to people and I write articles. I go home at 5.00, but I take work home. I finish work at 9.00 in the evening, then I go to bed.

Student B – Part 2

Sam Smith

I'm a sales rep. I get up at 5.30 in the morning. I have a shower, and I have a big breakfast. I leave the house at 8.30. From 9.00 to 12.30, I visit customers. I also call customers on my mobile phone. In the morning, I have meetings and make phone calls. I have lunch in my car – a sandwich or a burger. In the afternoon, I visit customers and I write reports. I go home at 6.00, but I take work home. I finish work at 11.00 in the evening, then I go to bed.

Student B – Part 1

1 What's her name?

_____

2 What's her job?

_____

3 What time does she get up?

_____

4 Does she have breakfast?

_____

5 What time does she start work?

_____

6 What does she do in the morning?

_____

_____

7 Where does she have lunch?

_____

8 What does she do in the afternoon?

_____

_____

9 Does she take work home?

_____

10 What time does she go to bed?

_____

Student A – Part 2

1 What's his name?

_____

2 What's his job?

_____

3 What time does he get up?

_____

4 Does he have breakfast?

_____

5 What time does he start work?

_____

6 What does he do in the morning?

_____

_____

7 Where does he have lunch?

_____

8 What does he do in the afternoon?

_____

_____

9 Does he take work home?

_____

10 What time does he go to bed?

_____

Jobs crossword

Pair A

Write crossword clues for these words.

Down

2 computer programmer _____

3 artist _____

4 chef _____

7 nurse _____

9 waiter _____

Across

1 police officer _____

5 shop assistant _____

6 reporter _____

8 school teacher _____

10 manager _____

Listen to the clues from pair B and complete the crossword.

Pair B

Write crossword clues for these words.

Down

1 personal assistant _____

4 sales rep _____

5 accountant _____

6 lecturer _____

Across

2 receptionist _____

3 designer _____

7 call centre worker _____

8 factory worker _____

9 builder _____

10 doctor _____

Listen to the clues from pair A and complete the crossword.

I'm here to see Bill Lee. ✂

Student A

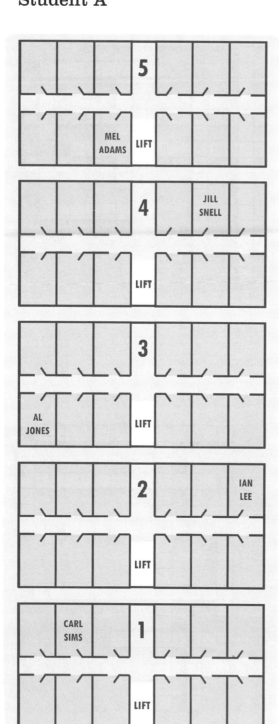

Student B

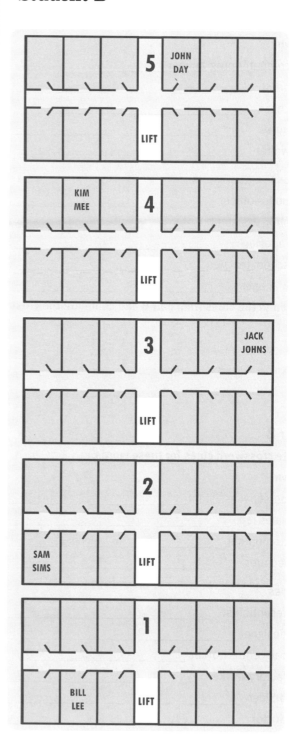

Ask to see:

- John Day
- Bill Lee
- Kim Mee
- Sam Sims
- Jack Johns

Ask to see:

- Carl Sims
- Al Jones
- Mel Adams
- Jill Snell
- Ian Lee

Hotel pairs

LIKE cycle	**HOTEL** You can borrow a bicycle at the Midtown Hotel.	**LIKE** shop for books	**HOTEL** The Downtown hotel is near the shops. There are a lot of bookshops.
LIKE eat Japanese food	**HOTEL** There's a Japanese restaurant in the Hotel Royal. You can eat there.	**LIKE** play football	**HOTEL** The Westside Sports Club has football matches on Saturdays.
LIKE play chess	**HOTEL** The City Hotel has a board games room. You can play a lot of games there.	**LIKE** go to the theatre	**HOTEL** The Broadway Inn is very near the theatres.
LIKE play tennis	**HOTEL** There's a tennis court at the Edgetown Spa Hotel.	**LIKE** do exercise	**HOTEL** There's a great fitness centre at the Mayfair. You can do exercise there.
LIKE I like going sightseeing.	**HOTEL** You can take a tour from the Mountain View Hotel. They've got a tour bus.	**LIKE** go swimming	**HOTEL** There's a pool at the Travel Rest hotel.
LIKE walk	**HOTEL** The Lakeside Hotel is in the mountains. You can walk from the hotel.	**LIKE** watch TV	**HOTEL** The Holiday Lodge has got a TV in every room.

Complete the sentences.

1 I like _____ chess.

2 I don't want _____ the presentation tomorrow.

3 We can _____ in the sea this afternoon.

4 I want _____ some books this weekend.

5 We can _____ sightseeing tomorrow.

6 I don't like _____ at 6.oo in the morning.

7 I want _____ a shower now.

8 We can _____ in that Italian restaurant tonight.

9 I don't like _____ reports.

10 Do you want _____ my mobile phone?

11 We can _____ a DVD tonight.

12 I like _____ in this town.

13 I don't want _____ my English homework tonight.

14 We can _____ work early tonight.

15 I don't like _____ to the radio.

read	go	listen	play	get up
swim	have	write	finish	give
eat	watch	do	live	use

Have you got a spare fridge?

Student A

dishwasher? · sofa? · table and chairs? · mirror?

Student B

cupboard? · coffee table? · bookcase? · bedside table?

Student C

fridge? · TV? · wardrobe? · lamp?

Student D

washing machine? · computer? · armchair? · bed?

Favourite cafés and restaurants

Restaurant	Student 1	Student 2	Student 3
Name?			
Location?			
Food?			
Your favourite food there?			
How often?			

Café	Student 1	Student 2	Student 3
Name?			
Location?			
Food/Drinks?			
Your favourite food/drink there?			
Good for reading? Chess? TV?			
How often?			

Famous birthdays

Student A

Albert Einstein 14 03 1879	Frank Sinatra 12 12 1915
Franklin Roosevelt 30 01 1882	Alfred Hitchcock 13 08 1899
Bette Davis 5 04 1908	Greta Garbo 18 09 1905
Mao Tse Tung 26 12 1893	Anna Freud 3 12 1895
Queen Elizabeth, the Queen Mother 4 08 1900	Indira Gandhi 19 11 1917

Margaret Thatcher   Mother Teresa of Calcutta   Martin Luther King

Marilyn Monroe   **Maria Callas**   Charlie Chaplin

Salvador Dalí   Ray Charles   Andy Warhol   Ernest Hemingway

Student B

Margaret Thatcher 13 10 1925	Mother Teresa of Calcutta 27 08 1910
Marilyn Monroe 1 06 1926	Martin Luther King 15 01 1929
Maria Callas 2 12 1923	Salvador Dali 11 05 1904
Andy Warhol 6 08 1928	**Ray Charles 23 09 1930**
Ernest Hemingway 21 7 1899	Charlie Chaplin 16 4 1889

Mao Tse Tung   Franklin Roosevelt   Greta Garbo

Anna Freud

Albert Einstein   Queen Elizabeth, the Queen Mother

Bette Davis

Frank Sinatra   Indira Gandhi   Alfred Hitchcock

Were you in New York last night?

Student A

You:
- in New York last year
- a good student when you were 10
- born in London
- good at music when you were a child
- born in 1980

Who was ...

- in New York last month?

_____

- an intelligent student when he/she was 10?

_____

- born in Berlin?

_____

- good at horse-riding when he/she was a child?

_____

- born in 1983?

_____

Student B

You:
- in New York last month
- a happy student when you were 10
- born in Delhi
- good at horse-riding when you were a child
- born in 1981

Who was ...

- in New York ten years ago?

_____

- a bad student when he/she was 10?

_____

- born in London?

_____

- good at singing when he/she was a child?

_____

- born in 1980?

_____

Student C

You:
- in New York ten years ago
- an intelligent student when you were 10.
- born in Boston
- good at singing when you were a child
- born in 1982

Who was ...

- in New York last night?

_____

- a good student when he/she was 10?

_____

- born in Delhi?

_____

- good at football when he/she was a child?

_____

- born in 1981?

_____

Student D

You:
- in New York last night
- a bad student when you were 10.
- born in Berlin
- good at football when you were a child
- born in 1983

Who was ...

- in New York last year?

_____

- a happy student when he/she was 10?

_____

- born in Boston?

_____

- not good at music when he/she was a child?

_____

- born in 1982?

_____

How was your holiday?

Student A

Part 1: Answer Student B's questions about your holiday. Use this information:	Part 2: Ask Student B questions about his/her holiday. Tick the picture that matches Student B's answer.	
• shops: not interesting • flight: great • hotel: not expensive • room: very nice • weather: awful • food: not very good • car: really nice • tourist attractions: boring	**flight** ☐☺ ☐☹	**weather** ☐☺ ☐☹
	food ☐☺ ☐☹	**tourist attractions** ☐☺ ☐☹
	hotel ☐£££ ☐£	**car** ☐☺ ☐☹
	room ☐☺ ☐☹	**shops** ☐☺ ☐☹

Student B

Part 1: Ask Student A questions about his/her holiday. Tick the picture that matches Student A's answer.		Part 2: Answer Student A's questions about your holiday. Use this information:
shops ☐☺ ☐☹	**weather** ☐☺ ☐☹	• flight: not very good • food: great • hotel: expensive • room: awful • weather: nice • tourist attractions: OK • car: not very good • shops: great
flight ☐☺ ☐☹	**food** ☐☺ ☐☹	
hotel ☐£££ ☐£	**car** ☐☺ ☐☹	
room ☐☺ ☐☹	**tourist attractions** ☐☺ ☐☹	

Grammar bets

1	Clark Gable was actor.
2	My mother were born in 1943.
3	When I was at school, I was good in mathematics.
4	My father not was born in London.
5	Billy Holiday and Maria Callas was singers.
6	When I was child, I was a good footballer.
7	We were in London ago two years.
8	Where you were last week?
9	Where were you yesterday night?
10	My sister was in home yesterday morning.
11	I don't know how play this game.
12	Was nice the weather yesterday?
13	Can you the window open?
14	When I was a child, I was bad on music.
15	We was good teachers.

Chat show

When you were a child ...

- play sports? Which sports? Now?
- like films? Which films? Favourite film?
- move house? From where to where?
- play an instrument? Which instrument? Now?
- start a hobby? Which hobby? Same hobby now?
- listen to music? Which music? Now?
- cook food? Which food? Now?
- talk on the phone a lot? Who with? Now?
- walk to school? How far?
- work around the house? Which jobs? Now?
- ask for a special birthday or Christmas present? What was it?
- live in a flat? Or a house? Where? Now?

Thank you for appearing on our show!

Quiz

Team A

1 Which city (live/Picasso) _____ in from 1904 to 1945?
   a Barcelona   **b** Paris   **c** New York

2 When (walk/astronaut Neil Armstrong) _____ on the moon?
   a 1963   **b** 1966   **c** 1969

3 Who (be) _____ Rose Maddox?
   a a singer   **b** a writer   **c** a poet

4 What (do/Julia Roberts) _____ before becoming an actor?
   a She was a model.   **b** She was a teacher.   **c** She was a singer.

5 When (die/Elvis Presley) _____?
   a 1974   **b** 1977   **c** 1979

6 Where (be/George W. Bush) _____ born?
   a California   **b** Texas   **c** Connecticut

7 Which English football club (play/David Beckham) _____
   for before going to Real Madrid?
   a Chelsea   **b** Manchester United   **c** Arsenal

8 How many children (have/Darwin) _____?
   a five   **b** ten   **c** one

✂ -

Team B

1 Where (die/Van Gogh) _____?
   a France   **b** Holland   **c** Belgium

2 When (live/Shakespeare) _____?
   a from 1564 to 1616   **b** from 1440 to 1590   **c** from 1621 to 1651

3 Who (be) _____ Wolfgang Amadeus Mozart's friend?
   a Franz Joseph Haydn   **b** Johann Sebastian Bach   **c** Johannes Brahms

4 What (invent/Philo Farnsworth) _____?
   a the television   **b** the radio   **c** the computer

5 How many husbands (have/Marilyn Monroe) _____?
   a two   **b** four   **c** three

6 When (move/Einstein) _____ to the United States?
   a 1942   **b** 1933   **c** 1955

7 Which famous university (work/Marie Curie) _____ at?
   a Oxford   **b** Heidelberg   **c** the Sorbonne

8 Where (be/Martina Hingis) _____ born ?
   a Slovakia   **b** the Czech Republic   **c** Switzerland

✂

Answers to Team A's questions	Answers to Team B's questions
1 He/Picasso lived in Paris.	1 He/Van Gogh died in France.
2 He/Neil Armstrong walked on the moon in 1969.	2 He/Shakespeare lived from 1564 to 1616.
3 She/Rose Maddox was a singer.	3 Franz Joseph Haydn was his/Mozart's friend *or* His/ Mozart's friend was Franz Joseph Haydn.
4 She/ Julia Roberts worked as a model.	4 He/Philo Farnsworth invented the television.
5 He/Elvis Presley died in 1977.	5 She/Marilyn Monroe had three (husbands).
6 He/George W. Bush was born in Connecticut.	6 He/Einstein moved there/to the United states in 1933.
7 He/David Beckham played for Manchester United.	7 She/Marie Curie worked at the Sorbonne.
8 He/Darwin had ten children.	8 She/Marina Hingis was born in Slovakia.

I'm going to have a holiday.

go to university	start a business	live abroad	move to a new house
past	past	past	past

change jobs	start a family	buy a painting	buy a boat
past	past	past	past

go to university	start a business	live abroad	move to a new house
future	future	future	future

change jobs	start a family	buy a painting	buy a boat
future	future	future	future

go to Las Vegas	go to Las Vegas	go to Hawaii	go to Hawaii
past	future	past	future

Question and answer dominoes

get up   be (x2)   move   want   not get up   not like   find   say
come   meet   take   love   not have   not be (x2)   have

| START | **A** Why did you stop smoking? | **B** Because I _____ cooking. | **A** Why are you so tired? |

| **B** Because I _____ to live longer. | **A** Why didn't you send the emails? | **B** Because I _____ really early this morning. | **A** Why was the teacher so angry with Pete? |

| **B** Because I _____ a problem with my computer. | **A** Why didn't they buy the house? | **B** Because he _____ to class late. | **A** Why didn't they come to the party yesterday? |

| **B** Because it _____ very small for them. | **A** Why did you go to London? | **B** Because they _____ very tired. | **A** Why didn't you get the job in England? |

| **B** Because my company _____ there. | **A** Why didn't you like the film? | **B** Because my English _____ good enough. | **A** Why was Jenny late for work? |

| **B** Because the actors _____ very good. | **A** Why didn't you buy that jacket? | **B** Because she _____ on time. | **A** Why did Carmen phone the police? |

| **B** Because I _____ the colour. | **A** Why didn't you get married to Sarah? | **B** Because a man _____ her handbag and her camera. | **A** Why was Pete so happy? |

| **B** Because she _____ that she didn't love me. | **A** Why didn't you do the shopping this morning ? | **B** Because he _____ ten pounds on the street. | **A** Why do you like Glasgow? |

| **B** Because I _____ time. | **A** Why did you open a restaurant? | **B** Because I _____ my wife there. | FINISH |

Teacher's notes
Photocopiable worksheets

Teacher's notes

UNIT 1 Vocabulary
The hotel game

- Use this activity after Lesson 1.1, Ex. 9 on page 11.
- New language: *I'm sorry, we're full.*

Procedure

Preteach the new language.

Sts work in groups of three. Give each group a copy of the board, a set of room number cards, a die and three counters. Sts decide which of them is visiting Canada, France and Australia.

Sts toss a coin to see who starts. They take it in turns to move across their section of the board – booking into hotels on the way. Use these scores for the die, so that the game takes some time to finish: 1 & 2 = move up one square; 3 & 4 = move up two squares; 5 & 6 = move up three squares. Shuffle the room cards and put them in a pile face downwards.

Using their own identities, sts must try to check into the hotels by introducing themselves to the student on their right: *Good morning, I'm … .* The student on their right picks up a room card. If there is a number on the card, a room is available and they welcome the person: *Good morning, Mr/Mrs/Ms Schmidt. Welcome to Hotel Perth. You are in room 265*. If the hotel is full (a card with a bed crossed out), the student says: *I'm sorry, Mr/Mrs/Ms Schmidt. We're full.* If the hotel is full, the student trying to check in must go back to the start square.

The first person to reach the end of the board wins.

UNIT 1 Grammar
Cities and countries

- Use this activity after Lesson 1.2 on page 13.
- New language: *Moscow*

Procedure

Preteach the new language.

Sts work in groups of three. Give each group a set of cards which are spread out face down. Ask sts to take turns choosing two cards and showing the cards to the group. The student showing the cards makes a sentence using the cards, for example *Warsaw is in Italy*. If the statement is true, the other sts say *Yes* and the student keeps the two cards. If it isn't true, the other sts say *No* and the student puts them back in the same place they were picked up from. If they are not sure who is right, they should call on you to be the final arbiter. After all of the cards have been picked up, the student who has the most pairs is the winner.

UNIT 1 Communication
Nice to meet you.

- Use this activity after Lesson 1.3 on page 15.

Procedure

Task 1

Use the core cards for real beginners and the core plus the extension cards for false beginners.

Divide sts into groups of three. Give each group a set of cards. Ask sts to put them in order to make a dialogue. If you want to make it competitive, set a time limit. The first group to order the dialogue correctly wins. Afterwards, sts act out the dialogue.

Answers

Core dialogue

Jaime: Hi, Natalia.

Natalia: Hi, Jaime. This is Birgit.

Jaime: Nice to meet you, Birgit.

Birgit: Nice to meet you, too.

Jaime: Where are you from, Birgit?

Birgit: I'm from Sweden.

Natalia: Where are you from in Sweden?

Birgit: I'm from Gothenburg. Where are you from?

Jaime: I'm from Spain.

Birgit: Where are you from in Spain?

Jaime: I'm from Vigo.

Extension

Birgit: Is Vigo in the south of Spain?

Jaime: No, it's in Galicia. Where exactly is Gothenburg?

Birgit: It's in the south west of Sweden. It's on the coast.

Jaime: Oh! Vigo's on the coast, too!

Birgit : Let's have a drink, Jaime.

Jaime: Great idea!

Task 2

Sts work in groups of eight. Give each student a different identity card. Explain that they are in a cocktail party and ask them to walk round the class introducing themselves to different people and finding out where they are from. With real beginners, you could elicit a simple example dialogue for two people and write it on the board, for example:

A: Hi, I'm … .

B: Hi … .

A: Nice to meet you.

B: Nice to meet you, too.

A: Where are you from?

B: I'm from … .

A: Where are you from in … ?

B: I'm from … . Where are you from?

A: I'm from … .

B: Where are you from in … ?

A: I'm from … .

With false beginners, allow sts freedom to use other relevant language they may know.

UNIT 2 Vocabulary
Family tree puzzle

• Use this activity after Lesson 2.1, Ex. 7 on page 21.

Procedure

Core version: Sts work in pairs. Hand out the family tree and one set of core cards, face down to each pair. Explain that they must use the information on their cards to complete the family tree.

Sts pick up the cards one by one and try to work out together what each card tells them. The first group to complete the family tree correctly wins.

Answers

(from top to bottom and left to right): Paolo 85; Elisabeta 82; Tomaso 41; Sofía 43; Carla 35; Luigi 34; Berta 27; Primo 29; Michaela 18; Gianni 16; Susana 10; Raffaella 8; Enzo 3

Extension: Same procedure as core version above. Use this version after sts have studied *his/her.*

Answers

(from top to bottom and left to right): James 84; Chloe 82; Mike 46; Melanie 47; Olivia 40; Tom 41; Jack 35; Emily 30; Sue 13; Daniel 11; Sophie 15; Ben 12; Joshua 4

As a follow-up activity to either version, sts can make sentences about the people in the family tree, e.g. *He's Carla's husband.* Their partner says who it is.

UNIT 2 Grammar
What's your email address?

• Use this activity after Lesson 2.3, Ex. 4d on page 25.

Procedure

Divide sts into pairs and hand out the worksheets.

Student A takes on the identity of Padma Gandhi and answers student B's questions. Afterwards, student B takes on the identity of John Brown and answers student A's questions.

With weaker sts, elicit the questions the sts will need and write them up on the board first. At this stage, sts find out about jobs with the question, *What's your job?*

UNIT 2 Communication
Who's Joe?

• Use this activity after Communication on page 26.

• New language: *relative, house, important, birthdate*

Procedure

Preteach the new language and ensure sts understand the categories on the card.

Sts work in pairs. Give each pair a Student A card and a Student B card. Ask sts first to think of an item for each of the eight categories and to write it in the appropriate place. You could write an example about yourself on the board.

After sts have filled in the chart, they should fold it so that only their answers are showing. Demonstrate with one student's card. They then exchange cards and take turns asking one another about each thing on the list, answering in as much detail as they can. Remind them that they use *Who's …* for people and *What's …* for everything else.

Example:

A: Who's Majid?

B: He's my uncle. He lives in Egypt. He's a doctor.

A: Oh, really? Where in Egypt does he live?

B: He lives in Cairo. … What's 73?

A: It's my house number.

B: Where do you live?

And so on.

For further practice, sts can do the exercise more than once, changing partners each time.

UNIT 3 Vocabulary
What's in your suitcase?

• Use this activity after Lesson 3.2, Ex. 5b on page 33.

Procedure

Sts work in pairs. Explain that they have to describe the contents of their suitcase to their partner, who must draw the contents inside the empty suitcase in the worksheet. Encourage them to ask the question, *What's in your suitcase?* before they start. They check the task by comparing their drawing to their partner's suitcase. Check pronunciation of plurals /s/ or /z/.

To make it slightly harder, you could give sts a minute to memorise the items in their case. Give sts B a minute after sts A have described their items and sts B have drawn them.

As a follow-up task for false beginners, you could ask the pairs to discuss what they would put in a suitcase for certain destinations, e.g. Oslo in the winter, Rome in the summer.

UNIT 3 | Grammar
Information swap

- Use this activity after Lesson 3.3 on page 35.
- New language: *library, famous for (clothes)*

Procedure

Preteach the new vocabulary.

Sts work in groups of four – A, B, C, D. Give each student their information and question sheets.

Explain that sts are going to ask and answer *Yes/No* questions about places. First, they make three *Yes/No* questions using the words on their question sheet. Give sts a few minutes to do this. You may wish to do some examples on the board first. Remind sts of the short answers. Ask them to give the correct information, e.g. if a student asks, *Is it a museum?* but the information says that it's a shop, answer *No, it isn't. It's a shop.*

A and C exchange information and B and D exchange information. When they have finished, A and B tell each other about the places they found out about; the same for C and D, e.g. *The Boquería is a market. It's in Madrid. It's open on Thursdays.* Together, they think of one more question to ask the other pair about their places, e.g. *Is it free?*

UNIT 3 | Communication
Where are you?

- Use this activity after Communication on page 36.
- New language: *traffic, hotel restaurant*

Procedure

Preteach the new language.

Sts work in pairs. Give each pair a Student A card and a Student B card. Student A and Student B take turns forming questions from the prompts and asking their partner. Their partner looks at the incomplete sentences and at the crossword puzzle, then answers the question by completing the sentence with an appropriate adjective and writing it in the crossword grid. When the puzzle is complete, the grey box on each puzzle will reveal each student's location.

Answers

Student A 1 big 2 modern 3 bad 4 hot 5 fine
6 small 7 old 8 beautiful 9 very 10 awful
Student A is in Bratislava.

Student B 1 bad 2 big 3 great 4 small 5 beautiful
6 fine 7 ugly 8 hot 9 awful 10 modern
Student B is in Birmingham.

UNIT 4 | Communication
Can I have a … , please?

- Use this activity after Lesson 4.1 on page 41.

Procedure

Divide sts into pairs and give them each their worksheet. Explain that sts are going to act out two restaurant dialogues using the words and pictures on their worksheets. In dialogue 1, student A is the waiter and student B is the customer. In dialogue 2, they swap roles.

UNIT 4 | Vocabulary
How much is … ?

- Use this activity after Lesson 4.2 on page 43.

Procedure

Sts work in pairs. Give each pair a Student A card and a Student B card. They should fold their cards and stand them up so that the clothing items with price tags are facing themselves with the items without prices angled so that both they and their partner can see them. Explain to sts that they have prices for four of the items on their own card and four of the items on their partner's card. They need to ask how much the items without prices are. Remind them to use *this/these* for items near them (that is, on their own card) and *that/those* for items further away (those on their partner's card), and to pay attention to whether there is one or more than one item. They should describe each item with its name and *black* or *white*. Encourage them to check that they have heard correctly, and to say *thank you* before writing the price next to the item. For example:

A: How much are those black trousers?

B: They're forty-four pounds ninety-eight.

A: Forty-four pounds ninety-eight?

B: Yes.

A: Thank you. How much is …?

Sts should ask and answer until they both have all of the price tags filled in. Then sts should compare pictures to check their answers.

UNIT 4 | Grammar

Answer the question.

• Use this activity after Lesson 4.3 on page 45.

Procedure

Sts work in pairs, A and B. Give each pair a copy of the board, two counters and the answers to their partner's questions.

Explain that sts are going to play a game that revises the language from the unit plus the verb *to be*. Show that there are two questions in each square – one for student A, one for student B.

Sts toss a coin to see who starts. Then they take it in turns to move across the board one square at a time, answering the questions. If they answer incorrectly, they miss a turn. The first student in each pair to reach the end of the board wins.

UNIT 5 | Communication

Where are you?

• Use this activity after Lesson 5.1 on page 51.

Procedure

Sts work in pairs. Give each student a copy of the worksheet. Explain that sts are on holiday. Ask them to choose which of the eight places they are in, but not to tell their partner. Sts then take turns describing this place to their partner, who listens to the description and tries to work out which of the eight places it is. The student listening may ask questions, but should not simply go through the list of place names and ask them one by one. For example:

A: There are some mountains, and there's a castle.

B: Is there a river?

A: Yes, there's a river and a lake.

B: Are you in Seatown?

A: No, I'm not. There's a museum.

B: Is there a beach?

A: Yes, there is.

B: Are you in Beachside?

A: Yes, that's right.

Rearrange sts into new pairs and repeat the activity.

UNIT 5 | Vocabulary

Find the differences.

• Use this activity after Lesson 5.2, Ex. 6b on page 53.

Procedure

Sts work in pairs. Give each student their town plan. Tell them to make sure their partner can't see it. Ensure that sts know the prepositions *next to, between, opposite, behind* and *in Corn Street, in Spring Street*.

Ask sts to find six differences between the town plans. They take it in turns to describe where places are on their plan and ask questions to clarify, using *there is/are, is/are there* and the prepositions. For example, student A: *There's a theatre next to the bank.* Student B: *Where's the bank?* Student A: *It's opposite the department store, in Corn Street.*

When they have finished, they compare plans to check their answers.

UNIT 5 | Grammar

Find a teacher.

• Use this activity after Lesson 5.3 on page 55.

Procedure

Sts work in groups of four – A, B, C, D. Give each student their worksheet.

Explain that sts are all teachers in a school and that they have to find someone to give the classes on their worksheets. First of all, they must find out if the other student has the ability to give the class, e.g. *Can you speak Italian?* or *Can you play the piano?* If the other student says *Yes, I can*, the first student must find out if he/she is available to give the class, e.g. *Are you free from 8.50 to 9.35?* The student who finds a teacher must write the teacher's name in the column provided:

Time	Class	Teacher
8.00–8.45	Italian	Renate
9.40–10.25	Dance	Peter

The student who is able to give the class must write down the subject in the free hours table:

Free Hours
8.00–8.45 Italian

The task finishes when everyone in the group has found someone to give the classes they cannot give.

Answers

Student A	Class	T	Student A teaches
8.00–8.45	Italian	B	8.50–9.35 Cooking
9.40–10.25	Dance	C	11.20–12.05 Piano
13.50–14.35	Golf	B	12.10–12.55 Football
16.20–17.05	Swimming	D	13.00–13.45 Football

Student B	Class	T	Student B teaches
10.30–11.15	French	D	8.00–8.45 Italian
11.20–12.05	Piano	A	9.40–10.25 Singing
14.40–15.25	Cooking	C	13.50–14.35 Golf
15.30–16.15	Dance	C	15.30–16.15 Singing

Student C	Class	T	Student C teaches
8.50–9.35	German	D	9.40–10.25 Dance
9.40–10.25	Singing	B	14.40–15.25 Cooking
13.00–13.45	Football	A	15.30–16.15 Dance
17.10–17.55	Golf	D	18.00–18.45 Italian

Student D	Class	T	Student D teaches
8.50–9.35	Cooking	A	8.50–9.35 German
12.10–12.55	Football	A	10.30–11.15 French
15.30–16.15	Singing	B	16.20–17.05 Swimming
18.00–18.45	Italian	C	17.10–17.55 Golf

UNIT 6 Communication
Friendfinders

• Use this activity after Lesson 6.1 on page 61.

Procedure

Hand out one copy of the worksheet to each student. You may wish to cut off the *Do you prefer?* section for real beginners. With false beginners, use the whole worksheet and preteach *Do you prefer ... or ...?* Divide sts into groups of six to eight.

Explain that each group is going to prepare a list of questions based on the worksheet for the other group to answer. Ask for one volunteer from each group to act as 'secretary'. Sts from each group suggest questions and the secretary writes them down. Afterwards, the sts copy the questions onto their own worksheets. Circulate and check that the questions are grammatically correct.

When everyone has copied the questions, make pairs (or threes) from different groups. In their pairs (or threes), sts ask each other the questions from their questionnaire and write down the replies.

Finally, sts return to their original groups and pool their answers. Ask them to decide which people in the other group would make good friends on the basis of the answers they have given.

UNIT 6 Vocabulary
What do builders do?

• Use this activity after Lesson 6.2, Ex. 2b on page 62.

• New language: *shoe designer*

Procedure

Sts work in pairs. Give each pair a set of 30 cards which are spread out face down. Sts take turns picking up and using the cards or putting them back where they were. To start, they must pick up and put back cards until one of them picks up an *A* or *An* card. When this happens, the student who picks up the card puts it aside, face up. It becomes the beginning of a sentence. That student then picks up another card. If it is a word that can come after *A* or *An*, then the student can add it to their sentence. If not, the card is replaced face down, and the other student draws. The card that completes each sentence is the picture of the job described. More than one sentence can be started by any player. If a student draws a word that cannot go on one of his/her own sentences, but can go on one of his or her partner's sentences, the word must be added to their partner's sentence.

At the end, the student with the most complete sentences wins. The following sentences will be made:

An architect designs buildings. (+ picture of architect)

A sales rep. sells things, for example computers and books. (+ picture of sales rep.)

A shoe designer designs shoes. (+ picture of designer)

A reporter writes articles. (+ picture of reporter)

A chef cooks food. (+ picture of chef)

A builder builds buildings. (+ picture of builder)

UNIT 6 Grammar 1
Question and answer bingo

• Use this activity after Lesson 6.3 on page 65.

Procedure

Divide the class into five teams. Give each student in a team a copy of the same bingo card. Explain that they are going to use the questions on their sheet as part of a game, but first they have to write out the questions correctly. Monitor and correct as necessary.

Explain that you are going to read out some sentences. Some of them are answers to the questions on their sheet. When sts hear an answer which matches one of their questions, they should cross the question out. When they have crossed out all their questions, they shout out *Bingo!* Give one or two example sentences first. Then read out the answers below in random order. Read out each answer twice and leave a few seconds for the sts to see whether they have the matching question.

When a student shouts *Bingo!*, check that you have read out the answers to all his/her questions. If so, he/she is the winner. If not, continue reading out more answers until someone else shouts *Bingo!*

Answers to read out

No, I go to bed late.   No, she works from home.   They are teachers.   She is 11.   She likes pasta.   He works for IBM.   He is 1 metre 80.   I'm tall and they are short.   It means *breakfast* and *lunch*.   No, she starts at 8 o'clock.   My favourite car is the Ferrari 360.   He's 72.   Yes, I like them a lot.   He's rich and I'm poor.   I like pizza.   No, I start at 7.45.   I work for IBM.   My favourite country is Greece.   My favourite actor is George Clooney.   No, I work from home.   I finish work at six o'clock.   No, she lives in France.   Yes, I like him a lot.

UNIT 6 | Grammar 2
Question race

• Use this activity after Communication on page 66.

Procedure

Sts work in pairs. Give each pair a game board and a Student A and Student B paper. Sts should not show their list of questions to their partner. Explain that some of the questions on the game board contain a mistake and some are correct. They put their counter in the 'Start' box and take it in turns to move their counters across the game board. As they move, they either correct the question or say: *It's correct.* Their partner tells them if they are correct, but doesn't give them the correct answer if they are wrong. If they are correct, they stay where they are until their next turn. If they are wrong, they move back one space, then try to correct the sentence again on their next turn. The winner is the first student to reach the 'Finish' box.

UNIT 7 | Grammar
Imperatives mime

• Use this activity after Lesson 7.1, Ex. 6 on page 71.
• New language: *newspaper, look left/right*

Procedure

Preteach the new language.

Divide sts into groups of four and subdivide each group into pairs. Explain that each pair is going to mime imperatives for the other pair to guess. Ask a pair to demonstrate to the class. For example, for the order *Please don't open the window*, one student could be opening a window when the other looks worried, mimes pushing it shut and shakes his/her finger.

Give each pair a different set of cards. They take it in turns to pick up a card and mime the order together – one person plays the part of the person who gives the order – the other receives the order. The sts in the other pair compete to see who can guess the imperative form correctly. Ask sts to show the difference between a firm command (with an exclamation mark) and a more polite one with *please*. The first student to guess correctly gets a point. Once all the cards have been used, the student with the most points wins.

If you have groups of three sts, ask them to work in different pairs each go.

UNIT 7 | Communication 1
Reading – writing relay

• Use this activity after Lesson 7.2, Ex. 2 on page 72.

Procedure

Sts work in pairs. Before the activity, stick the short text cards (Student A Part 1, Student B Part 2) to the wall – one set for each pair of sts. Ask sts to sit in pairs on the other side of the room (move the furniture away, if possible). Give sts B their questions for Part 1. When you say *go*, Student B reads out the first question on the list to Student A. Student A then runs across the room, reads the text to find the answer to the question and reports the answer back to Student B, who writes the answer down on his/her card. The procedure is repeated until all ten questions have been answered. The first team to finish, with all of the answers correct, is the winner. Sts then change roles and use the other text and questions.

Alternative procedure

If the above procedure is impossible because of space limitations, give each pair the Student A and Student B cards and ask them to complete the activity as a simple question and answer/reading and writing task. Sts should not look at each other's sheets.

Teacher's notes

UNIT 7 Vocabulary
Jobs crossword

• Use this activity after Lesson 7.2, Ex. 4 on page 73.

Procedure

Divide sts into groups of four. Give each pair a different worksheet. In pairs, sts prepare crossword clues for the words on the left of their worksheet. Explain that the clues should be two sentences and should be hints rather than definitions. Provide some examples for jobs that do not appear on the crossword, e.g. for *gardener*: *He/She works outside. He/She works with his/her hands.*

When both pairs have completed their clues, pair A read out their clues to pair B, who try to complete their crossword grid. If necessary, pair B can ask *Wh*-questions to find out more about the job. Don't allow *Yes/No* questions. Afterwards, pair B read out their clues and pair A try to complete the crossword grid.

Variation: Sts could work individually and compete with the other student in their pair to see who completes the crossword first.

UNIT 7 Communication 2
I'm here to see Bill Lee.

• Use this activity after Communication on page 76.

Procedure

Sts work in pairs. Give each pair a Student A and Student B role card. Sts take turns playing the role of a visitor and a receptionist. They should not show each other their cards. When they are given directions to an office, they should write the person's name in the correct office on their floor plan.

You could write a sample conversation on the board for extra support:

A: Hello. I'm here to see John Day.

B: What's your name, please?

A: I'm (own name).

B: OK, (Student A). Mr Day's office is on the fifth floor. Take the lift to the fifth floor and turn right. Mr Day's office is the first on the left.

A: Thank you.

When they have finished, sts compare floor plans to check their answers.

UNIT 8 Communication 1
Hotel pairs

• Use this activity after Lesson 8.1, Ex. 3 on page 80.

• New words: *fitness centre, borrow a bicycle, board games*

Procedure

Preteach the new language.

Sts work in pairs. Give each pair a set of 24 cards. Tell them to put the HOTEL cards face down in a pile on the table. Each student then takes 6 *LIKE* cards and holds them so that their partner cannot see them. Student A begins by choosing a *LIKE* card from his/her set, and saying a sentence, for example, *I like eating Japanese food*. He/She then picks up a *HOTEL* card from the pile. If the *HOTEL* card matches the *LIKE* card (for example, *There's a Japanese restaurant in the Hotel Royal. You can eat there.*), student A puts the pair down on the table. If the two cards don't match, student A must keep both cards. Student B then chooses a *LIKE* card and says a sentence about it. If student A is holding a matching *HOTEL* card, he/she must give it to student B to make a pair. If not, student B picks up a card from the *HOTEL* pile. As before, if a pair is made, the cards are put down. If not, student B keeps both cards. The game continues until one student uses all of his/her cards. Alternatively, you may wish to set a time limit and see who has the fewest cards when the time limit is reached.

UNIT 8 Grammar
Complete the sentences.

• Use this activity after Lesson 8.1, Ex. 6 on page 93.

• New language: *now, tonight, tomorrow*

Procedure

Preteach the new language.

Divide the class into pairs. Give each student a copy of the sentences and each pair a set of cards turned face down in a pile. Sts take it in turns to pick up a card and show it to their partner. They write the verb (in the correct form) into a sentence on the worksheet. Before they start, remind sts to use the infinitive after *can*, the *-ing* form after *like* and to + infinitive after *want*. Write some example sentences on the board. When all the cards have been used, sts check their answers with you. The student in each pair who has completed the most sentences correctly is the winner.

Answers

1 playing 2 to give 3 swim 4 to read 5 go
6 getting up 7 to have 8 eat 9 writing 10 to use
11 watch 12 living 13 to do 14 finish 15 listening

UNIT 8 Vocabulary
Have you got a spare fridge?

- Use this activity after Lesson 8.2, Ex. 7 on page 83.
- New language: *Have you got a spare …?/I've got a spare … .*

Procedure

Preteach the new language.

Sts work in groups of four. Explain that their flats are not properly furnished because they need certain items of furniture and have too many of other items. Say that the objective of the game is to refurnish their flats so that they end up with one of each item. They must try to find the items they need by asking and answering with the other sts in the group: *Have you got a spare …? Yes, I've got a spare … ./No, I haven't.* The game finishes when everyone in the group has successfully refurnished their flat.

UNIT 8 Communication 2
Favourite cafés and restaurants

- Use this activity after Lesson 8.3, Ex. 11 on page 85.
- New language: *location*

Procedure

Preteach the new language.

Sts work in pairs, then change partners twice. Give each student a copy of the activity. Begin by telling sts that they should use the prompts on the page to ask their partner questions about restaurants and cafés that they know. For example, *name?* should prompt sts to ask *What's the name of the restaurant? Location?* should prompt *Where is it?* and so on. Sts should complete the exercise with a partner, each answering the other's questions and talking about a different restaurant and café, then change partners and complete the exercise again with a different partner. If your sts come from a variety of places, encourage them to talk about restaurants and cafés in their home towns, to bring as much variety as possible to the activity.

UNIT 9 Vocabulary
Famous birthdays

- Use this activity after Lesson 9.1, Ex. 7 on page 91.

Procedure

Sts work in pairs. Give each student their set of date of birth cards face down in a pile and their list of names.

Sts take it in turns to pick up a date of birth card and say when the person was born: *He/She was born on*

… . They mustn't say who the person is. Their partner looks at the name list for clues and asks *Yes/No* questions to find out who it is, for example, *Was he a singer? Was he American,* etc. When they think they know the answer, they can ask: *Is it …?* If they get the answer right, they keep the date card. If they get the answer wrong, the date card is put in a separate pile and not used again during the game. The student who ends up with the greatest number of date cards wins.

UNIT 9 Communication 1
Were you in New York last night?

- Use this activity after Lesson 9.2, Ex. 3 on page 92.

Procedure

Sts work in groups of four – A, B, C, D. Give each student their information and question cards. Ask sts to imagine that they are at a party talking with friends, so the atmosphere is informal. Explain that they should ask and answer questions about the past, using the information on their role card to answer and the questions given. Do one or two examples to show how the activity works. For example, student A needs to find someone who was in New York last night. The question to ask is: *Excuse me, were you in New York last night?* The two possible answers are *Yes, I was* or *No, I wasn't.* If the answer is *Yes,* student A writes the name of that student, in this case student D. Sts continue until they have filled in all of the gaps. You can make it competitive by saying that the first person to complete their form is the winner. Rather than taking turns to ask questions around the group, they can compete for one another's attention, by saying *Excuse me …* or *Sorry …* if they are interrupting.

UNIT 9 Communication 2
How was your holiday?

- Use this activity after Lesson 9.3, Ex. 5b on page 95.

Procedure

Sts work in pairs. First, student B uses the prompts to ask student A about his/her holiday, for example, *How was the flight?* Student A uses the information on his/her card to answer the question, with a full sentence: *It wasn't very good.* student B ticks the picture on his/her card that corresponds to student A's answer. After student B asks about student A's holiday, they move on to Part 2, where the roles are reversed. At the end of the exercise, they should check that for each category, student A has ticked one picture and student B the other picture. Note that the pictures are not in the same order on both cards.

UNIT 9 Grammar
Grammar bets

• Use this activity after Communication on page 96.

Procedure

Sts work in pairs. Give each pair a copy of the worksheet. To develop interest in the activity, explain that they are going to bet on their knowledge of the grammar in the unit.

Ask sts to try to rewrite sentences 1–5 correctly. Afterwards, explain that they can 'place pretend bets' on their sentences: 10 euros/local currency if they are sure they have made the right corrections; five euros/local currency if they are not so sure; two euros/local currency if they are unsure. They write their 'bets' next to each sentence.

Write the correct version for each sentence on the board. If pairs have made the right corrections, they 'get' double the money they bet. If they have not corrected the sentence properly, they lose the money they 'placed' on it.

Repeat the same procedure with sentences 6–10, then with sentences 11–15. You can change the 'odds' by saying, for example, that a correct sentence wins three times the value of the bet. At the end of the game, sts count up the amount of money they have won or lost. The pair that has won the most money wins.

Answers

1 Clark Gable was **an** actor. **2** My mother **was** born in 1943. **3** When I was at school, I was good **at** mathematics. **4** My father **was not** born in London. **5** Billie Holiday and Maria Callas **were** singers. **6** When I was **a** child, I was a good footballer. **7** We were in London **two years ago**. **8** Where **were you** last week? **9** Where were you **last night**? **10** My sister was **at** home yesterday morning. **11** I don't know how **to** play this game. **12** Was **the weather nice** yesterday? **13** Can you **open the window**? **14** When I was a child, I was bad **at** music. **15** We **were** good teachers.

UNIT 10 Communication
Chat show

• Use this activity after Lesson 10.1 on page 101.
• New language: *chat show, host, guest*

Procedure

Preteach the new language.

Introduce the context by asking sts what chat shows they watch, and what sort of guests appear on the shows. Who have they seen interviewed? What did the guests talk about? Sts work in pairs. Give each student a copy of the worksheet. Sts take turns interviewing one another in the roles of chat show host and chat show guest, following the list of questions, and the examples. Encourage them to discuss the questions and answers in as much detail as they can. They can make up answers rather than answer about themselves if they prefer

UNIT 10 Grammar 1
Quiz

• Use this activity after Lesson 10.2 on page 103.
• New language: *die, When did … die?*

Procedure

Preteach the new language.

Explain to sts that they are going to take part in a quiz. Divide sts into groups of four and subdivide each group into two pairs. Give one pair the worksheet for team A and the other pair the worksheet for team B.

Ask each pair to complete the questions on their worksheet. Monitor and correct as necessary.

Give team A a copy of team B's answers and vice versa. Pair A asks its questions to pair B who have to agree on the answer. Explain that they must give a full sentence answer and use the past tense of the verb correctly. If they give the correct answer and make no grammatical mistakes, they get two points. If they give the correct answer but make a grammatical mistake, they get 1 point. Provide an example: *When did Monet paint the Folies Bergère?* a *in 1882* b *in 1850* c *in 1870* Answer: *He painted it/the Folies Bergère in 1882.* (2 points) *He paint it in 1882.* (1 point)

Then team B asks its questions to team A in the same way. The team that gets the most points wins the quiz.

UNIT 10 Grammar 2
I'm going to have a holiday.

• Use this activity after Lesson 10.3 on page 105.

Procedure

Sts work in groups of three or four. Give each group a set of cards, which they should place face down. One student begins by taking a card, looking at the words, and making a sentence, speaking either about the past or about the future, as indicated on the card, for example, *I'm going to go to Las Vegas* or *I went to Las Vegas*. The other sts then ask *Then what are you going to do?* for a 'future' statement or *Then what did you do?* for a 'past' statement. The student with the card must give a plausible answer, for example, *I'm going to win a lot of money* or *I won a lot of money*.

The second student then takes the next card from the pile, repeats what the first student said, for example, *Pierre went to Las Vegas and won a lot of money*, and adds his/her own statement, after which the other group members ask for the reason. Each student in turn repeats the previous student's 'story' before adding his or her own. Continue until all the cards have been used.

UNIT 10 Grammar 3
Question and answer dominoes

- Use this activity after Communication on page 106.

- New language: *good enough, tired, angry*

Procedure

Preteach the new language.

Sts work in groups of three or four. Give each group a set of dominoes and a list of verbs. Explain that their cards contain pairs of sentences A and B. The B sentences answer the questions in the A sentences. Give them an example to illustrate this: *A: Why didn't you get the job in England? B: Because my English wasn't good enough.*

The aim of the activity is for sts to join all the cards together. To help them, the first card is marked *Start* and the last card is marked *Finish*. Explain that they must add the past form of verbs from the list to the B sentences.

The first group to join all the sentences together and complete the B sentences with the right verb in its past form wins.

Answers

Because I **wanted** to live longer. Because I **had** a problem with my computer. Because it **was** very small for them. Because my company **moved** there. Because the actors **weren't** very good. Because I **didn't like** the colour. Because she **said** that she didn't love me. Because I **didn't have** time. Because I **loved** cooking. Because I **got up** at six o'clock this morning. Because he **came** to class late. Because they **were** very tired. Because my English **wasn't** good enough. Because she **didn't get up** on time. Because a man **took** her bag and her camera. Because he **found** ten pounds on the street. Because I **met** my wife there.

DVD worksheets

Before watching

1a Work with a partner. Write a response to the following phrases.

1 Good morning, I'm Simon Black.

2 Pleased to meet you.

3 This is Anna Reid.

4 Hi, Peter.

b Practise saying the phrases.

While watching

2 Watch the film and fill in the gaps.

Extract 1

John: Keira. This is Laurence.

Keira: 1 _ _ _ _ _ . Nice to meet you.

Laurence: Nice to meet you, too.

Extract 2

2 _ _ , Tommy? How are you?

Extract 3

Mits: My friends call me Mits.

Andy: And 3 _ _ _ _ _ are you from in Japan?

Extract 4

Man: How are you doing?

Anna: 4 _ _ _ _ _ , thank you.

Extract 5

Andy: OK, everyone, 5 _ _ _ _ is Mitsuru, our product specialist from Tokyo.

Everyone: Hi!

Andy: Oh, and 6 _ _ '_ Mits to his friends. So, Mits, let me introduce you to Mina – Mina Patel.

Mina: 7 _ _ _ _ _ . Nice to meet you.

Mits: Nice to meet you, 8 _ _ _ .

Extract 6

Anna: 9 _ '_ very pleased to meet you all, but please call me Anna.

After watching

3 Write the names of six famous people. Ask your partner to tell you where each of them is from.

1 _____

2 _____

3 _____

4 _____

5 _____

6 _____

Before watching

1 Complete the table with the capital cities, actors, writers and TV programmes.

Bruce Willis   Jane Austen   Angelina Jolie   Sydney

Jennifer Lopez   Rio de Janeiro   Big Brother   JK Rowling

Jerry Springer   Isabel Allende   Michael Douglas   Tokyo

Rome   Friends   Ian Fleming   Who wants to be a millionaire?

City	Actor	Writer	TV programme

While watching

2 Watch the film and fill in the missing information about Jennifer, Sean and Rachel.

> The Blue Planet   Toronto   Dr Who   Robert De Niro
> The Picture of Dorian Gray   Auckland   Henry Fonda   Oliver Twist
> London   Renee Zellweger   Agatha Christie   Mr Bean

1   Jennifer

Favourite city: _____

Favourite actor: _____

Favourite book: _____

Favourite TV programme: _____

2   Sean

Favourite city: _____

Favourite actor: _____

Favourite book: _____

Favourite TV programme: _____

3   Rachel

Favourite city: _____

Favourite actor: _____

Favourite book: _____

Favourite TV programme: _____

After watching

3 Ask three students the questions from the film. Complete the table below.

	Student 1	Student 2	Student 3
What's your favourite city?			
What's your favourite actor?			
What's your favourite book?			
What's your favourite TV programme?			

Before watching

1 Make 10 adjectives from the letters below:

1	lod	o _ _
2	nredmo	m _ _ _ _ _
3	ibg	b _ _
4	lalms	s _ _ _ _
5	tho	h _ _
6	dcol	c _ _ _
7	wne	n _ _
8	trgae	g _ _ _ _
9	tuefliabu	b _ _ _ _ _ _ _
10	guyl	u _ _ _

While watching

2 Watch the film and answer the questions.

1 What day is Gill in Peggy's Cove?
2 Is Peggy's Cove a small or big town?
3 Where is Kirsty's husband from?
4 Is Kirsty a famous actor?
5 Is Montreal an old city?
6 Is Gill in the Rockies on Thursday?
7 The mountains are g _ _ _ _ .
8 Is Vancouver ugly?
9 What is the last day of Gill's journey?
10 Where is Victoria?

After watching

3 Write five places to visit in your own country.

TOUR OF _____

Monday:

Tuesday:

Wednesday:

Thursday:

Friday:

Before watching

1a Work with a partner. Write five useful phrases to use in a shop.

1 _Can I help you?_ _____

2 _____

3 _____

4 _____

5 _____

b Practise saying each of the phrases.

While watching

2 Watch the film and answer the questions.

1 Who is the big bunch of flowers for?

2 Who is the small bunch of flowers for?

3 Who is Lisa?

4 Who is Lisa's father?

3 Watch again and write the prices.

1 red flowers   £ _____

2 pink flowers   £ _____

3 white flowers   £ _____

4 all the flowers   £ _____

5 cappuccino and carrot cake   £ _____

After watching

4 Work with a partner. Write a short dialogue in a clothes shop.

Before watching

1 Work with a partner. Fill in the box with words to describe each of the places. For example, *places, food, cities, tourist attractions, adjectives.*

Cornwall, UK	New Zealand	New York, USA

While watching

2 Watch the film and answer the questions.

Cornwall

1 Where is Cornwall?

2 Are there a lot of big hotels?

3 Is the coast ugly?

4 Are the breakfasts big or small?

New York

5 Where is New York?

6 What food can you eat in New York?

7 Are there a lot of languages in New York?

8 The speaker says, 'New York is _ _ _ _ _ for culture.'

Murawhai, New Zealand

9 Is Murawhai in the countryside or on the coast?

10 Is it a popular place for holidays?

11 Are there a lot of people in Murawhai?

12 Murawhat is great for three things: _____, _____ and _____ .

After watching

3a Describe your favourite place for a weekend holiday. Write five sentences and use *there is/there are* when possible.

1 _____

2 _____

3 _____

4 _____

5 _____

b Read your sentences to your partner.

Before watching

1a Work with a partner. Complete the five questions below for an interview with a singer.

1 What _____?

2 Where _____?

3 Who _____?

4 What's your favourite _____?

5 Can you _____?

b Ask your partner the questions.

While watching

2 Watch the film and then answer the questions below.

1 Andy Platz is
   a) a singer.   b) a writer.   c) an actor.

2 Andy's mum is from
   a) Hong Kong.   b) England.   c) the Philippines.

3 Andy plays the
   a) guitar, piano and saxophone. b) flute, piano and drums. c) flute, piano and violin.

4 Andy listens to music
   a) in the evenings.   b) in the morning and afternoon. c) all day.

5 Andy works
   a) 4–5 hours a day in the studio. b) 14–15 hours a day in the studio. c) 14–16 hours a day in the studio.

6 In his spare time, Andy goes to
   a) the theatre.   b) football matches.   c) the cinema.

7 Andy can cook
   a) French and Chinese food. b) Italian and Chinese food. c) French and Italian food.

8 How often does Andy travel?
   a) never   b) a lot   c) sometimes

After watching

3 Work with a partner. Write five sentences to describe the daily routine of a famous singer.

1 _____
2 _____
3 _____
4 _____
5 _____

Before watching

1   Write six sentences using an adverb of frequency and a work phrase for each of the jobs.

Adverb of frequency	never not often/not usually sometimes often usually always
Work phrases	call customers answer the phone take work home work outdoors travel abroad work from home

1   A receptionist *never takes work home.*
2   A manager _____
3   An artist _____
4   A nurse _____
5   A teacher _____
6   A shop assistant _____

While watching

2   Watch the film and write true (T) or false (F) next to each of the sentences.

1   About 5,000 people work in this company.   ____

Sarah, the receptionist

2   Sarah is the second person visitors meet.   ____
3   Her job is easy.   ____
4   She likes helping people.   ____

Michael, the chef

5   The first meal Michael cooks is lunch.   ____
6   He orders food for the next week.   ____
7   He doesn't like his job.   ____

Yemi, the designer

8   Yemi looks at photos and pictures for the books.   ____
9   He doesn't work with many people.   ____
10   He always finishes at 5.   ____

Derek, the post room worker

11   Derek doesn't like the people he works with.   ____
12   They sometimes open the bags of mail in the morning.   ____
13   They usually get 20–25 bags of post a day.   ____

After watching

3   Write six more sentences about the work routines of the people in the film. Use an adverb of frequency for each sentence.

Before watching

1a Ask your partner if they like each of the activities in the box using *Do you like ...?*

b Ask your partner to use an adjective to describe their answer: *boring, exciting, difficult, interesting, fun, easy.*

Example

Do you like eating out?

Yes, I like eating out. It's fun.

go cycling   eat out   play chess   play tennis   go sightseeing   go for a walk   read a book   play football   go to the theatre   do exercise

While watching

2 Watch the film and fill in the gaps.

1 Windsurfing is like sailing with no b _ _ _ .

2 Skateboarding is like s _ _ _ _ _ _ .

3 You can snowboard inside or outside on real m _ _ _ _ _ _ _ _ .

4 Bungee jumping is e _ _ _ , but it isn't boring.

5 BMX r _ _ _ _ _ is exciting.

6 You can do in-line skating in the s _ _ _ _ _ .

7 When you go scuba diving, the f _ _ _ are beautiful.

8 Canoeing on a r _ _ _ _ is fun.

9 Can you climb t _ _ _? Then you climb a w _ _ _ .

10 When you parascend the c _ _ _ _ _ _ _ _ _ _ is beautiful.

After watching

3 Interview your partner about one of the adventure activities above. Think of five questions to ask them.

1 _____

2 _____

3 _____

4 _____

5 _____

Before watching

1 What do you think people did or didn't do in the UK 100 years ago?

100 years ago:

1 people *did/didn't* play football.
2 people *did/didn't* go to the cinema.
3 there *were/weren't* lots of cars on the roads.
4 there *were/weren't* lots of shops.
5 people *did/didn't* watch TV.
6 people *did/didn't* go to the beach on holiday.

While watching

2 Choose the correct answer for the following questions.

1 The UK was a very different place in
   a) 1801.   b) 1911.   c) 1901.

2 Only 1% of the population was over
   a) 55.   b) 66.   c) 65.

3 People were at work for
   a) 11 hours a day.   b) 12 hours a day.   c) 10 hours a day.

4 Lots of children were only 10 when they were
   a) factory workers.   b) street cleaners.   c) shop assistants.

5 The streets were quite
   a) noisy.   b) exciting.   c) quiet.

6 The new technology was
   a) motor car, electric tram and bicycle with one wheel.   b) motor car, electric tram and train.   c) motor car, electric tram and bicycle with two wheels.

7 According to the film, there weren't any
   a) computers.   b) cookers.   c) books.

8 Popular sports were
   a) football and cricket.   b) football and rugby.   c) football and tennis.

After watching

3 How do you think the following things were in your country 100 years ago?

Working life	Life was hard. Many people worked long hours. Women did not work.
Towns and streets	
Transport	
Free time activities	
Sports	

4 Show your answers to your partner, and ask each other questions.

Before watching

1 Work with a partner. Write five sports that we play on grass.

1 _____

2 _____

3 _____

4 _____

5 _____

While watching

2 Watch the film and write true (T) or false (F) *next* to each of the sentences.

1 The four ladies say 'Afternoon', 'Good afternoon' to each other.

2 The teams are from North London and South London.

3 The ladies wear white.

4 The ladies are shy.

5 The ladies drink coffee.

6 A lady moves a ball with her shoe.

7 The ladies are not competitive.

8 Patricia and Marion win the match.

After watching

3 Work with a partner. Write six sentences about the film in the past simple. Use the verbs in the box.

win   lose   say   move   play   have

1 _____

2 _____

3 _____

4 _____

5 _____

6 _____

1 Saying hello

Before watching

1 a/b ▶ Sts work with a partner to write a response to each of the phrases. More than one response might be possible. False beginners could develop the exchange into a mini-dialogue. Circulate and monitor, supporting as necessary. Elicit feedback from the class. Sts then practise saying the phrases to each other.

> **Suggested answers:** 1 Good morning, I'm …
> 2 Pleased to meet you, too./Nice to meet you, too.
> 3 Hi/Hello, Anna. /I'm … . Nice to meet you.
> 4 Hi, … .

While watching

2 ▶ Tell sts they are going to watch a series of short introductions and their task is to complete some of the phrases. Ask sts to read the gapped sentences and ask if they have any questions. Play extracts 1–3, allowing sts to make notes. Play the extracts again for sts to check their answers. Discuss the answers together. Write the sentences on the board and ask different sts to complete the missing words. Proceed in the same way with extracts 4–6.

> **Answers:** 1 Hello 2 Hi 3 Where 4 Great 5 This
> 6 It's 7 Hello 8 too 9 I'm

After watching

3 ▶ Sts choose six well-known people and ask their partner where each of them is from. Encourage sts to use the contracted form *he's/she's from* in their answers. Circulate and monitor as they work, and correct grammatical mistakes. Ask some pairs to demonstrate their exchanges.

2 Favourites

Before watching

1 ▶ Check that sts understand the following vocabulary: *cities, actors, writers* and *TV programmes*. Put sts into pairs or small groups. Sts then complete the table. Check answers as a class, and ask if sts can give you any information about the places and people.

> **Answers:** City: Rome   Sydney   Rio de Janeiro
> Tokyo   Actor: Bruce Willis   Jennifer Lopez
> Michael Douglas   Angelina Jolie   Writer: Isabel
> Allende   Jane Austen   JK Rowling   Ian Fleming
> TV programme: Big Brother   Friends   Who wants
> to be a millionaire?   Jerry Springer

While watching

2 ▶ Give sts some time to read the information boxes. Ask if anyone has any questions about vocabulary. Then play the film extract right through, pausing between each monologue for sts to make notes. Sts watch the extract again to check their answers. Elicit the answers from the class.

> **Answers:** Jennifer: London   Robert De Niro
> Murder on the Orient Express   The Blue Planet
> Sean: Auckland   Renee Zellweger   The Picture of
> Dorian Gray   Mr Bean
> Rachel: Toronto   Henry Fonda   Oliver Twist
> Dr Who

After watching

3 ▶ Sts read the questions in the table, which are exactly the same as the questions asked in the film extract. Sts then interview three other sts. They note down their answers in the table. Circulate and monitor. Make notes of errors for a correction spot later. Ask for feedback from one or two individual sts, in full sentences, e.g. *His favourite actor is Bruce Willis.* Pool information and compile class statistics.

3 Across Canada

Before watching

1 ▶ Explain to sts that the adjectives are all mixed up and they need to reorder them to spell 10 of the adjectives they have learnt in the SB. Elicit answers from the class.

Answers: 1 old   2 modern   3 big   4 small   5 hot
6 cold   7 new   8 great   9 beautiful   10 ugly

While watching

2 ▶ Ask sts to read the questions and check they understand them all. Play the film extract, allowing sts to make notes. Play it again for sts to check their answers. Ask sts to check their answers with a partner, then go over them as a class. Ask for complete sentences.

Answers: 1 Gill is in Peggy's Cove on Monday.
2 Peggy's Cove/It is small.   3 Kirsty's husband's/
He's from Canada.   4 No, she isn't.   5 No it isn't.
It's modern.   6 No, she isn't. She's in the Rockies on Wednesday.   7 The mountains are great.
8 No it isn't. It's beautiful.   9 Friday is the last day of Gill's journey.   10 It's on Vancouver Island/near the Pacific Ocean.

(*Optional extension:* If there is time, play the extract a final time for sts to decide which is their favourite place in the film. Pool feedback and compile class statistics.)

After watching

3 ▶ Put sts into pairs and ask them to write five places to visit during a week's tour of their own country. Encourage them to write short descriptions of the places using the adjectives from the unit. Circulate and support, giving additional vocabulary as necessary.

OPTIONAL EXTENSION

Sts find another pair and describe their five-day trip around a country using the adjectives they have written down.

4 The flowers

Before watching

1 ▶ Sts work with a partner and brainstorm five phrases to use in a shop. Encourage them to write more if they can. Elicit answers from the class and write them on the board in two columns: *customer* and *shop assistant*. Ask sts to practise saying the phrases, taking turns to be the shop assistant and the customer.

Possible answers: Shop assistant: Can I help you?   It's/They're (£1.20).   Anything else?   Sure.
Certainly.   Here you are.   That's (£2.50).
Customer: How much is this/that ...?   How much are those/these ...?   Can I have a/an/two ...,
please?

While watching

2 ▶ Explain the task and teach any new vocabulary. Play the film and ask sts to make notes. Play the film once again for sts to check their answers. Go through the answers together, identifying the four people in the film and their relationship to each other.

Answers: 1 his mother   2 his girlfriend   3 his girlfriend   4 the shop assistant/florist/man in the shop

3 ▶ Ask sts to read through the list of items and recap the story together to remind sts about each item. Play the extract and pause after the prices for sts to take notes. Play the extract one more time, pausing before each price and asking individual sts for the answer.

Answers: 1 £2 (each)   2 £1.50 (each)   3 £1.99 (a bunch)   4 £22.99   5 £3.80

After watching

4 ▶ Sts can choose another type of shop if they prefer. Brainstorm more phrases and write them on the board. Include phrases with *this, that, these, those*. Put sts in pairs. Circulate and support as necessary. Ask them to act out the dialogues.

5 Holiday places

Before watching

1 ▶ Sts work in pairs to write as many words as possible connected with each of the three places. They can write adjectives, places, cities or cultural references. Pool ideas and write them on the board.

While watching

2 ▶ Give sts some time to read the questions. Check understanding. Play the film extract through once, allowing sts to make notes. Play it again for sts to check their answers. Elicit answers from the class.

> **Answers:** 1 It's in the south west of England.
> 2 No, there aren't. 3 No, it's beautiful. 4 They're big (and very good). 5 It's on the east coast of the US. 6 You can eat Chinese, Spanish and Italian food. 7 Yes, there are. 8 great 9 It's on the (northwest) coast. 10 Yes, it is. 11 No, there aren't. 12 fishing, surfing, relaxing

After watching

3a ▶ Sts write five simple sentences to describe their favourite holiday destination. Encourage them to include *there is/there are* and *some/a lot of* to consolidate grammar studied in the unit and to use the adjectives they know. Circulate and monitor, correcting grammar.

b ▶ Ask sts to work with someone they haven't worked with yet during this unit. Encourage them to ask questions to find out more about the place their partner has chosen.

6 The interview

Before watching

1a ▶ Sts work in pairs to choose a famous singer (they can select from the list on the board from the warmer activity) and then decide on five questions to ask this person. Support sts by suggesting question topics such as cars, music, food, fashion, holidays, films, TV, sport. Circulate and monitor, checking accuracy of question forms. Elicit questions and write some on the board for pairs to add to their lists if they wish.

> **Possible questions:** What do you eat and drink before a concert? Where do you live? What's your favourite song? Who's your favourite singer? What's your favourite city? Can you dance?

b ▶ Sts then role play an interview with a famous singer. They should swap roles so each has a chance to ask and answer. Ask a few pairs to role play their interview to the class.

While watching

2 ▶ Ask sts to read through the questions and ask about vocabulary if they wish. Explain that they are going to watch the film and need to choose the correct answer to each question. Play the film once, allowing sts to make notes. Play again for sts to check their answers. Ask sts to check their answers with a partner before going through them as a class.

> **Answers:** 1 a   2 c   3 b   4 c   5 b   6 c   7 a
> 8 b

After watching

3 ▶ Sts work together to write five sentences to describe a day in the life of a famous singer (or an invented one if they don't have enough information). Refer sts back to lesson 6.3 for a reminder on Present Simple with *he/she/it*. Circulate and monitor. Afterwards, if sts have written about a real person, they can join with another pair, read out their sentences and ask the other sts to guess who the singer is.

7 The company

OPTIONAL WARMER

Sts work in pairs to describe a job to each other using the Present Simple and vocabulary from unit 7. Their partner has to try and guess what their job is by asking *Yes/No* questions, e.g. *Do you work in an office?*

Before watching

1 ▶ Ask sts to work individually first, then compare their sentences with a partner. Elicit suggestions and write a few on the board, correcting grammar as you do so.

Possible questions: 1 A receptionist never works from home.   2 A manager sometimes calls customers.   3 An artist often works from home. 4 A nurse doesn't usually work outdoors. 5 A teacher usually takes work home.   6 A shop assistant doesn't often travel abroad.

While watching

2 ▶ Ask sts to read the statements. Check they understand and explain as necessary. Play the film, stopping at the end of each speaker/job to allow sts to make notes. Play the whole film through once again. Go through the answers as a class, asking sts to correct the false statements.

Answers: 1 F – About 500 people work in this company.   2 F – She is the first person visitors meet. (**Note:** Ordinal numbers are introduced in 7.3. If the activity is used after 7.2, give a brief explanation of *first* and *second*.) 3 T   4 T   5 F – The first meal he cooks is breakfast.   6 T   7 F – He likes his job. 8 T   9 F – He works with lots of people.   10 F – He never finishes at 5.   11 F – He likes the people he works with. They're nice.   12 F – They always open the mail bags in the morning.   13 T

After watching

3 ▶ Sts make more sentences about the work routines of the people in the film, based on what they've seen. Sts can guess if necessary. Support with vocabulary as necessary. Encourage sts to refer back to the unit. Circulate and support as necessary. Ask sts to read out their sentences starting *This person...* . The rest of the class guesses who it is.

8 Change your life

OPTIONAL WARMER

Write *adventure activities* on the board. Elicit what this means and ask students to name some. Write them on the board. Put sts in pairs and ask them to write a list of adventure activities and any words which are associated with them. Pool ideas and add more activities and relevant vocabulary for each one to the list on the board.

Before watching

1a/b ▶ Check that sts remember all the activities in the box from the unit. Sts work in pairs and ask each other if they like each of the activities. Monitor this activity and encourage sts to ask more questions if they want. Encourage fluency. Encourage them to talk about the activities on the board as well. Ask sts to feed back to the class about what activities their partner likes.

While watching

2 ▶ Ask sts to read the sentences to see if they have any questions. You may wish to preteach the adventure activities: *wind surfing, skateboarding, snowboarding, bungee jumping, BMX racing, in-line skating, scuba diving, canoeing, rock climbing, parascending.* Play the film, allowing sts to make notes. Play it again for sts to check their answers. Go over the answers as a class. Elicit other information given about each activity.

Answers: 1 boat   2 surfing   3 mountains   4 easy 5 racing   6 streets   7 fish   8 river   9 tree 10 countryside

After watching

3 ▶ Ask sts to choose the adventure activity that interested them most. Ask them to write five questions to ask their partner. Circulate and support as necessary. Then ask pairs to interview each other.

OPTIONAL EXTENSION

Ask sts to get up and walk around the class and interview each other with their questions. Explain that they must find an adventure enthusiast who loves the activity. Encourage sts to ask further questions. Invite one or two pairs to role play an interview with an adventure enthusiast in front of the class.

9 100 years ago

OPTIONAL WARMER

Sts work in pairs. Ask them to think of what things were different 100 years ago, e.g. clothes, types of food, work, music, education, travel, houses, free time activities. Elicit ideas and pool them on the board.

Before watching

1 ▶ Sts think of how the UK may have been 100 years ago by underlining or circling one of the options given in each statement. Ask them to compare their answers with a partner. Monitor and encourage sts to add any information they can to the statements. Go through the statements as a class, eliciting further information where possible.

While watching

2 ▶ Ask sts to read the questions and check if they have any vocabulary queries. Play the film through once, allowing sts to make notes. Play it again for sts to check their answers, then go over them as a class.

Answers: 1 c   2 c   3 b   4 a   5 c   6 c   7 a   8 b

After watching

3 ▶ Sts fill in the table describing what they think the aspects of life listed were like in their own country. Circulate and support with vocabulary.

4 ▶ Sts swap with their partner and ask each other questions about what they've written. Ask one pair to model some questions and answers for the class first. Pool feedback and build up a picture of what life was like.

OPTIONAL EXTENSION

Sts write a description of their country 100 years ago from their notes, adding information which other sts gave if they wish.

10 Cucumber sandwiches

OPTIONAL WARMER

Ask sts to tell each other about traditional snacks in their own country, for example strong coffee early in the morning, a cappuccino at 11a.m., etc. Pool ideas.

Before watching

1 ▶ Sts work in pairs to write down games played on grass. Allow sts to use their dictionaries if necessary. Ask for class feedback.

Possibe answers: tennis, football, rugby, hockey, cricket, some athletics events, horse riding

While watching

2 ▶ Preteach vocabulary items: *wear*, *shoe* and *match*. Ask sts to read the sentences. Check understanding.

Play the film and ask sts to make notes. Play the film again for sts to check their answers. Elicit answers from the class. Ask sts to correct the false items, using whole sentences.

Answers: 1 F – The ladies/They say *Morning, Good Morning* to each other.   2 W   3 W   4 F No, they're not. They're confident.   5 F No, they drink tea. 6 W   7 F The ladies are/They're competitive. 8 F No, they don't. Gladys and Edna win the match.

After watching

3 ▶ Sts work with a partner to write six simple sentences about the film in the Past Simple. Encourage them to infer what the ladies felt about the game as well as writing about the events. This also revises the skill of a simple summary from unit 10. Circulate and monitor as sts work giving support as necessary. Pool ideas on the board. Ask for other sentences which describe

Possible answers: Gladys and Edna won the match. Patricia and Marion lost the match.   The ladies said Good Morning to each other.   The umpire said, 'Tea ladies!'   A lady moved a ball with her shoe/foot. The ladies played bowls.   They had tea to drink.

Tests

Grammar

I'm/you're

1 Complete the sentences with *I'm* or *You're*.

I'm Mercedes Garcia.

A: Good morning. (1) ___ Scott Handy.

B: Good morning, Mr Handy. (2) ___ in room 121.

A: Thank you.

C: Hello. (3) ___ Erika Espen.

D: Nice to meet you, Ms Espen. (4) ___ Marco Mariani.

C: Nice to meet you, too, Mr Mariani.

E: (5) ___ Adreas Talesa.

F: Hello, Mr Talesa. (6) ___ in room 551.

(**3 points**)

he's/she's/it's

2 Write sentences about the words.

Melbourne/in Australia
It's in Australia.

1 Milan/in Italy

_____

2 Victoria Beckham/from the UK

_____

3 Antonio Banderas/from Spain

_____

4 The Eiffel Tower/in Paris

_____

5 Cristina Branco/from Portugal

_____

6 the Taj Mahal/in India

_____

(**3 points**)

Who ...?; my

3 Complete these dialogues.

A: *Who's she?*
B: *She's my sister.*

A: Who's (1) _____ ?
B: (2) _____ my father.
A: (3) _____ she?
B: She's (4) _____ mother.
A: Who's (5) _____ ?
B: (6) _____ my sister.

(**3 points**)

What's your ...?; his/her

4 Write questions for these answers.

What's her phone number?
Her phone number is 0191 449 0032.

1 _____

My name's Anne Jones.

2 _____

My mobile number is 07730 288099.

3 _____

My address is 12 New Road, Durham.

4 _____

His name's Ian.

5 _____

She's Alice Simmons.

6 _____

His email address is luke@starmail.com.

(**3 points**)

to be

5 Complete the sentences. Use contractions.

Ellie   She's my daughter.

1 Cecile and Celine _____ from Canada.
2 You _____ great.
3 The gallery _____ in New York.
4 John _____ my father.
5 I _____ in the photo.
6 Rebecca and I _____ in Paris.

(**3 points**)

the verb *to be: negative*

6 Write negative sentences.

You're a doctor.   You aren't a doctor.

1 They're in room 445.

_____

2 You're from Australia.

_____

3 He's my father.

_____

4 She's from Berlin.

_____

5 It's my car.

_____

6 We're in Paris.

_____

(**3 points**)

this, that, these, those

7 Choose the correct word in *italics*.

How much are/is those blue T-shirts?

1 How much is *these/this* brown dress?
2 How much *is/are* that red T-shirt?
3 How much are *those/that* dresses?
4 How much *is/are* these bags?
5 How much are *that/those* shirts?
6 How much *is/are* those bracelets?

(3 points)

possessive

8 Choose the correct option for each sentence.

What's __c__ phone number?
a) Ann   b) hers   c) his

1 She's _____ sister.
   a) Angela's   b) hers   c) his's
2 They're _____ train tickets.
   a) Sam   b) Sams   c) his
3 It's _____ aspirin.
   a) her's   b) Mike's   c) Lee
4 What's _____ email address?
   a) she   b) is   c) her

(2 points)

there is/are

9 Underline the correct sentences.

a) *There are good museums in Paris.*
b) *There's a good museums in Paris.*
c) *There's good museum in Paris.*

1 a) There are nice café near my house.
   b) There's a nice café near my house.
   c) There's nice café near my house.
2 a) There are nice beaches in Florida.
   b) There's nice beaches in Florida.
   c) There are a nice beach in Florida.
3 a) There are spice market in Istanbul.
   b) There spice market in Istanbul.
   c) There's a spice market in Istanbul.
4 a) There's a nice hotel on 4th Street.
   b) There are nice hotel on 4th Street.
   c) There's a nice hotels on 4th Street.

(2 points)

Total: 25 points

Pronunciation

1 Underline the stressed syllable in each word.

India

1 Delhi   2 Sydney   3 Berlin
4 Brazil   5 Poland   6 Australia

(3 points)

2 How is the *'s* pronounced? Tick the correct box.

	/s/	/z/
My father's in the garden.	☐	☑
1 My brother's name is Tom.	☐	☐
2 What's your phone number?	☐	☐
3 My sister's 17 years old.	☐	☐
4 Her mother's an architect.	☐	☐
5 Where's your coat?	☐	☐
6 My wife's an actor.	☐	☐

(3 points)

3 Write the words in the correct column.

pairs maps tops cameras shoes books
trousers skirts students friends

/s/	/z/
students	*friends*

(4 points)

Total: 10 points

Vocabulary

1 Complete the table.

Room 506   *Room five oh six*

1	Room 219	_____
2	Room ____	Room three four eight
3	Room 114	_____
4	Room ____	Room five oh nine
5	Room 708	_____
6	Room ____	Room two six five

(3 points)

2 Write the greeting for each time.

8:30 Good morning.

1 9:30 _____

2 14:30 _____

3 18:30 _____

4 22:30 _____

(2 points)

3 Use the words in the box to complete the conversation.

| sorry | Excuse | Nice | thank |
| please | meet | Pardon | you |

A: (1) _____ me.

B: Yes?

A: I'm Christos Chandos. Are you Sarah Potter?

B: No, I'm not. I'm Millie Jones.

A: Oh, (2) _____ !

B: This is Sarah.

A: Hello, Sarah. (3) _____ to (4) _____ you.

C: Nice to meet (5) _____ , too.

B: Christos, would you like a coffee?

A: (6) _____ ?

B: Would you like a coffee?

A: No, (7) _____ you.

B: Sarah, would you like a coffee?

A: Yes, (8) _____ .

(4 points)

4 Underline the correct answer.

74 = seventy-four/forty-seven

1 34 = forty-four/thirty-four

2 12 = twelve/twenty-one

3 80 = eighty/eighteen

4 15 = fifty/fifteen

5 25 = fifty-two/twenty-five

6 67 = sixty-seven/seventy-seven

(3 points)

5 Which word in each group is different?

accountant/actor/map/engineer

1 teacher/camera/MP3 player/suitcase

2 artist/sales assistant/book/doctor

3 shirt/shoes/student/trousers

4 old/skirt/small/ugly

5 Monday/manager/Tuesday/Friday

6 beautiful/modern/police officer/big

(3 points)

6 Put the letters in the correct order to write eight colours and clothes.

a elub hirts   a blue shirt

1 a raip fo owrnb ohess

_____

2 a elbu trisk

_____

3 a cbalk taoc

_____

4 a neegr resds

_____

5 a tewhi gba

_____

6 an roaneg tha

_____

7 a welloy T-hirts

_____

8 a prai fo der routsers

_____

(4 points)

7 Complete the table.

a sandwich	two *sandwiches*
a person	two (1) _____
a (2) _____	three men
a woman	five (3) _____
a (4) _____	six babies
a child	four (5) _____
a (6) _____	two wives

(3 points)

8 Choose the correct word in *italics*.

He's from Mexico/Mexican.

The Taj Mahal is an (1) *India/Indian* restaurant, but the chef is from (2) *China/Chinese*. It's next to a (3) *France/French* café called Bonjour. They have coffee, and they also have cakes from (4) *England/English*. It's opposite the (5) *China/Chinese* restaurant. But the chef is from (6) *Italy/Italian*!

(3 points)

Total: 25 points

Reading

1 Read the email.

> Hi Ian and Jill
> How are you? Mike and I are fine. We're in Bangkok
> at the Mandarin Oriental Hotel. It's really modern.
> Our room is beautiful. Bangkok is big! And it's hot!
> Mitch and Suzanne are in the Mandarin Oriental
> Hotel, too. They're our friends. They're from the UK.
> Mitch is an actor and Suzanne's a doctor. They're
> great!
> Love
> Simone

2 Answer the questions.

1 How are Mike and Simone?

_____

2 Where are Mike and Simone?

_____

3 Is Bangkok hot?

_____

4 Where are Mitch and Suzanne from?

_____

5 What's Suzanne's job?

_____

(**5 points**)

3 Write true (T) or false (F).

1 The hotel is old. ____

2 Bangkok is small. ____

3 The hotel room is ugly. ____

4 Mitch and Suzanne are Mike
and Simone's friends. ____

5 Mitch is a doctor. ____

(**5 points**)

Total: 10 points

Listening

Listen and complete the table.

Name	Country	City	Age	Job	Where now?
Tania	Russia			engineer	
Sam	the US		40		Australia
Henri	France			student	
Adrienne	the UK		30		China
Pedro			20	student	
Donatella	Italy	Rome			London

(**15 points**)

Writing

Write a personal profile of yourself. Write full sentences about: your name; where you are from;
your age; your job; some of your favourite things.

(**15 points**)

100 points

Grammar

I'm/you're

1 Complete the sentences with *I'm* or *You're*.

I'm Ursula Winger.

A: Hello. (1) ___ Samia Apavu.

B: Nice to meet you, Ms Apavu. (2) ___ Marcus Oliver.

A: Nice to meet you, too, Mr Oliver.

C: (3) ___ Adrea Teller.

D: Hello, Ms Teller. (4) ___ in room 301.

E: Good morning. (5) ___ Priscilla Hardy.

F: Good morning, Ms Hardy. (6) ___ in room 211.

(**3 points**)

he's/she's/it's

2 Write sentences about the words.

The Eiffel Tower/in Paris
It's in Paris.

1 Angela Merkel/from Germany

_____

2 The Taj Mahal/in India

_____

3 Antonio Banderas/from Spain

_____

4 The London Eye/in London

_____

5 David Beckham/from the UK

_____

6 Melbourne/in Australia

_____

(**3 points**)

Who ...?; my

3 Complete these dialogues.

A: *Who's he?*   **A:** (3) _____ he?

B: *He's my brother.*   **B:** He's (4) ____ brother.

A: Who's (1) _____ ?   **A:** Who's (5) _____ ?

B: (2) _____ my mother. **B:** (6) _____ my father.

(**3 points**)

What's your ...?; his/her

4 Write questions for these answers.

What's your email address?
My email address is eugene@fujiyama.com

1 _____

He's Adam Simmons.

2 _____

My address is 12 Old Court Road, Oxford.

3 _____

Her name's Jan.

4 _____

His phone number is 344 0990.

5 _____

My name's Edmond Lange.

6 _____

My mobile number is 07720 288 099.

(**3 points**)

to be

5 Complete the sentences. Use contractions.

Ernie   He's my son.

1 Sally and I _____ in Rome.

2 Pedro and Juan _____ from Mexico.

3 The gallery _____ in Boston.

4 You _____ great.

5 Joanna _____ my mother.

6 Mr Anderson _____ in the photo.

(**3 points**)

the verb *to be*: negative

6 Write negative sentences.

You're an actor.   You aren't an actor.

1 They're from Montreal.

_____

2 She's in room 244.

_____

3 It's your car.

_____

4 I'm from Australia.

_____

5 We're in London.

_____

6 She's my mother.

_____

(**3 points**)

this, that, these, those

7 Choose the correct word in *italics*.

How much *is/are* those bracelets?

1 How much *is/are* these shoes?
2 How much is *these/this* brown T-shirt?
3 How much are *that/those* T-shirts?
4 How much *is/are* that red dress?
5 How much *are/is* those blue dresses?
6 How much are *those/that* green shoes?

(3 points)

possessive

8 Choose the correct option for each sentence.

He's __c__ brother.
a) his's   b) hers   c) Ann's

1 It's _____ car.
   a) her's   b) Lees   c) Mike's
2 She's _____ sister.
   a) hers   b) his's   c) Ed's
3 They're _____ train tickets.
   a) Joes   b) her   c) Joe
4 What's _____ phone number?
   a) his   b) she   c) is

(2 points)

there is/are

9 Underline the correct sentences.

a) *There are good museums in New York.*
b) *There's a good museums in New York.*
c) *There's good museum in New York.*

1 a) There are spice market in Delhi.
   b) There spice market in Delhi.
   c) There's a spice market in Delhi.
2 a) There's nice café near my hotel.
   b) There are nice café near my hotel.
   c) There's a nice café near my hotel.
3 a) There's a nice restaurant on 6th Street.
   b) There are nice restaurant on 6th Street.
   c) There's nice restaurant on 6th Street.
4 a) There are nice beaches in Portugal.
   b) There nice beaches in Portugal.
   c) There are a nice beach in Portugal.

(2 points)

Total: 25 points

Pronunciation

1 Underline the stressed syllable in each word.

Poland

1 London   2 Berlin   3 Tokyo
4 Argentina   5 Australia   6 India

(3 points)

2 How is the 's pronounced? Tick the correct box.

	/s/	/z/
My mother's in Italy.	☐	☑
1 My wife's name is Alicia.	☐	☐
2 His sister's a student.	☐	☐
3 My father's 78 years old.	☐	☐
4 What's your name?	☐	☐
5 My husband's a doctor.	☐	☐
6 Where's your bag?	☐	☐

(3 points)

3 Write the words in the correct column.

| pairs   maps   tops   books   students |
| friends   trousers   skirts   cameras   shoes |

/z/	/s/
pairs	*maps*

(4 points)

Total: 10 points

Vocabulary

1 Complete the table.

Room 206   *Room two oh six*

1 Room 231	_____
2 Room _____	Room three five seven
3 Room 564	_____
4 Room _____	Room five oh five
5 Room 798	_____
6 Room _____	Room four six three

(3 points)

2 Write the greeting for each time.

8:00 Good morning.

1 8:30 _____

2 15:30 _____

3 19:30 _____

4 23:30 _____

(2 points)

3 Use the words in the box to complete the conversation.

> sorry   me   Nice   No   please   meet
> Pardon   you

A: Excuse (1) _____ .

B: Yes?

A: I'm Chris Berger. Are you Sandy Peters?

B: No, I'm not. I'm Pat Jameson.

A: Oh, (2) _____ !

B: This is Sandy.

A: Hello, Sandy. (3) _____ to meet (4) _____ .

C: Nice to (5) _____ you, too.

B: Chris, would you like a coffee?

A: (6) _____ ?

B: Would you like a coffee?

A: (7) _____ , thank you.

B: Sandy, would you like a coffee?

A: Yes, (8) _____ .

(4 points)

4 Underline the correct answer.

47 = seventy-four forty-seven

1 50 = fifty/fifteen

2 44 = thirty-four/forty-four

3 52 = fifty-two/twenty-five

4 21 = twelve/twenty-one

5 77 = sixty-seven/seventy-seven

6 18 = eighty/eighteen

(3 points)

5 Which word in each group is different?

accountant/actor/map/engineer

1 modern/skirt/big/ugly

2 doctor/camera/MP3 player/book

3 Monday/teacher/Wednesday/Friday

4 artist/sales assistant/suitcase/doctor

5 beautiful/old/police officer/small

6 shirt/trousers/student/shoes

(3 points)

6 Put the letters in the correct order to write eight colours and clothes.

a der hirts   *a red shirt*

1 a neerg gba

_____

2 a raip fo elub ohess

_____

3 a hiewt tha

_____

4 a welloy trisk

_____

5 a dre T-hirts

_____

6 an ongera taoc

_____

7 a prai fo cklab routsers

_____

8 a wrobn resds

_____

(4 points)

7 Complete the table.

a sandwich	two *sandwiches*
a wife	two (1) _____
a (2) _____	five women
a baby	six (3) _____
a (4) _____	two people
a man	three (5) _____
a (6) _____	four children

(3 points)

8 Choose the correct word in italics.

She's from *Spain/Spanish.*

Red Square is a (1) *Russia/Russian* restaurant, but the chef is from (2) *Japan/Japanese.* It's next to a (3) *France/French* café called La Parisienne. They serve (4) *Turkey/Turkish* coffee. It's opposite the (5) *Italian/ Italian* restaurant. The chef is from (6) *China/Chinese*!

(3 points)

Total: 10 points

Reading

1 Read the email.

Hi Jim and Susan
How are you? Bill and I are great! We're in Singapore
at the Marriott Hotel. It's really modern. Our room
is beautiful. Singapore is big! And it's hot!
Milo and Edith are in the Marriott Hotel, too.
They're our friends. They're from New York. Milo is a
doctor and Edith's an engineer. They're nice!
Love
Emma

2 Answer the questions.

1 How are Bill and Emma?

_____

2 Where are Bill and Emma?

_____

3 Is Singapore hot?

_____

4 Where are Milo and Edith from?

_____

5 What's Edith's job?

_____

(5 points)

3 Write true (T) or false (F).

1 The hotel is modern. ____

2 Singapore isn't hot. ____

3 The hotel room is beautiful. ____

4 Milo and Edith are Bill and Emma's friends. ____

5 Milo is an engineer. ____

(5 points)

Total: 10 points

Listening

Listen and complete the table.

Name	Country	City	Age	Job	Where now?
Tania	Russia			engineer	New York
Sam	the USA		40		
Henri	France		20	student	London
Adrienne	the UK			actor	
Pedro			20		Rome
Donatella	Italy	Rome			London

(15 points)

Writing

Write a personal profile of yourself. Write full sentences about: your name; where you are from;
your age; your job; some of your favourite things.

(15 points)

100 points

Grammar

me, you, him, her, it, us, them

1 Complete the answers using *me, you, him, her, it, us, them*.

Do they like you?
Yes, they like *me.*

1 Do her parents like you and your brother?
No, her parents don't like _____ .

2 Does Sally know you?
Yes, she knows _____ .

3 Do you like your new shoes?
No, I don't like _____ .

4 Do you like Mr Dylan?
No, I don't like _____ .

5 Does Mike know Mrs Smith?
No, Mike doesn't know _____ .

6 Do you know me?
Yes, I know _____ ! You're Tom!

(**3 points**)

Present Simple *he/she/it*

2 Complete the sentences with the words in the box.

> like   watch   work   starts   finish   watches
> likes   start   works

Does your work *finish* at 5:00?

1 Does she _____ Mexican food?
2 She _____ Japanese food.
3 He doesn't _____ TV.
4 Does he _____ for Citibank?
5 He _____ for KLM.
6 She _____ a lot of TV.
7 Does it _____ at 9:00?
8 It _____ at 10:00.

(**4 points**)

imperatives

3 Delete one incorrect word in each sentence.
Don't to eat ice cream for breakfast.

1 Turn it off your mobile phone.
2 Please don't to be late!
3 Speak the English in class.
4 Don't is watch TV all day.
5 For eat a sandwich for lunch.
6 Come to in, please.

(**3 points**)

would like

4 Put the words in the correct order to make sentences.

you what drink to would like?
What would you like to drink?

1 biscuits would some you like?
_____

2 you would like to what eat?
_____

3 a tea I'd cup like of.
_____

4 and do sugar you milk want?
_____

5 a cup like of you tea would?
_____

6 please I'd water, like mineral a.
_____

(**3 points**)

have got/has got

5 Choose the correct word in *italics*.
Have/Has they got a big house?

1 I *hasn't/haven't* got a television.
2 He *has/have* got a new car.
3 *Have/Has* you got a small house?
4 We *has/have* got a big car.
5 They *hasn't/haven't* got a garage.
6 *Have/Has* she got a new bicycle?

(**3 points**)

question words

6 Write a question for each answer.

Where is it?
It's in the house.

1 _____

He's my brother.

2 _____

I live in New York.

3 _____

I like the Chinese restaurant. The Italian restaurant
is too expensive.

4 _____

She's 24 years old.

5 _____

I'm a doctor.

6 _____

They like Indian food, Italian food ... everything!

(3 points)

past of *to be* (affirmative)

7 Complete the sentences with *was* or *were*.

I *was* a great singer when I was a child.

1 The party _____ great!

2 We _____ very happy.

3 I _____ a good football player at school.

4 Simon _____ born in 1990.

5 They _____ doctors in Paris.

6 Phil and Angela _____ in London last year.

(3 points)

Past Simple (irregular verbs)

8 Complete the conversations with the correct verb.

A: *Did they come to your house for lunch?*
B: *Yes, they did. They came on Sunday.*

1 A: _____ Mike _____ to Belarus?
   B: Yes, he did. He went last week.

2 A: Did Begonia and Andres take a lot of photos?
   B: No, they _____ any photos.

3 A: _____ you _____ the lottery?
   B: Yes, I did. I won £15,000!

4 A: Did we lose the game?
   B: Yes, we _____ . We _____ 3–0.

5 A: _____ you _____ '18'?
   B: No, I didn't. I said '80'.

6 A: _____ she _____ a new car?
   B: Yes, she did. She bought a BMW.

(3 points)

Total: 25 points

Pronunciation

Put the verbs in the correct column.

visited	asked	started	moved
lived	finished	played	worked
arrested	cooked	closed	wanted

/ɪd/	/t/	/d/
visited	asked	

(5 points)

Vocabulary

1 Which word in each group is different?

~~chef~~/sells/writes/designs

1 architect/sales rep./designs/builder

2 sell/write/build/designer

3 builder/articles/buildings/clothes

4 chef/cook/food/reporters

5 designs/builds/cooks/architect

6 write/reporter/chef/designer

(3 points)

2 Match the words to make verbs of routine.

eat salad

1 get   **a** fast food
2 eat   **b** a shower
3 watch   **c** TV
4 go   **d** up
5 start   **e** to bed
6 have   **f** work

(3 points)

3 Complete the months of the year.

January
February

1 M_____		**6** A_____	
2 A_____		**7** S_____	
3 M_____		**8** O_____	
4 J_____		**9** N_____	
5 J_____		**10** D_____	

(5 points)

4 Unscramble the work phrases.

eiwrt rtrepos *write reports*

1 krow morf meho _____

2 evah teeminsg _____

3 vegi tipresonsenta _____

4 ktae wrok hemo _____

5 arensw het oneph _____

6 orwk stooroud _____

(3 points)

5 Write each word in the correct list.

> coffee table   sink   sofa   fridge
> wardrobe   bath   cooker   bed   basin

1 kitchen:

washing machine, *sink*, _____ , _____

2 living room:

armchair, lamp, _____ , _____

3 bathroom:

toilet, _____ , _____

4 bedroom:

mirror, _____ , _____

(2 points)

6 Fill in the gaps with an appropriate word.

John F. Kennedy was born *in* Brookline, Massachusetts (1) _____ the 29th (2) _____ May, 1917. When he was a child, he was good (3) _____ playing American football. He got married (4) _____ Jacqueline Bouvier (5) _____ 1953. He was president (6) _____ the US from 1961 to 1963.

(3 points)

7 Use the words in the box to complete the menu.

> Green   Main   soup   beef
> chops   cake   cocktail

> **Starters**
> Seafood *cocktail*
> Fish (1) _____
> (2) _____ salad
>
> (3) _____ **courses**
> Roast (4) _____
> Lamb (5) _____
> Vegetable pasta
>
> **Desserts**
> Ice cream
> Chocolate (6) _____

(3 points)

8 Complete the sentences with *yesterday*, *last* or *ago*.

I went to the cinema *yesterday*.

1 I was in Hong Kong three weeks _____ .

2 Mike was in an Italian restaurant _____ night.

3 My parents were at my house _____ .

4 Keith was in Morocco _____ year.

5 Millie and Don were late for work _____ .

6 My first flight was ten years _____ .

(3 points)

Total: 25 points

Reading

1 Read the three short stories below.

> It was a good week for waitress Sally Caruthers, 35. She went to her favourite restaurant and did karaoke singing. Jez Simpson was there. He liked her singing. Who is Jez Simpson? Jez plays guitar for the band Badboy. He asked Sally to sing on their new CD!
>
> It started as a good week for Emilio Sanchez, a doctor from Texas. He found an old gold coin near his house ($5,000!). And then he lost it. 'I looked and I looked, but I didn't find it again. I can't understand it.' Never mind, Emilio.
>
> It was a good week for Erik Van Espen. He went to the supermarket and won a new car. 'I went to buy some milk. When I bought it, I was the 1,000,000th customer. The prize was a new car. It was a great day!' Not bad, Erik!

2 Are the following sentences true (T) or false (F)?

Sally had a bad week. *F*

1 Jez didn't like Sally's singing. ___

2 Jez is in a band. ___

3 Sally wasn't lucky. ___

4 Emilio lost something and then found it. ___

5 Emilio is a doctor. ___

6 Emilio stole $5,000. ___

7 Erik bought a new car. ___

8 Erik wasn't happy. ___

9 Erik bought some milk. ___

(**9 points**)

3 Answer the questions.

1 Who won something?

_____

2 Who went to the supermarket?

_____

3 Where did Sally Caruthers go?

_____

4 What's Sally's job?

_____

5 Where is Emilio Sanchez from?

_____

6 What did Emilio lose?

_____

(**6 points**)

(**Total: 15 points**)

Listening

Listen to four people (Paul, Betty, Jim and Louise) talking about where they live. Complete the table.

	Paul	Betty	Jim	Louise
House or flat?	house		flat	
Bedroom			1	1
Living room	2		1	
Bathroom		1		1
Garage	1	0	0	
Garden		0		0
Car	2		0	
Bicycle		0	1	

(**15 points**)

Writing

Write a paragraph about your school days. What sports were you good at? What subjects did you like? Who were your friends? Where did you go together?

(**15 points**)

100 points

Test B Units 6–10

Grammar

me, you, him, her, it, us, them

1 Complete the answers using *me, you, him, her, it, us, them*.

Do they like your brother?
Yes, they like him.

1 Do you like Mrs Smithfield?
    No, I don't like _____ .
2 Do her parents like you and your sister?
    Yes, her parents like _____ .
3 Does Rodney know Mr Kent?
    No, Rodney doesn't know _____ .
4 Does Roberto know you?
    Yes, he knows _____ .
5 Do you know me?
    Yes, I know _____ ! You're Roy!
6 Do you like your new trousers?
    No, I don't like _____ .

(3 points)

Present Simple *he/she/it*

2 Complete the sentences with the words in the box.

like	watch	work	starts	finish
watches	likes	start	works	

Does your work finish at 5:00?

1 She _____ for United Airlines.
2 Does he _____ Japanese food?
3 He _____ a lot of TV.
4 He _____ Chinese food.
5 They don't _____ TV.
6 Does it _____ at 7:30?
7 It _____ at 12:00.
8 Does she _____ for HSBC?

(3 points)

imperatives

3 Delete one incorrect word in each sentence.

Please don't to eat chocolate for breakfast.

1 Please don't is watch TV all day.
2 Turn it off your mobile phone.
3 For eat a sandwich for lunch.
4 Please don't to be late!
5 Come to in.
6 Speak the English in class, please.

(3 points)

would like

4 Put the words in the correct order to make sentences.

you what drink to would like?
What would you like to drink?

1 and do sugar you milk want?

    _____

2 water mineral would some you like?

    _____

3 a cup like of you coffee would?

    _____

4 you would like to what drink?

    _____

5 please I'd like biscuit, a.

    _____

6 a coffee I'd cup like of.

    _____

(3 points)

have got/has got

5 Choose the correct word in *italics*.

Have/Has they got a big car?

1 We *has/have* got a big house.
2 I *hasn't/haven't* got a garage.
3 They *hasn't/haven't* got a television.
4 He *has/have* got a new bicycle.
5 *Have/Has* she got a new house?
6 *Have/Has* you got a small car?

(3 points)

question words

6 Write a question for each answer.

Where is it?
It's in the house.

1 _____

He's 27 years old.

2 _____

She's my sister.

3 _____

I'm a manager.

4 _____

I live in London.

5 _____

They like Chinese food, Indian food ... everything!

6 _____

I like the Italian restaurant. The French restaurant is too expensive.

(3 points)

past of *to be*: affirmative

7 Complete the sentences with *was* or *were*.

I was a great football player when I was a child.

1 Felix _____ born in 1987.
2 My holiday _____ great!
3 They _____ actors in Paris.
4 We _____ very happy.
5 Paolo and Andrea _____ in Rio last year.
6 I _____ a good singer at school.

(3 points)

Past Simple (irregular verbs)

8 Complete the conversations with the correct verb.

A: *Did they come to your house on Saturday?*
B: *No, they didn't. They came on Sunday.*

1 **A:** Did we win the game?
  B: Yes, we _____ . We _____ 3–0.

2 **A:** _____ Mike _____ to Argentina?
  B: Yes, he did. He went last week.

3 **A:** _____ you _____ '15'?
  B: No, I didn't. I said '50'.

4 **A:** Did Tim and Kim take a lot of photos?
  B: No, they _____ any photos.

5 **A:** _____ he _____ a new car?
  B: Yes, he did. He bought a Volkswagen.

6 **A:** _____ you _____ your wallet?
  B: Yes, I did. I lost it yesterday.

(3 points)

Total: 25 points

Pronunciation

Put the verbs in the correct column.

visited	moved	talked	started
finished	lived	listened	walked
arrested	cooked	closed	wanted

/ɪd/	/d/	/t/
visited	*moved*	

(5 points)

Vocabulary

1 Which word in each group is different?

chef/sells/writes/designs

1 chef/cook/food/reporters
2 architect/sales rep./designs/builder
3 designs/builds/cooks/builder
4 sell/cook/build/designer
5 designer/write/reporter/chef
6 chef/clothes/articles/buildings

(3 points)

2 Match the words to make verbs of routine.

eat fast food

1 eat	**a** up
2 get	**b** salad
3 start	**c** to bed
4 go	**d** work
5 watch	**e** a shower
6 have	**f** TV

(3 points)

3 Correct the spelling mistakes.

Janury   <u>January</u>
Fibruary   <u>February</u>

1 March _____   **6** Aujust _____

2 Appril _____   **7** Septimber _____

3 Mey _____   **8** Oktober _____

4 Jone _____   **9** Novembur _____

5 Juli _____   **10** Dicember _____

(5 points)

4 Unscramble the work phrases.

krow morf meho   <u>work from home</u>

1 eiwrt rtrepos   _____

2 etak rokw ohem   _____

3 warens hte honep   _____

4 ehva meeinsgt   _____

5 orkw stodorou   _____

6 iveg attipresonsen   _____

(3 points)

5 Write each word in the correct list.

> coffee table   armchair   fridge   wardrobe
> bath   cooker   bed   toilet   washing machine

1 bathroom:

   basin, *toilet*, _____

2 kitchen:

   sink, _____ , _____ , _____

3 bedroom:

   mirror, _____ , _____

4 living room:

   sofa, lamp, _____ , _____

(2 points)

6 Fill in the gaps with an appropriate word.

Bill Clinton was born *in* Hope, Arkansas (1) _____ the 19th (2) _____ August, 1946. When he was a child, he was good (3) _____ playing the saxophone. He got married (4) _____ Hillary Rodham (5) _____ 1975. He was president (6) _____ the US from 1993 to 2001.

(3 points)

7 Use the words in the box to complete the menu.

> salad   courses   soup   beef
> chops   cream   cocktail

Starters
Seafood <u>cocktail</u>
Fish (1) _____
(2) Green _____

(3) **Main** _____
Lamb (4) _____
Roast (5) _____
Vegetable pasta

Desserts
Ice (6) _____
Chocolate cake

(3 points)

8 Complete the sentences with *yesterday, last* or *ago*.

I went to London *yesterday*.

1 Kevin was in France _____ year.

2 I was in New York three weeks _____ .

3 Emma and Ben were late for work _____ .

4 Kim was in a Chinese restaurant _____ night.

5 My first flight was eight years _____ .

6 Emily was at my house _____ .

(3 points)

Total: 25 points

Reading

1 Read the three short stories below.

> It was a good week for designer Elsie Foster. She went to the supermarket and won a new car. 'I went to buy some bananas. When I bought them, I was the 1,000,000th customer. The prize was a new car. It was a great day!' Not bad, Elsie!
>
> It started as a good week for Peter Laroche, an actor from New York. He found an old gold coin near his house ($7,000!). And then he lost it. 'I looked and I looked, but I didn't find it again. I can't understand it.' Never mind, Peter.
>
> It was a good week for waitress Elizabeth Regis, 25. She went to her favourite restaurant and did karaoke singing. Mick Axe was there. He liked her singing. Who is Mick Axe? Mick plays guitar for the band Thiefboy. He asked Elizabeth to sing on their new CD!

2 Are the following sentences true (T) or false (F)?

Sally had a bad week. _F_

1 Elsie bought a new car. ___
2 Elsie wasn't happy. ___
3 Elsie bought some bananas. ___
4 Peter lost something and then found it. ___
5 Peter is an actor. ___
6 Peter stole $7,000. ___
7 Mick didn't like Elizabeth's singing. ___
8 Mick is in a band. ___
9 Elizabeth wasn't lucky. ___

9 points

3 Answer the questions.

1 What's Elizabeth's job?

_____

2 Who won something?

_____

3 Where is Peter Laroche from?

_____

4 Who went to the supermarket?

_____

5 What did Peter lose?

_____

6 Where did Elizabeth go?

_____

6 points

Total: 15 points

Listening

Listen to four people (Paul, Betty, Jim, and Louise) talking about where they live. Complete the table.

	Paul	Betty	Jim	Louise
House or flat?			flat	house
Bedroom	6			1
Living room	2	1	1	1
Bathroom	2			1
Garage		0	0	
Garden		0	0	
Car	2			2
Bicycle				0

15 points

Writing

Write a paragraph about your school days. What sports were you good at? What subjects did you like? Who were your friends? Where did you go together?

15 points

100 points

Test A Units 1–5
Grammar

1 *I'm/you're*

1 I'm 2 You're 3 I'm 4 I'm 5 I'm 6 You're

2 *he's/she's/it's*

1 It's in Italy. 2 She's from the UK. 3 He's from Spain.
4 It's in Paris. 5 She's from Portugal. 6 It's in India.

3 *Who ...?; my*

1 he 2 He's 3 Who's 4 my 5 she 6 She's

4 *What's your ...?; his/her*

1 What's your name? 2 What's your mobile phone number?
3 What's your address? 4 What's his name? 5 What's her
name? 6 What's his email address?

5 *to be*

1 They're 2 You're 3 It's 4 He's 5 I'm 6 We're

6 *the verb to be: negative*

1 They aren't in room 445. 2 You aren't from Australia.
3 He isn't my father. 4 She isn't from Berlin. 5 It isn't my
car. 6 We aren't in Paris.

7 *this, that, these, those*

1 this 2 is 3 those 4 are 5 those 6 are

8 *possessive*

1 a 2 c 3 b 4 c

9 *there is/are*

1 b 2 a 3 c 4 a

Pronunciation

1 1 <u>D</u>elhi 2 <u>S</u>ydney 3 <u>B</u>erlin 4 <u>B</u>razil 5 <u>P</u>oland 6 Aust<u>r</u>alia

2 1 /z/ 2 /s/ 3 /z/ 4 /z/ 5 /z/ 6 /s/

3 /s/ maps, tops, books, skirts

/z/ pairs, cameras, shoes, trousers

Vocabulary

1 1 Room two one nine 2 Room 348 3 Room one one four
4 Room 509 5 Room seven oh eight 6 Room 265

2 1 Good morning. 2 Good afternoon. 3 Good evening.
4 Good night.

3 1 Excuse 2 sorry 3 Nice 4 meet 5 you 6 Pardon
7 thank 8 please

4 1 thirty-four 2 twelve 3 eighty 4 fifteen 5 twenty-five
6 sixty-seven

5 1 teacher 2 book 3 student 4 skirt 5 manager
6 police officer

6 1 a pair of brown shoes 2 a blue skirt 3 a black coat
4 a green dress 5 a white bag 6 an orange hat 7 a yellow
T-shirt 8 a pair of red trousers

7 1 people 2 man 3 women 4 baby 5 children 6 wife

8 1 Indian 2 China 3 French 4 England 5 Chinese 6 Italy

Reading

2 1 They're fine. 2 They're in Bangkok (in the Mandarin
Oriental Hotel). 3 Yes, it is. 4 They're from the UK.
5 She's a doctor.

3 1 F 2 F 3 F 4 T 5 F

Listening

Tapescript

I'm Tania. I'm from Russia. Do you know Moscow? I'm from
Moscow. It's a big city. I'm 35 years old. I'm an engineer. I'm in
New York. New York is my favourite city!

Hello. My name's Sam. I'm from the US. I'm from New York
City. I'm 40 years old. I'm a doctor. Right now, I'm on holiday in
Australia.

Hi. My name's Henri. I'm from France – Paris. I'm 20 years old.
I'm a student. I'm in London. My father is from England.

Hello. My name's Adrienne. I'm from the UK. I'm from London.
I'm 30 years old. I'm an actor. Right now, I'm on holiday in China.

Hi. My name's Pedro. I'm from Mexico – Mexico City. I'm 20 years
old. I'm a student. I'm in Rome. My father is from Italy.

I'm Donatella. I'm from Italy. Do you know Rome? I'm from Rome.
It's a big city. I'm 32 years old. I'm a teacher. I'm in London.
London is my favourite city!

Name	Country	City	Age	Job	Where now?
Tania	Russia	Moscow	35	engineer	New York
Sam	the US	New York	40	doctor	Australia
Henri	France	Paris	20	student	London
Adrienne	the UK	London	30	actor	China
Pedro	Mexico	Mexico City	20	student	Rome
Donatella	Italy	Rome	32	teacher	London

Writing

Sts' own answers.

Test B Units 1–5
Grammar

1 *I'm/you're*

1 I'm 2 I'm 3 I'm 4 You're 5 I'm 6 You're

2 *he's/she's/it's*

1 She's from Germany. 2 It's in India. 3 He's from Spain.
4 It's in London. 5 He's from the UK. 6 It's in Australia.

3 *Who ...?; my*

1 she 2 She's 3 Who's 4 my 5 he 6 He's

4 *What's your ...?; his/her*

1 What's his name? 2 What's your address? 3 What's her
name? 4 What's his phone number? 5 What's your name?
6 What's your mobile number?

5 *to be*

1 We're 2 They're 3 It's 4 You're 5 She's 6 He's

6 *the verb to be: negative*

1 They aren't from Montreal. 2 She isn't in room 244.
3 It isn't your car. 4 I'm not from Australia. 5 We aren't in
London. 6 She isn't my mother.

7 *this, that, these, those*

1 are 2 this 3 those 4 is 5 are 6 those

8 **possessive**

1 c 2 c 3 b 4 a

9 *there is/are*

1 c 2 c 3 a 4 a

Pronunciation

1 1 London 2 Berlin 3 Tokyo 4 Argentina 5 Australia
6 India

2 1 /s/ 2 /z/ 3 /z/ 4 /s/ 5 /z/ 6 /z/

3 /z/ friends, trousers, cameras, shoes
/s/ tops, books, students, skirts

Vocabulary

1 1 Room two three one 2 Room 357 3 Room five six four
4 Room 505 5 Room seven nine eight 6 Room 463

2 1 Good morning. 2 Good afternoon. 3 Good evening.
4 Good night.

3 1 me 2 sorry 3 Nice 4 you 5 meet 6 Pardon 7 No
8 please

4 1 fifty 2 forty-four 3 fifty-two 4 twenty-one 5 seventy-
seven 6 eighteen

5 1 skirt 2 doctor 3 teacher 4 suitcase 5 police officer
6 student

6 1 a green bag 2 a pair of blue shoes 3 a white hat 4 a
yellow skirt 5 a red T-shirt 6 an orange coat 7 a pair of
black trousers 8 a brown dress

7 1 wives 2 woman 3 babies 4 person 5 men 6 child

8 1 Russian 2 Japan 3 French 4 Turkish 5 Italian 6 China

Reading

2 1 They're great. 2 They're in Singapore. 3 Yes, it is.
4 They're from New York. 5 She's an engineer.

3 1 T 2 F 3 T 4 T 5 F

Listening

Tapescript

I'm Tania. I'm from Russia. Do you know Moscow? I'm from
Moscow. It's a big city. I'm 35 years old. I'm an engineer. I'm in
New York. New York is my favourite city!

Hello. My name's Sam. I'm from the US. I'm from New York
City. I'm 40 years old. I'm a doctor. Right now, I'm on holiday in
Australia.

Hi. My name's Henri. I'm from France – Paris. I'm 20 years old.
I'm a student. I'm in London. My father is from England.

Hello. My name's Adrienne. I'm from the UK. I'm from London.
I'm 30 years old. I'm an actor. Right now, I'm on holiday in China.

Hi. My name's Pedro. I'm from Mexico – Mexico City. I'm 20 years
old. I'm a student. I'm in Rome. My father is from Italy.

I'm Donatella. I'm from Italy. Do you know Rome? I'm from Rome.
It's a big city. I'm 32 years old. I'm a teacher. I'm in London.
London is my favourite city!

Name	Country	City	Age	Job	Where now?
Tania	Russia	Moscow	35	engineer	New York
Sam	the US	New York	40	doctor	Australia
Henri	France	Paris	20	student	London
Adrienne	the UK	London	30	actor	China
Pedro	Mexico	Mexico City	20	student	Rome
Donatella	Italy	Rome	32	teacher	London

Writing

Sts' own answers.

Test A Units 6–10
Grammar

1 *me, you, him, her, it, us, them*

1 us 2 me 3 them 4 him 5 her 6 you

2 **Present Simple** *he/she/it*

1 like 2 likes 3 watch 4 work 5 works 6 watches
7 start 8 starts

3 **imperatives**

1 it 2 to 3 the 4 is 5 for 6 to

4 *would like*

1 Would you like some biscuits? 2 What would you like to
eat? 3 I'd like a cup of tea. 4 Do you want milk and sugar/
sugar and milk? 5 Would you like a cup of tea? 6 I'd like a
mineral water, please.

5 *have got/has got*

1 haven't 2 has 3 Have 4 have 5 haven't 6 Has

6 **question words**

1 Who is/Who's he? 2 Where do you live? 3 Which
restaurant do you like? 4 How old is she? 5 What do you
do? 6 What kind of food do they like?

7 **past of** *to be*: **affirmative**

1 was 2 were 3 was 4 was 5 were 6 were

8 **Past Simple (irregular verbs)**

1 Did, go 2 didn't take 3 Did, win 4 did, lost 5 Did, say
6 Did, buy

Pronunciation

/ɪd/	/t/	/d/
visited	asked	moved
started	finished	lived
arrested	worked	played
wanted	cooked	closed

Vocabulary

1 1 designs 2 designer 3 builder 4 reporters 5 architect
6 write

2 1 d 2 a 3 c 4 e 5 f 6 b

3 1 March 2 April 3 May 4 June 5 July 6 August
7 September 8 October 9 November 10 December

4 1 work from home 2 have meetings 3 give presentations 4 take work home 5 answer the phone 6 work outdoors

5 1 fridge, cooker 2 sofa, coffee table 3 basin, bath 4 bed, wardrobe

6 1 on 2 of 3 at 4 to 5 in 6 of

7 1 soup 2 Green 3 Main 4 beef 5 chops 6 cake

8 1 ago 2 last 3 yesterday 4 last 5 yesterday 6 ago

Reading

2 1 F 2 T 3 F 4 F 5 T 6 F 7 F 8 F 9 T

3 1 Erik 2 Erik 3 to a restaurant 4 She's a waitress. 5 Texas 6 a gold coin

Listening

Tapescript

Paul: I'm Paul. I live with my parents and my brothers and sisters in a big house. We've got six bedrooms, a big kitchen, two big living rooms and two bathrooms. We've got a big garage, and we've got a really big garden. We've got two cars, and we've got seven bicycles.

Betty: My name's Betty. I live in my sister's flat. She's got three bedrooms, a living room, a kitchen and one bathroom. She hasn't got a garage or a garden. We haven't got a car or a bicycle.

Jim: My name's Jim. I live alone in a small flat. I've got one bedroom, a living room, a kitchen and a bathroom. I haven't got a garage, and I haven't got a garden. I've got a bicycle, but I haven't got a car.

Louise: I'm Louise. I live with my husband in a small house. We've got a bedroom, a living room, a kitchen and a bathroom. We've got a small garage, but we haven't got a garden. We've got two cars. We haven't got any bicycles.

	Paul	Betty	Jim	Louise
House or flat?	house	flat	flat	house
Bedroom	6	3	1	1
Living room	2	1	1	1
Bathroom	2	1	1	1
Garage	1	0	0	1
Garden	1	0	0	0
Car	2	0	0	2
Bicycle	7	0	1	0

Writing

Sts' own answers.

Test B Units 6–10
Grammar

1 *me, you, him, her, it, us, them*
1 her 2 us 3 him 4 me 5 you 6 them

2 **Present Simple *he/she/it***
1 works 2 like 3 watches 4 likes 5 watch 6 start 7 starts 8 work

3 **imperatives**
1 is 2 it 3 for 4 to 5 to 6 the

4 *would like*
1 Do you want milk and sugar/sugar and milk? 2 Would you like some mineral water? 3 Would you like a cup of coffee? 4 What would you like to drink? 5 I'd like a biscuit, please. 6 I'd like a cup of coffee.

5 *have got/has got*
1 have 2 haven't 3 haven't 4 has 5 Has 6 Have

6 **question words**
1 How old is he? 2 Who is she? 3 What do you do? 4 Where do you live? 5 What kind of food do they like? 6 Which restaurant do you like?

7 **past of *to be*: affirmative**
1 was 2 was 3 were 4 were 5 were 6 was

8 **Past Simple (irregular verbs)**
1 did, won 2 Did, go 3 Did, say 4 didn't take 5 Did, buy 6 Did, lose

Pronunciation

/ɪd/	/d/	/t/
visited	moved	talked
started	lived	finished
arrested	listened	walked
wanted	closed	cooked

Vocabulary

1 1 reporters 2 designs 3 builder 4 designer 5 write 6 chef

2 1 b 2 a 3 d 4 c 5 f 6 e

3 1 March 2 April 3 May 4 June 5 July 6 August 7 September 8 October 9 November 10 December

4 1 write reports 2 take work home 3 answer the phone 4 have meetings 5 work outdoors 6 give presentations

5 1 bath 2 washing machine, fridge, cooker 3 bed, wardrobe 4 armchair, coffee table

6 1 on 2 of 3 at 4 to 5 in 6 of

7 1 soup 2 salad 3 courses 4 chops 5 beef 6 cream

8 1 last 2 ago 3 yesterday 4 last 5 ago 6 yesterday